LISBON

LISBON

WAR IN THE SHADOWS
of the
CITY OF LIGHT,
1939–1945

NEILL LOCHERY

PUBLICAFFAIRS
New York

Published in the United States by PublicAffairs™,
a Member of the Perseus Books Group

PublicAffairs books are available at special discounts for bulk
purchases in the U.S. by corporations, institutions, and other
organizations. For more information, please contact the Special
Markets Department at the Perseus Books Group, 2300 Chestnut
Street, Suite 200, Philadelphia, PA 19103, call (800) 810–4145,
ext. 5000, or e-mail special.markets@perseusbooks.com.

Book Design by Brent Wilcox

The Library of Congress has cataloged the printed edition as follows:
Library of Congress Cataloging-in-Publication Data
Lochery, Neill.
    Lisbon : war in the shadows of the City of Light, 1939–1945 /
Neill Lochery.—1st ed.
        p.   cm.
    Includes bibliographical references and index.
    ISBN 978–1-58648–879–6 (hardcover)—
ISBN 978–1-58648–880–2 (electronic)   1. World War, 1939–
1945—Portugal—Lisbon.   2. World War, 1939–1945—Secret
service.   3. World War, 1939–1945—Military intelligence.
4. Espionage—Portugal—Lisbon—History—20th century.
5. Neutrality—Portugal—Lisbon—History—20th century.
6. World War, 1939–1945—Economic aspects—Portugal.
7. Lisbon (Portugal)—History—20th century.   I. Title.
    D763.P82L556 2011
    946.9'4209044—dc23

                                            2011021792

First Edition
10 9 8 7 6 5 4 3 2 1

For Emma, Benjamin, and Hélèna

CONTENTS

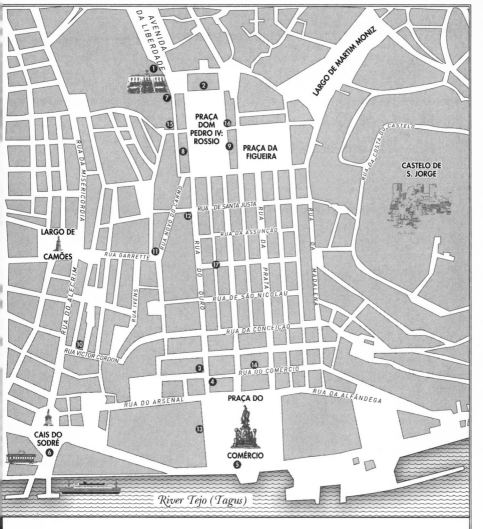

CENTRAL LISBON

1. Rossio train station
2. Teatro Nacional (National Theatre)
3. Bank of Portugal
4. Headquarters of Banco Espírito Santo
5. Government Ministries at Praça do Comerical
6. Trains to Belém, Estoril and Cascais from Cais do Sodré train station
7. Café Chave d'Ouro
8. Hotel Pensão Rocio
9. Hotel Francfort (hotel to Peggy Guggenheim, Arthur Koestler)
10. P.V.D.E (Secret Police) Headquarters

11. German propaganda shop
12. Elevador Santa Justa
13. Government Ministry balcony from where Salazar gave his speech in 1941
14. PanAm ticket office
15. Café Leão d'Ouro (frequented by Peggy Guggenheim and other refugees)
16. Café Sueca
17. Offices of the American Jewish Joint Distribution Committee

0		.05		.10 miles
0		.05		0.10 kilometers

LISBON

1. Rossio train station
2. National Assembly (Parliament)
3. Prime Ministers Official Residence (São Bento)
4. Government Ministries at Praça do Comerical
5. Trains to Belém, Estoril and Cascais from Cais do Sodré train station
6. Harbour & Docks at Alcântara: from where the refugees departed
7. British Embassy
8. American Embassy (Legation)
9. P.V.D.E (Secret Police) Headquarters
10. Século Newspaper
11. German Propaganda Shop
12. World Jewish Congress offices
13. German Embassy
14. Buick Car Dealership
15. American Consulate General
16. Diário de Notícias Newspaper
17. Castelo de São Jorge
18. American Jewish Joint Distribution Committee
19. HICEM – offices of the Hebrew Immigration Aid Services
20. Brazilian Embassy
21. Hotel Tivoli

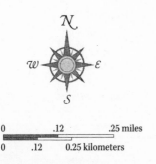

0   .12   .25 miles
0   .12   0.25 kilometers

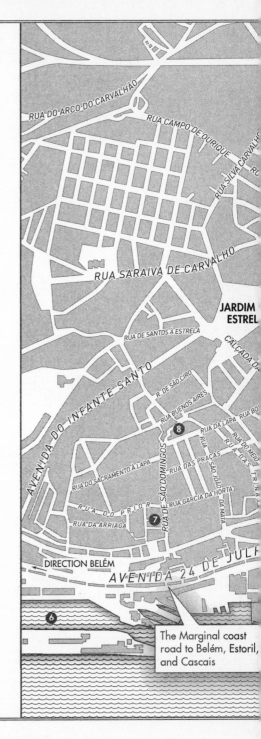

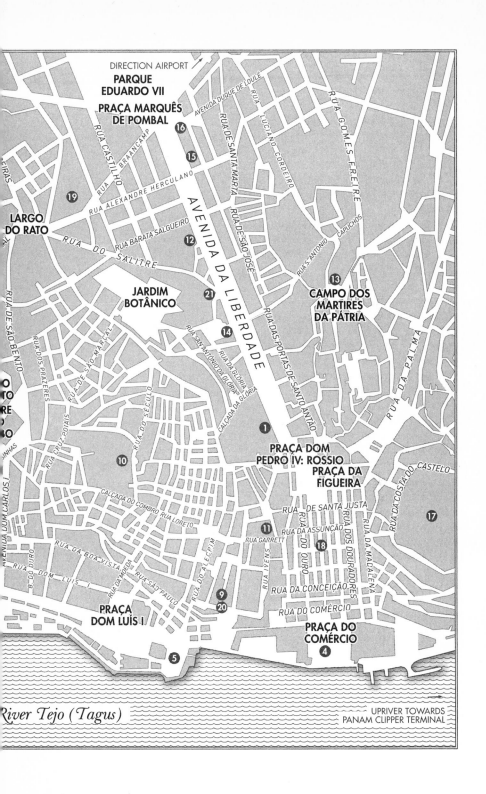

Introduction

A T THE END OF THE MOVIE *CASABLANCA,* AS RICK
Blaine and Captain Louis Renault head off to start their
"beautiful friendship" by joining the Free French Garrison at
Brazzaville, the plane carrying Victor Laszlo and Ilsa Lund takes
off into the fog. It is to "neutral" Lisbon that they are headed with
their letters of transit. In real life, the city of Lisbon during World
War II more than resembled the film set; to many people who
worked in the city during the latter stages of the war, Lisbon became affectionately known as "Casablanca II." The real-life version had all the ingredients of the fictional storyline: broken
romances; desperate refugees trying to obtain the correct paperwork and selling the family jewels to finance their onward passage; a thriving black market as supply dictated that the prices of
diamonds and other rare stones fell to record low levels; cafés
and hotel bars full of refugees and spies scattered across the city
center and along Lisbon's coastline resorts.

There was also a real-life Captain Renault in Lisbon: the
greatly feared head of the Portuguese Secret Police, Captain
Agostinho Lourenço. Senior figures of the German Reichsbank
were in the city from time to time, busy arranging payment terms
for Portuguese goods. The city had the last great gambling house

1

in wartime Europe, located along its coastline at Estoril.[1] Here, the roulette wheel was spun long into the night with the exiled royalty of much of Europe playing blackjack at the tables, or engaged in private sessions of poker in the discrete side rooms. It was here that wealthy Jewish refugees gambled against suntanned German Gestapo agents dressed in badly cut civilian clothes, with the house taking 5 percent of everybody's winnings.[2]

During the years of World War II, Lisbon was at the very center of world attention, and was the only European city where both the Allies and the Axis powers openly operated. Lisbon's story was set within the context of a country that was frantically trying to hold on to its self-proclaimed wartime neutrality, but which, in reality, was increasingly caught in the middle of the economic, and naval, wars between the Allies and the Nazis. It was not, however, a conventional tale of World War II: Barely a shot was fired, or a bomb dropped. Instead, it was a tale of intrigue, betrayal, opportunism and double dealing, all of which took place in the Cidade da Luz (City of Light), and along its idyllic Atlantic coastline.

Ultimately a relatively poor European country not only survived the war physically intact, but came out at the end of it in 1945 much wealthier than it had been when war had broken out in 1939. Although much of this wealth was considered by the Allies to be "ill-gotten gains," the Portuguese were allowed to retain the vast majority of it as post-1945 Cold War political realities reemphasized the importance of the country, and its Atlantic Islands (the Azores), to the cause of the Western Powers.

Lisbon was a city in which an apparent German plot to kidnap the Duke and Duchess of Windsor was foiled. They were among the more exotic refugees, many of them Jewish, who flooded into the city seeking a passage to the United States or Palestine on one of the ships that sailed from the neutral port, or for the super rich, via the Azores on the Pan-American Boeing Clipper "flying boat" service to New York. Most refugees, however, had to wait months, or even years, in the city before securing their onward passage. On the run from the Germans since the fall of France in the summer of 1940, many of the refugees survived on a clandestine network of financial and organizational support, which originated from the offices of wealthy American Jews in New York City. The not so fortunate had to rely on the limited help from the British, the Portuguese authorities, and locally run rescue organizations.

Allied and German agents operated openly in the city and monitored every move of the "enemy." Their role was to log enemy shipping movements in and around the busy, deep-water port of Lisbon, to spread propaganda, and to disrupt the supply of vital goods to the enemy. Among the agents who visited Lisbon was a young Ian Fleming, busy devising Operation Golden Eye and playing blackjack at the Estoril Casino—a location that was to later provide the inspiration for a James Bond film. The Iberian Desk of the British Special Operations Executive (SOE) was led by the brilliant spy chief, and traitor, Kim Philby, who controlled the British agents operating in the city from London. The writers Graham Greene and Malcolm Muggeridge worked at the same desk as Philby, before Muggeridge was briefly posted to Lisbon and eventually on to the Portuguese colonies.

As the British and German agents watched each other, their movements were, in turn, shadowed and recorded by Captain Agostinho Lourenço's Portuguese secret police, the Polícia de Vigilância e Defesa do Estado (PVDE). Lourenço's reports and decisions determined which espionage activities in the city the authorities tolerated, and which they did not. As a number of British, German, and Italian secret agents, and journalists (including the local correspondent of the London *Times*) found to their cost, if you tried to cross Captain Lourenço, your stay in Portugal was severely shortened.

Lisbon was also the end of the line for escaped Allied prisoners of war (POWs) who arrived in the city to be flown back to

England on the three-times-per-week BOAC-operated flights from Lisbon to Whitchurch, near Bristol. The passenger lists of the flights were a who's who of the senior network of British spies in the city, as well as shadowy Allied industrialists involved in the trade war with the Germans. Competition for places on the planes was strong with various British agencies fighting for the limited number of seats. There were also instances when wealthy members of Lisbon's large Anglo community were caught trying to use the service to transport their maids down to Lisbon. The much loved British Hollywood actor, and star of *Gone with the Wind*, Leslie Howard, would fatefully take one of those flights. Allied and Axis agents operated at the airport twenty-four hours a day bribing local customs officials to gain access to the cargo and passenger lists of the enemy. Both BOAC and Lufthansa operated flights out of the city's airport, with their aircraft parked almost next to one another on the tarmac. Writing in 1944, the chief BOAC operations officer in the city described the daily scene at Lisbon's airport as being like the movie *Casablanca*, but twentyfold. During the hours of darkness, Lisbon Airport was highly susceptible to mist from the river, which added to its atmospheric mystery.

Central to the story of Lisbon is the Portuguese leader, António de Oliveira Salazar, who had come to power with the establishment of the *Estado Novo* in 1932. For Salazar, World War II presented a potentially lethal challenge to his regime, and to Portugal in general. Such was the concentration that Salazar devoted to steering Portugal through the war that, in addition to serving as prime minister for the duration of the war, he also served as minister of foreign affairs, minister of war, minister of the interior, and for the first part of the war, minister of finance. Salazar viewed it as his personal mission, and challenge, to prevent Portugal from being dragged into the war and repeating the mistakes of World War I.

Salazar believed that World War II brought two major threats to Portugal: a potential German, or Spanish invasion, and the possibility of Portugal losing its empire. Portugal had backed General Franco in the Spanish Civil War: Lisbon was used as a supply port for Franco's forces, and Salazar sent Portuguese brigades to fight on Franco's side. Despite this, there was still a feeling in Lisbon that Franco, and some of his key supporters, harbored territorial ambitions over Portugal. Recent unpublished documents indicate the existence of very detailed Spanish military plans for the invasion of Portugal during World War II.

The changing order of priorities for Salazar during World War II fit into two fairly distinct time periods. The first part of the war, 1939–1942, was devoted to preventing the threat of Axis (or proxy) invasion. The second part of the war, 1943–1945, was spent dealing with increasing Allied demands on Portugal, particularly over the Portuguese Atlantic Islands (the Azores)—where both the British and Americans planned secret invasions if Portugal did not comply with Allied demands. Although Salazar initially feared a German victory, as the war developed he became increasingly apprehensive about the prospects of a total Allied victory. Two issues worried him about this: what such an outcome would mean for Portugal and its colonies; and equally worryingly, what it would mean in terms of the power of the Soviet Union.

The Portuguese leader saw the major enemy of his regime, and indeed the coming threat to Europe as a whole, to be not Nazism but Communism, and specifically the Soviet Union. Salazar showed a cold war mentality well before the iron curtain fell over Eastern Europe. He believed that the internal Portuguese communist opposition would use the war (as indeed it did in 1944/45 with strikes and mass protests) as a means to mount a challenge against him. At different times during the war Salazar also suspected that Portugal's oldest ally, Britain, would prefer to see the back of his authoritarian regime and replace it with a more democratic government linked to the return of the Portuguese monarchy.

There was an additional crucial economic element to the role of Lisbon during World War II, which came to dominate Salazar's thinking during the war, and was to eventually lead to the country making a small fortune out of the war. Wolfram (also known as tungsten) was mined in Portugal. It was a vital ingredient of the German war machine. By 1943 the Germans and their European allies were almost totally dependent on Portuguese and Spanish wolfram to keep their armaments industry functioning. They threatened military action if Portugal bowed to Allied pressure to cut its sales to the Nazis. Given that the German army and air force were located only 270 miles from Portugal's eastern border, this threat was taken seriously in Lisbon.

The exporting of wolfram became conditional on payment in gold, and so another layer of intrigue entered Lisbon. During the war, gold was a far safer form of payment than paper currencies, but the Allies disputed the origins of a large percentage of the gold. They argued that gold had been looted by the Germans from the countries they had occupied, and later taken from the victims of the Holocaust. At the end of the war, Nazis smuggled gold into Lisbon on its way out to Brazil and from there dispersed it across South America to help finance their postwar Nazi communities in the region. To this day, the vaults of the Bank of Portugal are alleged to still contain gold bars stamped with the Nazi insignia. In an embarrassing revelation, the Catholic Church in Portugal was forced to admit that rebuilding work at the Catholic shrine in Fatima (north of Lisbon) was paid for with Nazi gold bars that the church had mysteriously acquired from the Bank of Portugal.

After the war, the Allies, while insisting that the actions of the Portuguese government in selling wolfram had, in effect, prolonged the war, did not make Portugal return the Nazi gold it had received in payment. Instead, a quiet accord was reached in which Portugal was allowed to keep nearly all of the gold in return for allowing the United States continued access to an airbase on the Azores. The Allies' decision was in stark contrast to the hard-line policy they adopted toward other neutral countries that had received Nazi gold and were made to return virtually all of it.

For Portugal, and the regime, the war represented as great an existential challenge as a literal battle for their lives would be, even though in practice no battlefield ever came to Portugal. The drama was to maneuver the country away from the attention of either of the warring powers. It was a policy of knife-edge neutrality, a poker game for the future. And in Salazar, Portugal possessed as wily a player as any of the belligerent nations. By 1945, Lisbon, and the wider country, not only emerged physically unscathed, but also much richer. Salazar was able to continue to rule Portugal until a stroke incapacitated him in 1968 and eventually led to his death in 1970. The Nazi gold remained largely untouched in Portuguese accounts scattered across the globe. This is the story of how Salazar and Lisbon got away with it, navigating the shadowy back alleys of wartime subterfuge to outwit fiercer and larger opponents.

CHAPTER 1

Sitting Out the War

LISBOETAS, SITTING AT PACKED PAVEMENT CAFÉS sipping coffee from tiny cups, learned of the outbreak of World War II from the morning newspapers, which were conveniently attached in each café to bamboo frames.[1] Smoking cigarettes while their shoes were vigorously polished by one of the grubby boys who hung around the central square known as Rossio, the almost exclusively male café goers digested the latest proclamation of the Portuguese government carried on the front page of every newspaper. The proclamation warned that, while the seat of war was distant, it could not be a matter of indifference to Portugal.[2] It went on to caution that the country could not expect to escape the reactions of a long and terrible war, and the government called upon the population to bear with fortitude the inevitable sacrifices and difficulties that lay ahead.[3]

Of greatest significance, however, was the confirmation that despite the defense obligations of an ancient alliance with England—the Anglo-Portuguese treaty of 1373, the oldest extant alliance in the world, which the government claimed it had no wish to refrain from confirming at so grave a moment—Portugal was not obliged to abandon its position of neutrality in the present emergency.[4] The statement did not amount to a formal declaration of neutrality, but its intent was obvious to all.[5] The dictatorship in Lisbon hoped to

quietly sit out the war.[6] Among the café goers in Rossio, and in the
wider country, there was widespread support for this policy of un-
declared neutrality.[7] The German minister in Lisbon made it clear
that, for the time being, such a policy was also acceptable to Berlin,
provided that Lisbon did not try to meet any of its "special obligations" to Britain.[8]

Decaying, shabby, and in desperate need of reinvention, Lisbon
in September 1939 was a neglected sleeping beauty of a city. A few
minutes' walk away from the glamour of Rossio café society, even
the spectacular deep blue autumn sky could not hide the truth that
many of the city's once beautiful buildings were revealing the consequences of decades of poor upkeep.

Plaster fell off houses in increasingly large chunks, to expose the
dirty gray interior cement work that lay beneath. Cracked ornate
blue decorative tiles urgently needed to be replaced. Broken windows were left unrepaired, the paint peeling from their rotting
frames. Shutters were covered in a layer of sandy-colored dirt from
the rain which, in the absence of any guttering, fell straight off the
overhanging roof tiles. Drying linen was hung from the increasingly rusty iron railings of balconies.[9] A strong smell of damp emanated from poorly maintained communal entrances to apartment
buildings, and many of the steep wooden staircases, which wound
up five or six floors, were caked in dust with rickety banisters that
had seen better days.

By day, Lisbon was full of deep rich colors, and despite the long
hot summer of 1939, the grass was a surprisingly dark and lush
shade of green. Orange, purple, and red flowers grew everywhere
and provided a sweet smell in contrast to the petrol-induced
smoggy haze that hung over the city on certain early autumn morn-
ings.[10] In the center of the city, strange looking trolley-trams rattled
over the rails, ringing their high-pitched bells. Speeding taxis
screeched as they crossed and recrossed the highly polished tram
rails that had warped in the heat.[11] In Lapa, the diplomatic area
and smart suburb to the west of the city center with superb vistas

to the river below, there was the constant noise of crane sirens and ships' horns emanating from the busy docks at the foot of the hill.[12] Foreign diplomats sat in shaded embassy gardens awaiting instructions from their respective governments, while continuing to mingle and party with Lisbon's small elite.[13]

During the hours of darkness, Lisbon was a noisy city, dogs barked and cocks crowed almost all night.[14] While the lights were going out across the rest of Europe, Lisbon remained brightly lit, with neon advertising signs glowing from the top of buildings lending additional illumination to the brilliant white light of the street lamps.[15] River mist and fog often rolled in at night, giving a distinctly noir movie atmosphere. The city, with its narrow streets and high-walled gardens, resembled Naples or Sicily more than any city in neighboring Spain.[16]

The Avenida de Liberdade, which ran out of the top of the Rossio climbing gently straight up towards the city park, was the Champs-Élysées of Lisbon. The Avenida had opened in 1882 and was the finest road in Lisbon. It was 1,500 meters long and 90 meters wide, and was home to two theaters, four cinemas, and several streetside cafés. Many of the city's glamorous luxury hotels such as the Hotel Tivoli and Hotel Aviz were located along, or close to, its wide tree-lined boulevards.[17]

The Hotel Aviz became the permanent home of the financial refugee, Calouste Gulbenkian, known as Mr. Five Percent for the share of oil wealth that accrued to him from deals across the Middle East. Gulbenkian was reputed to be the richest man in the world. He arrived in Lisbon during the war, after the Portuguese had provided him with assurances about his financial empire. More often than not, Gulbenkian dined alone in the hotel with his secretary and valet sitting at a table close by, in case their services were required.[18] Later in the war, Gulbenkian would run into trouble with the Allies over the attempted sale of a 2 percent stake that he owned in the Reichsbank.[19] He claimed improbably that he needed to sell these shares, valued at 3 million marks, in order to meet his personal and business needs in Portugal.[20]

Using his considerable wealth, which was readily available to him, Gulbenkian bought art from Jews who were in financial distress in Lisbon. The American embassy in Lisbon reported that he purchased a number of masterpieces from Henry Rothschild, who was a refugee in the city.[21] The works came from the National Gallery in London, and according to Allied sources, Gulbenkian made three payments to Rothschild totalling 1,355,000 escudos (approximately $54,200).[22] Working away in his hotel suite, Gulbenkian was uninterrupted in his business transactions during the war, although he was closely monitored by the British embassy in Lisbon and by the Treasury in London.[23]

The summer of 1939 had not been a vintage year for Lisbon hotels. Room occupancy rates were down, due in part to the small number of foreign visitors to the city, and also to the aftereffects of a difficult decade that saw Portugal struggle to emerge from the economic depression.[24] Lisbon in 1939 was well off the beaten track for most foreign tourists. Those who did venture to Lisbon flocked to its coast and, in particular, the seaside resort of Estoril, complete with its casino and mild year-round climate. Everything, however, was about to change, as within one year Lisbon's hotels would be full to overflowing with refugees, diplomats, and spies from both sides in the war. Hotels had to open additional wings, or annexes, to try to meet the increased demand. Even so, finding a room in a Lisbon hotel from 1940 to 1942 was no easy task.

Almost overnight, after the outbreak of the war, Lisbon became one of the major centers of world affairs: Its geographical position; its excellent shipping facilities for traffic to the Mediterranean, and to North and South America; the strategic importance of the Azores and the Portuguese colonies in Africa and the Far East; and the existence in Portugal of vitally needed raw materials such as wolfram gave Lisbon a sudden importance to the plans of both sides in the war.[25] Naturally, all of this newfound importance had a potential downside: If Lisbon did not reassure each side of its neutrality, then it faced at least economic sanctions from the Allied powers, and outright invasion by the Germans, possibly with the help of the Spanish. One man, as a result, faced the ultimate challenge of trying to successfully navigate Portugal, and its colonies, through the geopolitics of World War II.[26]

CHAPTER 2

The Most Beautiful
Dictator

PORTUGAL'S LEADER, DR. ANTÓNIO DE OLIVEIRA
Salazar, whom one senior British official described as the most
physically beautiful of all the European dictators, sat alone in his
sparsely furnished office in the prime minister's residence behind
the magnificent Palace of São Bento, assessing the international
situation on a daily basis.[1] As usual his desk was crammed with well
ordered piles of official papers and correspondence. A photograph
of a sombre looking Benito Mussolini sat on the right. When later
Salazar became disillusioned with Mussolini, the picture was replaced by one of the pope.

Salazar was frugal; he didn't use heating.[2] Instead, he worked
with a rug round him and, to further insulate himself from the cold
Lisbon winter, he also wore his overcoat when he worked at his
desk.[3] Salazar's thrifty and simple approach to his work life was
heavily highlighted in Portuguese newspapers of the era such as *O
Seculo*.[4] The idea was to try to install the values of Salazar into the
ordinary Portuguese.

A man hugely dedicated to his job and country, Salazar was determined that his carefully crafted policy of neutrality would save
the nation, and the Portuguese empire, from the horrors of war.

At the start of World War II, Salazar served as the president of the Council (prime minister), a position that he had occupied since 1932. Salazar, however was no believer in primus inter pares and he simultaneously also held the cabinet portfolios of war, foreign affairs, and finance. In this respect, his style of rule resembled more that of Benito Mussolini of Italy, who also held multiple portfolios during times of crisis, than the Spanish dictator General Francisco Franco, who never headed a ministry.[5]

Political power, as a result, was almost totally centralized in Salazar's hands, whose love of detail, ability to work long hours, and apparent lack of interest in a social life or family allowed him to deal personally and directly with issues, which other leaders would have delegated to their lieutenants.[6] The huge amount of personal and political correspondence that Salazar got through during this period is testament to his ability to take an interest in managing almost all affairs of state.

Salazar's typical working day started with breakfast at eight-thirty, during which he read the newspapers, after which he worked, usually in his office, until two.[7] Between two and four, he took a fifteen-minute lunch, a walk, and met with visitors.[8] From four until six, he rested and took a walk in the gardens of his residence at São Bento and from six until nine, he was back at his desk. After this he had a light supper by himself before returning to work until midnight.[9] He rarely changed his routine. He wasn't teetotal—with his meals, he enjoyed a glass of wine from the Dão region where he had been born—he never smoked, and he enjoyed reading the latest editions of economic journals in order to relax and keep abreast of developments in the academic study of the economy.[10]

Salazar was clearly one of the most intellectually gifted men of his generation. A university professor at Coimbra, he stood head and shoulders above the other political and economic personalities of the day in Lisbon.[11] He remains, however, one of the most divisive figures in Portuguese history. Given Salazar's continued controversial status in Portugal, and internationally, it comes as little surprise that his wartime policies remain misrepresented, misinterpreted, or simply misunderstood in many of the accounts of Portugal and World War II.[12]

Salazar was the son of a small freeholder in the hamlet of Vimieiro, near the dreary town of Santa Comba Dão in the province of Beira Alta in central Portugal. He was originally destined to become a priest, and undertook much of the required training and learning to fulfil this aim.[13] Although Salazar gave up on his attempt to join the Catholic Church, he never really left it. The influence of the church could be seen in both his personal conduct and also in the philosophy and policies of the governments he led. The powerful role of the church among Portugal's mainly peasant rural population was a central feature of Portuguese society.

After studying law at Coimbra University, Salazar accepted a teaching position. He never married, although he evidently enjoyed the company of women. There is a story that his first, and perhaps greatest, love ended badly when her parents thought that Salazar, the son of a peasant, had few future prospects and forbade the girl to see him anymore.[14] It is said that when he returned to Santa Comba Dão for the funeral of his mother—he was already prime minister—he spoke to the girl, but not to her parents.

This setback came as something of a jolt to the academically brilliant and socially confident Salazar. It was a stark reminder to him of the existing social order of the day.[15] For much of his life, a peasant girl, Dona Maria, who went with Salazar to Lisbon and served as a type of housekeeper, looked after him. She was said to be familiar with some of the affairs of state, but had little influence over Salazar's thinking. She remained with him throughout his thirty-six years as prime minister, and until his death in 1970.

———

It was during his time in Coimbra that Salazar met Manuel Cerejeira, a priest from the Minho district in northwestern Portugal. The two men came to share a house in what was a usual arrangement at Coimbra University in a *republica* (a house where students live). Salazar and Cerejeira lived together from 1915–1928, a period that covered their student days and the early part of their respective careers.

Years later, while talking about Salazar to the French writer Christine Garnier, Cerejeira described him as a man of many contrasts.[16] He argued that Salazar enjoyed the physical beauty of women, but lived the life of a monk.[17] He also pointed out that there was always a sense of conflict going on in Salazar's head between skepticism and passion and between kindness and harshness.[18] In truth, Salazar's friendship with Cerejeira was an important stage in helping him develop his academic power base within the University in Coimbra.[19] In later years however, the friendship of the two old housemates would be placed under great stress.

Both men were destined to eventually leave the comfort and ordered life of Coimbra University and came to Lisbon. Once in Lisbon they were to move up rapidly through the respective ranks of the political and church hierarchies to assume the two central positions in Portugal: head of the government, and head of the Catholic Church. Cerejeira rose the through the ranks of the Catholic Church to become initially, in 1929, the patriarch of Lisbon. A month after becoming patriarch, he was appointed cardinal and served for nearly forty-eight years.

In 1928, Salazar arrived in Lisbon, very much an outsider to the establishment, to be appointed minister of finance. As the British noted from the moment he entered the government armed with dictatorial powers, Dr. Salazar addressed himself to the task of regenerating his country.[20] Working with incredible zeal and showing great stamina, Salazar tried, almost unaided, to turn the economy around. He wrote up his own reports, carefully studied economic conditions, and personally went through the books of each government department to see if it were possible to make major improvements and savings.[21]

Eventually, with a series of well-planned reforms, and without course to foreign borrowing, he succeeded in placing the public finances on a sound footing.[22] Salazar had also endowed the country with a long period of internal political stability, unknown during the previous Republican epoch.[23] Even when governments fell he remained in place as minister of finance before finally being appointed to lead the country in 1932.

There is some debate as to how original his economic reforms really were, and also some disputes over the authenticity of the economic data of the era, but it is clear that his policies helped save Portugal from virtual collapse. Indeed, the resulting legitimacy of the dictatorship he eventually formed and led was based on economic successes rather than personal charisma or military victories. This type of legitimacy set him aside from the other European dictators of the era.

Despite these economic successes, the agricultural workers and industrial wage earners who continued to have to live on their meager wages did not regard his regime with any enthusiasm. His loftily worded addresses explaining his ideology and rationale for policy went over their heads. As a result of his failure to connect with the masses or overtly improve their economic lot, there was a large degree of widespread opposition to the regime, and to Salazar in particular, from divergent forces, many of which were related to the communists.[24]

For Salazar, the onset of World War II was not just about a challenge to the sovereignty of the nation but also, given his belief that opposition forces would use the war as a catalyst to attempt to overthrow him, to the future survival of the regime. This internal dimension to the war was never far from Salazar's mind and to some extent drove his policies towards the war.

The British Foreign Office characterized "Salazar the man" as having the shrewdness and parsimonious habits of the peasant; the native caution of the village dweller who mistrusts the prattle of the marketplace and the motives of others; and the cold detached outlook of the scholastic churchman who has been taught to appraise the puppet show of human endeavor sub specie aeternitatis. Added to the principles of canon law and of orthodox political and economic theory imbedded in his student days at Coimbra, moreover, was the pedagogic training acquired after graduation, during the years when Salazar joined the university faculty in the inbred intellectual atmosphere of this ancient and very old-fashioned seat of learning.[25]

Flatteringly, the Spanish leader, General Francisco Franco, stated in an interview with *Le Figaro* that Salazar was the most complete statesman, and the one most worthy of respect, that he had known.[26] Franco went on to say that he regarded him as an extraordinary personality for his intelligence, his political sense and his humanity. Salazar's only defect, he added, was his modesty.[27]

By the end of the 1930s Salazar had clearly developed into a respected international statesman, and the majority of the Portuguese population were either generally supportive of his regime or saw it simply as inevitable. The country remained terribly poor, but there was a degree of economic and political stability. Salazar understood, however, that all his accomplishments were imperiled if the country had to participate in a costly war.

CHAPTER 3

Preparing for the Worst

AS A MAJOR WAR LOOKED EVER MORE LIKELY, SALAZAR spent much of the first part of 1939 carefully planning how Portugal would respond to such a development. In meetings with officials, and in long solo walks in the large secluded garden that surrounded his office, Salazar had thought through a policy that, in the event of war, would see Portugal attempt to stay neutral. Salazar's famed analytical and intellectual skills were hardly required to arrive at such a policy. With a small and badly equipped military force, and with its old ally, Britain, unable or unwilling, to formally guarantee its sovereignty, Lisbon had no real means of defense and therefore its best option appeared to try to remain outside of the fray.[1] The notion of neutrality was a logical policy option, but what was going to prove more challenging for Salazar was how to maintain this position of neutrality as Portugal, and its colonies, became ever more important to both warring sides.

Salazar proudly proclaimed to the National Assembly in a speech on October 9, 1939, that on no account would Portugal take advantage of its position of neutrality to make business out of the war.[2] It is clear, however, that, for a variety of reasons, including his own strong economic instincts, Salazar could not resist the temptation of breaking this promise at almost every stage.[3]

Salazar's speech, and especially the promise not to cash in on the war, was widely reported in the British press. Among many British newspaper readers there remained a sense of mystery as to how Britain's oldest ally should, in the hour of need, choose to remain neutral. During the speech, Salazar had strongly reaffirmed the Anglo-Portuguese alliance, and had explained how England approved of Portugal's neutrality.[4]

The speech did reveal another vital part of Salazar's priorities, the importance of the maintenance of the integrity of the Portuguese empire.[5] In truth, despite his ice coolness in dealing with diplomatic matters, Salazar had been extremely irritated by the British government, and the consequences for Lisbon of Neville Chamberlain's policy of appeasement towards Germany—a policy that led the government in London to offer parts of the Portuguese empire to Germany without the consent of Lisbon.

The British double dealing involved an offer reputedly made by an increasingly desperate Chamberlain to Adolf Hitler the previous year to try to resolve the German colonial issue once and for all. Among other concessions to Germany, Chamberlain offered Portuguese-controlled Angola. Hitler was reportedly initially interested in the offer and asked what would happen if the Portuguese objected. Chamberlain said that, in the end, Portugal and the other colonial powers involved would cooperate. He went on to argue, however, that it was vital to keep the plan secret from Lisbon and the other powers at the present. Great effort was made to brief the British press to keep the proposals quiet, but there was a strong suspicion in Lisbon of what the British were up to with Hitler. In the end, Chamberlain's offer came to nothing: The Fuhrer rejected the offer arguing that the colonial question could wait for up to ten years to be resolved.[6]

Lisbon's irritation with the British over the colonial issue could be traced back further, to the Peace Conference that followed the end of World War I. Portugal had started the war as a neutral, but later its forces joined the fighting. Portugal's ill-trained and poorly equipped soldiers suffered heavily in France with around 700 killed and 33,000 total casualties.[7] In percentage terms, total fatalities amounted to 7 percent of the total mobilized Portuguese fighting force.[8] Although these figures are not as dramatic as those from the major participants in the war, the resulting political instability in Lisbon after the war was profound. To add to the injuries, during the Peace Conference, the Portuguese correctly suspected that the Allies were proposing to transfer a part of Angola to Belgium in order to give the Belgian Congo an Atlantic Coast.[9] At the conference, the Portuguese had also failed to secure additional lands from German East Africa to add onto Mozambique.[10] In Lisbon, the British were old—but not entirely trustworthy—allies.

The British ambassador in Lisbon, Sir Walford Selby, was a regular visitor to Salazar's office and enjoyed a somewhat distant workmanlike relationship with the Portuguese leader. By his own admission, Selby was in the twilight of his diplomatic career and represented the old school of the Foreign Office.[11] He had previously served as a private secretary to five foreign ministers, and Lisbon was to be his last job before he retired at the age of sixty.[12]

Selby was viewed as bureaucratically sound but, according to a colleague, he lacked self-confidence and did not have good oral skills or powers of persuasion. In times of peace, Selby, the old-fashioned English gentleman who got on well with Portuguese officials, was more than competent, but amid the intrigues of war he lacked the stamina and dynamism to be head of mission in a city that moved to the center stage of world events.[13] As David Eccles, who worked for the Ministry of Economic Warfare out of Lisbon and Madrid suggested, it was not in the wartime interest of His Majesty's Government (HMG) to be represented by someone who couldn't deal effectively with Dr. Salazar.[14]

Selby's opposite number, the Portuguese ambassador to London, Armindo Monteiro, was nearly as British as Selby. He spoke better English than most Englishmen, and had all the mannerisms of an old–fashioned, public school–educated, upper-class English gent. It will come as little surprise that Monteiro was a highly popular personality with leading conservative politicians and the British Foreign Office. Monteiro, a former Portuguese foreign minister, was a strong Anglophile who had spent the prewar period developing close personal relationships with the political and diplomatic elite in London. He was skeptical of General Francisco Franco, and believed that the Falangists posed a major threat to Lisbon's independence.

In Monteiro's opinion, Portugal's best course of action was to tie itself closely into the old alliance with England. As World War II developed, Monteiro's role became central to Lisbon's relationship with London, and he would increasingly come to disagree with Salazar's wartime policy. The detailed and, at times, passionate correspondence between Salazar and Monteiro remains one of the most interesting chronicles of Lisbon's role in the war.

At the start of the war, both Monteiro and Selby noted a growing number of misunderstandings between Lisbon and London over the question of Portuguese neutrality.[15] For Salazar the aims of neutrality were clear. He did not view neutrality as a rigid policy, but rather one that could be adapted to events and changing circumstances during the war. Salazar understood that to some extent, he would have to play both sides and also that he would in turn, be played by both sides. What was more important for Salazar was achieving his own wartime objectives: to prevent an invasion of Portugal by Germany or Spain or both, which would result in the occupation of his Lisbon and his having to flee and lead a government in exile. He also wanted to avoid Portugal being used as a battleground by foreign armies. The Peninsular Wars between Britain and France in the nineteenth century led to large parts of the Portuguese royal family, and economic and political elite fleeing to Brazil, where they set up court and helped to develop their new home.[16] Many never returned; the detrimental impact on the pace of development in Portugal, and increase in political instability, was felt for decades.[17]

Two additional aspects of the Peninsular Wars were not forgotten in Lisbon. The British destroyed much of the center of the country with their "scorched earth" policy against Napoleon's armies, an action that took away some of the country's best agricultural lands.[18] While the war almost bankrupted Portugal, the Rothschild family, and in particular Nathan Rothschild, made a fortune out of it by effectively bankrolling the Duke of Wellington's campaign.[19] Part of Nathan Rothschild's process of getting money to Wellington involved the smuggling of gold bullion.

Even a less gifted student than Salazar would have been able to quote the more recent example of Portugal's involvement in World War I as a rationale for remaining neutral in World War II. Portugal initially declared its neutrality at the start of that war, but eventually joined the Allies in 1916 with disastrous consequences for the internal political, social, and economic stability of Lisbon. In truth, the link between external events and challenges to the continued rule of his authoritarian regime was never far from Salazar's mind. In the autumn of 1939, while devoting considerable time to the present, Salazar also had an eye on the future, and what Europe and the world would resemble at the conclusion of the war.

Salazar's worldview had not been developed through visits to foreign lands—he had rarely traveled out of Portugal—but through scholarly reading and good old rational thought.[20] The major challenge during the early part of the war was to deal with the perceived threat of an invasion of Portugal by Germany, or a proxy one by Spain. The British Chiefs of Staff calculated that if Spain launched a military invasion of Portugal it would take them just under three weeks to reach Lisbon and, in effect, take over the country.

Salazar was aware that there were elements within Spain who saw the takeover of Portugal as a major part of Spanish imperialist territorial ambitions. These claims were widely disseminated in Falangist propaganda against Lisbon.[21] On June 16, 1939, for example, the London *Evening Standard* had reported a story that Spanish "fascists" had urged the seizure of Portugal. The fascists correctly claimed that Portugal had no effective military power to defend her home or colonial territory.

The story was in turn picked up by the Portuguese Secret Police, the PVDE (*Polícia de Vigilância e de Defesa do Estado*) and was cataloged in their reports of external propaganda, then subsequently passed onto the Portuguese leadership. [22] That would not happen until May 1941, however, when Spain drew up formal preliminary detailed plans for the invasion of Portugal. At the time, one of General Franco's aides suggested to a German diplomat that a war against Portugal would be a useful diversion from Spain's internal political troubles.[23]

CHAPTER 4

Mixed Messages

SALAZAR, SITTING IN HIS LISBON OFFICE AT THE outbreak of World War II, was not unduly fearful of the imperialist agenda of General Franco towards Portugal, at least compared to his concern that Spain might declare support for the Germans and join the Axis powers. Here Salazar found common ground with the British, who were desperately concerned that Spain would throw its lot in with Germany—which, like Salazar, had supported Franco during the Spanish Civil War. In Germany, there was growing frustration that Spain had not immediately joined the Axis powers, and Hitler brought strong pressure to bear on Franco to fall into line. Unwittingly, Salazar had found a vital role for himself and Lisbon: to persuade Franco to remain out of the war.

During the initial stages of the war, the British used Salazar's relationship with Franco to relay messages to the Spanish leader, and to help convince him to accept specific British economic and political policies towards the Iberian Peninsula. Ambassador Selby passed on requests from the Foreign Office and the Ministry of Economic Warfare. After the war, historians and participants hotly debated the role Salazar played in ensuring Spanish neutrality. Many factors contributed to the Spanish decision, not least the tide of war turning from 1942 onwards against the Axis powers, but the role of Salazar in reassuring and, at times, convincing Franco that neutrality remained the best policy and should not be underestimated. Salazar's role appears all the more remarkable given that his country was under direct threat of invasion from its bigger neighbor.

By the spring of 1940 Lisbon was starting to experience the impact of both the Allied and German propaganda campaigns to try to curry favor with the Portuguese. Salazar was somewhat irritated by the efforts of both sides.[1] He tried—largely in vain—to prevent some of their media activities through his state censor, who blocked the publication of offensive articles or certain films. Early German efforts were largely conducted by mail in an attempt to try to evade the censor.[2] Pamphlets depicting German war successes were produced locally and sent from Madrid.[3]

British propaganda in Lisbon was initially limited: London didn't produce much and the Lisbon-based reporters of British newspapers had difficulty interesting their respective editors in Lisbon. When the British propaganda machine did eventually grind into gear, much of the material produced resembled their German counterparts' material in style and layout. Later in the war, Malcolm Muggeridge, who was based in Lisbon while working for British intelligence, noted on his walks two adjoining shops that were exhibiting British and German propaganda pictures and publications, which he felt rather oddly resembled one another.[4] Different brands of the same commodity, he suggested, like Coke and Pepsi.[5]

During this "phony" stage of the war in late 1939, the German propaganda machine in Lisbon attempted to convince Salazar that the British were planning to try to overthrow him and his authoritarian government.[6] Indeed, German propaganda went further, suggesting that the British were threatening the life of Salazar.[7] For some time before, Salazar had suspected, wrongly, that the British were growing increasingly frustrated with his regime, and wanted to replace it with a return of the Portuguese monarchy and some form of democratic government.[8] Salazar was right about the

British frustration, but wrong about any concerted or coordinated British plot to get rid of him.

The Germans' efforts to sow the seeds of paranoia in Salazar's head were part of a wider scheme employed by both the Allies and Axis powers operating in Lisbon to try to convince the Portuguese of the true identity of their real enemies. Both the Allies and Axis powers believed that Salazar could be brought more onto their respective side once he understood where Lisbon's best interest lay. In reality, Salazar proved far too clever for most of these plots to stand any chance of success.

At the early stage of the war there was growing concern among the large and vocal Anglo community in Lisbon that the Germans were winning the propaganda battle. As one British expat noted, German propaganda was as fierce as ever. He went on to warn that the Germans were spreading ridiculous rumors about the British and the French, and that the Portuguese were not at all sure which was the winning side. Another British resident suggested that while Germany gained ground and conquered further sympathies, Britain was losing ground.[9]

Under pressure from London, Selby raised the issue of German propaganda, and other activities, with the Portuguese on May 8, 1940, and received a lame assurance that any foreigner abusing the hospitality afforded him would be punished accordingly.[10] Subsequently, German activity in Lisbon intensified rather than dwindled, and by June 1940 there were calls from some senior figures in Lisbon's Anglo community for a change of policy at the British embassy in the city.[11]

The German ambassador to Portugal, Baron Oswald von Hoyningen-Huene was playing the game very cleverly.[12] A man of the old aristocratic school of the German diplomatic service, Hoyningen-Huene had been busy developing closer ties between Berlin and Lisbon during the prewar period. He studied, and understood, Portuguese history and culture, and appealed to the nationalist sentiments of Salazar and other senior Portuguese personalities.[13] He gave talks at universities in Lisbon and Coimbra on the past glories of the Portuguese Empire and positioned himself as a strong supporter of the culture and symbols of the Portuguese *Estado Novo*. Naturally, all of this was designed to appeal to Salazar, who, to some extent, took the bait without ever developing close personal ties with the ambassador. After the war, however, Salazar allowed Hoyningen-Huene to settle permanently in the Lisbon area, where he lived out his retirement.

Sharp, clever, and diplomatically astute, Hoyningen-Huene was good at socializing and an obsessive networker. He was a regular guest at the high table of the dinner parties of the Portuguese and international elite in Lisbon during the war, and saw his mission as trying to loosen Anglo-Portuguese ties. Hoyningen-Huene was to play a central role in Lisbon as the war developed, and in particular in the negotiations over vitally important wolfram supplies from Portugal to Germany. The British duly noted that he was a very able man, and his impressive performance led, in part, to the decision to replace Selby with a more suitable ambassador to deal with the German propaganda onslaught.[14]

In the early stages of the war the German propaganda effort in Lisbon was best served by the continued military successes of Hitler.[15] The greater the success, the more reluctant the Portuguese were becoming to mention the old alliance with Britain for fear of antagonizing the Germans. The government in Lisbon, simply, was showing signs of wanting to back the side that looked most likely to win the war. On the ground, Muggeridge noted that when the war was going badly for the Allies, the Portuguese fell over themselves trying to please the Germans.[16] He also observed that the number and rank of Portuguese officials that would show up at a garden party at British Consulate-Generals rose and fell in relation to the latest communiqués from the front.[17]

As the war developed, so the quantity and quality of the propaganda from both sides increased. In newspapers, at newsstands, and in dedicated shops, the Allies and Germans competed for people's attention. There is little evidence, however, to suggest that all the effort, time, and money that both sides put into their campaigns led to any major change of public sentiment in Lisbon towards the warring sides.

The more pressing issue for Salazar than propaganda was the organization of the defense of Lisbon and Portugal. This issue had become something of another prewar bone of contention between Lisbon and London. There were two important related problems. The first centered upon a potential renegotiation of terms of the historic alliance between the two countries, modifying Britain's obligation to defend Portugal and encouraging Portugal to become more self-reliant. The second concerned the sale of arms by Britain to Portugal. The British had hoped to sell Lisbon arms in order to help develop the Portuguese armed forces and increase the Portuguese army's ability to defend the country. At various stages of the negotiations over arms sales, Salazar procrastinated, arguing that many of the arms that the British were trying to sell were overpriced and already obsolete. The process was torturous and created a degree of ill feeling between the two countries. In the end, and much to British annoyance, Salazar looked to other countries to supply much of Portugal's arms—including Germany.

During the spring of 1940, the ongoing question of the best way to defend Lisbon was set against the backdrop of French reports of Spanish troop movements towards the Portuguese border.[18] In the atmosphere of nervousness in Lisbon, such rumors and reports added to the already high state of anxiety. The British added to the paranoia by accusing the Axis powers of attempting to create the conditions for a coup, which would be used as the trigger for Spanish intervention in Portugal.[19]

In fact, the War Office in London viewed the original French source of the reported Spanish troop concentration with a degree of skepticism.[20] In Lisbon, Walford Selby thought the rumors unduly alarmist, unless Italy joined the war.[21] The British War Cabinet accepted his judgment, but did call for a paper on the prospects of potential Axis intervention in Portugal.[22] The reports, however, did help focus minds on how best to defend Lisbon and what options there were for both the leadership in Lisbon and for the Allies if the country was invaded by a hostile power. For Salazar personally it was a stark reminder that one of the warring powers could use internal opposition to his regime as a pretext for taking over the country.

Just as the Lisboeta café goers in the Rossio were becoming increasingly apprehensive about the war—which had initially appeared so distant but now seemed to be involving Portugal, just as Salazar had warned—Salazar offered the people of Lisbon something to take their minds off the war: a huge exhibition and fair to celebrate Portugal's past glories as well as salute the achievements of his regime. It was pure political theater, and its timing, in helping to reassure the local population, was perfect. The message was clear: While France might be on fire, all was well in Lisbon during the long hot summer of 1940.

CHAPTER 5

Forget About Your Troubles

T HE EXPOSIÇÃO DO MUNDO PORTUGUÊS (PORTUGUESE World Exhibition) marked the anniversary of the founding of the Portuguese nation in 1140, and its independence from Spain in 1640. It was an ambitious project that reflected the attempt by Salazar to remind the Portuguese people of the historic role of Portugal in the world. It also served the purpose of being a major propaganda boost for the ideology, values, and symbols of the Estado Novo.[1]

There is a famous black-and-white photograph of Salazar taken during the opening ceremony of the exhibition. Salazar is giving instructions to a group of men with a portly man with a huge smile looking on at the scene.[2] One of the men to whom Salazar was giving instructions was Duarte Pacheco, the most important figure behind the public works program and the man responsible for the physical side of the exhibition. The gentleman looking on was António Ferro, a former journalist and biographer of Salazar, who was charged with crafting the philosophy of the Estado Novo and its implementation. Pacheco was the visionary, the translator of lofty projects into reality and Ferro the spin doctor in charge of developing propaganda and spreading the message. Both men were close to Salazar, had played roles in bringing him to the leadership and were vital to the exhibition, and to all the projects and propaganda of the Estado Novo.

Duarte Pacheco had become president of the Lisbon Municipality at the end of 1938. He also served at various times as minister of public works and communications.[3] One of the most colorful characters in the regime, he was known to have great charm and enjoyed a reputation for being a man who got things done.[4] His charm was lost on some, however, particularly the landowners whose land the Estado Novo took, at prices well below the market rate.[5] His public works projects changed the physical landscape of Lisbon and the surrounding areas.

Exposição do Mundo Português was a project on a grand scale and was very much in tune with the intensive program of public works that the Estado Novo was undertaking in the Lisbon area. The Estrada Marginal, a major road linking the city with its coast out to the fishing village of Cascais, was opened. The first motorway was built, the city's international airport opened in October 1942, and new ferry port terminals linked the city with its satellites across the river.[6] New housing projects were begun in the suburbs, which aimed to transform the generally poor housing conditions in Lisbon. Water supplies were brought to parts of the city for the first time, solving a long-standing problem. Critics of the public works programme argued with some merit that these grand projects were never brought in on anything approaching budget, and that the process of awarding contracts was used to reward the friends of the regime.[7] The Portuguese secret police, the PVDE, reported that there was a feeling of resentment among many ordinary Portuguese about the cost of the projects and the lack of improvement in the economic and housing conditions for the majority of the city's inhabitants.[8] Salazar quickly dismissed these, and other rumors, as communist propaganda.[9]

Duarte Pacheco died on November 16, 1943, the victim of a horrific car crash the previous day. His funeral was a large state affair in which Salazar led the mourners. Writing in his diary on that day, Salazar nostalgically recalled that it had been Pacheco who had originally come to Coimbra in 1928 to offer him the post of minister of finance when others wanted somebody else to take the post.[10] He also admitted how much he would miss him. Pacheco had been with Salazar since the start, and his death left Salazar more internally isolated. Much of Pacheco's legacy can still be viewed in contemporary Lisbon. The chances are that any visitor to the city today will use the airport and the roads that were part of Pacheco's vision and projects of the late 1930s and early 1940s.

Pacheco's exhibition was built near the bank of the River Tagus in Lisbon at Belém. The choice of the location was deliberately highly symbolic.[11] The area represented the "Golden Age" in the eyes of the Portuguese, when their maritime power was at its height. The building works for the exhibition took over two years to complete and involved, at its peak, some 5,000 workers. No doubt mindful of the costs of the project, Salazar took a close interest in the planning and construction of the exhibition, making sure that everything would be ready on time.

Construction work was temporarily halted for a month when World War II broke out, but a decision was taken that the exhibition should go ahead despite the war. The exhibition site was comprised of a series of pavilions that were dedicated to the founding of the nation, the discoveries, and the independence of the nation from Spain. There was also a large pavilion dedicated to the achievements of the Estado Novo as well as its future plans. Other parts of the exhibition highlighted traditional Portuguese villages, costumes, and culture.

The newly created buildings and monuments aimed at reflecting the memory of the past glories of the country and linking it to the present works and ideological narrative of the dictatorship. Put simply, it was intended to reflect the attempt of Salazar, and Ferro, of creating a single version of history and linking this to the modern in order to reinforce a collective national culture based on the values of the Estado Novo.[12] It was opened in June 1940, and by the time it closed its doors on December 2, 1940, nearly 3 million people had visited the site.[13] On the surface, this appears to be a satisfactory number, but it masks the fact that there were very few foreign visitors. Since the opening of the exhibition coincided with the German advance on France, almost no visitors from abroad were able to see it.

Despite the timing, the opening ceremony of the exhibition was a lavish affair with much pomp and ceremony. Formally dressed political and church leaders enjoying the fine weather toured the exhibition site. In the evening there was a colorful fireworks display that lit up the skies above much of the city and the river. The images of Salazar and the various VIPs touring the site appeared almost surreal, as at that very moment fighting raged in France, and German soldiers marched towards the French-Spanish border.

The Duke of Kent represented the British royal family at the Exposição do Mundo Português and paid an extended visit to Lisbon in the summer of 1940. Salazar personally handled the arrangements for the duke's visit to Lisbon, and both the British and the Portuguese saw his trip as a propaganda opportunity.[14] Indeed, the British keenly noted and reported Portuguese praise for the duke's visit and in the local press.[15] While the duke's visit did little to reduce the increasing tension in Anglo-Portuguese relations, it offered a reassuring reminder of Britain's engagement with Portugal, where it was seen as a huge success.

The Duke of Kent's tour guide around the various exhibits and monuments was a close friend of Salazar, the Portuguese banker and head of Banco Espírito Santo (BES), Ricardo Espírito Santo e Silva. If Salazar was the leading Portuguese political personality of the era in Lisbon, so Ricardo Espírito Santo was the major financial figure of the same period. The two men were close and the unusually intimate tone of correspondence from Espírito Santo to Salazar reflected this friendship.

Handsome, suave, always beautifully dressed in Savile Row suits, and fluent in several European languages, Ricardo Espírito Santo played a major role in the wartime dealings between Portugal and the Axis powers. He was married to the daughter of a prominent Jewish family from Gibraltar. He had built the championship golf course at Estoril and was himself a national golf champion. The golf course was one of the many venues he used to mix with the Portuguese and international elite. The British famously described him as a man of undoubted ability and of boundless ambition in financial and social spheres. They went on to suggest that he was very much addicted to all the amusements of international society and was agreeable, clever, and cultivated, but self-seeking above all. His ruling passion in life was described as making money.[16]

In truth, Espírito Santo was more than simply a leading banker. He was, to some extent, Salazar's eyes and ears among the families of the Portuguese elite, as well as the foreign diplomats and royals who found themselves temporarily (or permanently) based in the Lisbon area. He was also an informal adviser to Salazar on a number of issues, and this point provided him and his business empire a degree of political cover, which proved useful when the British and the American governments grew increasingly critical of his financial dealings with the Germans.[17]

Espírito Santo's professional and personal relationship with Salazar was naturally also a source of jealousy among many other of the wealthy banking and industrial families in Lisbon. During the war, in the arena of economic warfare, it is clear that on several occasions Espírito Santo and his empire were targeted by rivals keen to see him and his bank placed on the blacklist of companies that the British Ministry of Economic Warfare (MEW) had introduced. The story of Ricardo Espírito Santo and BES remains very much at the center of the tale of Lisbon during the war. Like Salazar, Espírito Santos's role in the war remains very much misrepresented and misunderstood by many people.

The summer of 1940 brought the war to Lisbon. The attempt of Salazar to quietly sit out the war quietly appeared to have failed. The German invasion of France took its army to the French-Spanish border. For Lisboetas taking advantage of the early summer warm weather to sunbathe on the beaches at Estoril and Cascais, the war had become a major topic of conversation. There was much talk about the operation at Dunkirk and the stoic virtues of the British in general.[18]

Before the fall of France there had been widespread indifference towards the war from Lisbon's chattering classes, but afterwards, there was a feeling of deep anxiety and fear.[19] Among parts of the local economic elite, there was also a sense that there was money to be made out of the war, and this opportunism was privately encouraged by the regime. Double dealing was to become heavily institutionalized during the war years as Lisbon sought to reverse its slow decline and state of decay. In the summer of 1940, Lisbon was a city in deep transformation, from being a spectator in the war to a center of wartime activities and intrigues.

CHAPTER 6

Wartime Refugees

DURING THE WARM SUMMER EVENINGS OF 1940, THE lights of Lisbon continued to shine brightly with the neon signs on top of buildings advertising goods from Sandeman port wine to Omega watches. In the Rossio, rows of black cars were parked around the entire area, and the local taxi drivers continued to do good business shuttling people from cafés to local homes or hotels. Rossio remained the beating heart of the city. It was the square that the majority of the tram routes passed through. It also had a great number of cafés, shops, and moderately priced hotels. The city's busy Central Station was located by the northwestern end of the square, and passengers would descend from the platforms high above the Rossio and come down past the ticket offices towards the square at street level. In the middle of the Rossio stood the statue of D. Pedro IV, erected in 1870. The monument was twenty-seven meters tall, and dominated the square. It was an ideal place to arrange to meet friends.

Outwardly there was little change in Rossio in the summer of 1940 from the previous year. Rationing hadn't yet been introduced and the cake stands in the various cafés were still full of a wide choice of delightful sweet pleasures. The beautifully pristine white café tablecloths remained the same, as were the slightly grumpy aging waiters, some of who appeared to have spent an entire lifetime working in the same café. The large billiard saloon and the biggest café in Rossio, Chave d'Ouro, continued to be packed with locals playing at its nine full-sized tables. The summer of 1940, however, was very different from the previous one.

The first noticeable change was the sound that emanated from the Chave d'Ouro café. The nasal tone of the Portuguese language was still present, but it was matched now by the sounds of languages from across Europe. English, French, German, Polish and even Russian voices could be detected. The male-dominated Portuguese café society had been replaced by something much more cosmopolitan, and more family oriented. The foreign refugees usually spoke in hushed tones, leaning forward at tables in case their conversations were overheard.[1] There was good reason to speak quietly. The much-feared Portuguese secret police, the PVDE, were responsible for watching the foreigners during their stay in Lisbon, and many of them were under close surveillance by PVDE agents.

The refugees who sat at the tables looked and dressed completely differently from the Lisboetas. Most of the men still wore suits, but the cut was invariably different from the locals, more relaxed and slightly baggier—usually French influenced. The women looked from a different era than the locals in their conservative old-fashioned buttoned-up style. Dressed in slacks the female refugees stood at street bars where only men stood before. At night they often went out by themselves, and without hats, which in Lisbon society was the mark of a prostitute. Lisboetas looked at the uninvited guests with a sense of sad and passive wonderment. Too reserved to protest, they were nonetheless deeply shocked by the intrusion of the refugees on their social custom and values. [2]

Despite the uncertainty of their future, and the difficulties they had encountered in reaching Lisbon, the refugees brought a degree of elegance that had hitherto been missing from the city. It was in the cafés that the writer Arthur Koestler, himself a refugee in Lisbon for seven weeks, would find the inspiration for his book, *Arrival and Departure*, in which Lisbon was referred to not by name but rather by the term "Neutralia." As Koestler noted, the refugees were creatures of habit, always frequenting the same cafés and taking the same promenades.[3] Despite its relatively large size, the center of Lisbon was very compact, squeezed between hills on each side with little opportunity for natural expansion. While the foreigners frequently ran into one another in street cafés or at the British or United States consulates, there was little direct contact between the Lisboetas and the new temporary foreign residents of the city.

Many of the thousands of refugees that arrived in Lisbon during the long hot summer of 1940 had fled Paris and traveled to the South of France, then through Spain and across into Portugal. As Arthur Koestler put it,

> Lisbon was the bottle-neck of Europe, the last open gate of a con-
> centration camp extending over the greater part of the Continent's
> surface. By watching that interminable procession, one realised that
> the catalogue of possible reasons for persecution under the New
> Order was much longer than even a specialist could imagine; in fact,
> it covered the entire alphabet, from A, for Austrian Monarchist, to
> Z, for Zionist Jew. Every European nation, religion, party was rep-
> resented in that procession, including German Nazis of Strasser's
> oppositional faction and Italian Fascists in disgrace.[4]

Of the original refugees, most were Jewish, and were looking to collect the relevant and complex paperwork needed to get to America or Palestine. A large number of the Jewish refugees were wealthy former residents of Paris and the surrounding areas, and were using their funds in the best way they could to secure their onward passage. Other refugees were less financially well off and needed support from the Portuguese authorities or the British.

What nearly all the refugees had in common was the wait. Nothing happened quickly in Lisbon.

Both the American consulate and the British embassy were initially hugely understaffed to deal with the influx. The completion of paperwork and the gathering of the correct stamps in passports all took time. On top of this, onward travel arrangements had to be made and funds secured to pay for the trip—usually in cash or, for the lucky ones, funds wired from family or patrons based abroad. Among the refugees were the rich, the famous, and royalty, all of whom had to experience the uncertainties of Lisbon life for a few difficult weeks or months.

The refugee crisis that gripped Lisbon during the summer of 1940 was, in part, caused by the actions of one man, Aristides de Sousa Mendes, the Portuguese Consul in Bordeaux. Like Salazar, Aristides de Sousa Mendes had graduated in law from Coimbra University. Sousa Mendes, however, came from a markedly higher social background than Salazar. He was the son of a highly regarded court judge of Beira, and was considered to be from a moderately aristocratic family.[5] He enjoyed a relatively low level diplomatic career, during which he experienced several brushes with the authorities. In truth, his career up to this point had largely been overshadowed by that of his twin brother, César, who was a senior ambassador and had served, briefly, as Salazar's first foreign minister. César also studied law at Coimbra University and the twin brothers graduated before both deciding to choose the path of the diplomatic service.

In June 1940, thousands of refugees had gathered in Bordeaux in the hope of fleeing the German advance through France. With the fall of Paris, Bordeaux had become the temporary French capital. It was from Bordeaux that on the morning of June 17, 1940, Charles de Gaulle climbed aboard a small airplane and left the country, as Winston Churchill put it, "carrying the honour of

France."[6] In his cramped office on a first floor building in the Quai Louis XVIII, Aristides de Sousa Mendes was working long days and well into the night issuing transit visas to refugees who had to remain in France until their turn came to plead their case.

By the middle of June the situation had become chaotic with soldiers imposing discipline and order on the queues of increasingly desperate people. According to his nephew, Sousa Mendes became ill, exhausted, and had to lie down.[7] At this point he considered what to do and whether he should enforce the strict criteria imposed by Salazar and the Ministry of Foreign Affairs regarding who should be allowed to enter Portugal. In the end, he decided to issue visas to all without distinguishing on the grounds of nationality, race, or religion. This went against the policy that Lisbon had been trying to carefully enforce, which was particularly aimed at trying to keep the Jews fleeing the Germans out of Portugal.

The previous year, on November 13, 1939, Aristides de Sousa Mendes, like all other Portuguese consuls around the world, had received a circular from the Portuguese Foreign Ministry. Known as Circular 14, it for the first time introduced a racial or religious criterion to the question of temporary immigration to Portugal. Circular 14 instructed the consuls that any stateless person or Jew would need to have their case referred directly to the Portuguese Foreign Ministry.[8]

Sousa Mendes noted that this new process would have been difficult to implement at the best of times, and given the situation in Europe in 1940 it made for impossible delays.[9] He was also aware that the Foreign Ministry was turning down nearly all the requests by Jews for visas to enter Portugal. Sousa Mendes was not blind to the peril that the Jews found themselves in in Bordeaux. The consul, and his team of helpers (including a rabbi), understood that if the Jews failed to get out of Bordeaux in time, the chances were that they would be deported to a concentration camp.

Circular 14 was not issued out of thin air. Throughout the 1930s, the dictatorship had made efforts to erect barriers to any refugees staying in Portugal. This type of action was, of course, not unique to Portugal, but with the country's very limited economic means it was viewed as necessary. Refugees who did manage to enter Portugal during this time were not generally treated badly. Efforts were made to house them in tourist areas away from Lisbon, but the country was not able, without support from outside parties, to do much. Put simply, during this period it was primarily economic constraints rather than political ideology that made the Portuguese reluctant to accept more refugees. Those that did come were not usually allowed to enter the Portuguese job market, nor were they able to claim the meager state benefits open to Portuguese citizens.

Initial estimates put the number of visas that Sousa Mendes signed at around 30,000. On the basis of these numbers, Sousa Mendes came to be known as the Portuguese version of Raoul Wallenberg, who saved around 100,000 Jews in Hungary between 1944 and 1945, before he was arrested and imprisoned by the Soviets. For a number of reasons, however, the comparison is not particularly valid.[10] The number of 30,000 refugees that Sousa Mendes was thought to have saved has been widely quoted by both journalistic and academic sources.[11]

The real number, however, was considerably lower. The report of the Portuguese secret police, the PVDE, who were responsible for controlling Portugal's borders, puts the total number of refugees from the whole of Europe in 1940 as follows: entry by land 30,854, by sea 6,843, and by air 5,843 making a total of 43,540. The PVDE also recorded the numbers of departures: by land 13,991, by sea 17,452, and by air 5,136 making a grand total of 36,579. There were 6,961 remaining in the country.[12] According to the records of the Consulate in Bordeaux the number of visas granted by Sousa Mendes between January 1 and June 22 (when he was recalled to Lisbon) was 2,862. The vast majority of these visas (1,575) were granted between June 11 and June 22.[13]

In terms of the number of Jews among this group, it is clear, according to official estimates of Jewish rescue groups operating in the city, that in the second half of 1940 some 1,500 Jews who had come to Portugal without onwards visas sailed from Lisbon.[14] We need to add to this figure those Jews who were not dependent on the rescue groups operating in the city and therefore not registered with them. Even allowing for this group there is a large gap between the reality of the actual number that Sousa Mendes saved and the myth of the 30,000 figures. Most of the Jewish refugees who escaped France and came through Spain to Portugal during the summer of 1940 clearly did so as the result of the work of Sousa Mendes, but the numbers were much lower.

It would be more prudent, if a little cynical, to regard Sousa Mendes as a "Wallenberg Lite" rather than to talk of him in the same context as the Swedish diplomat. Regardless of this, there are streets today in both Lisbon (and the Lisbon coast) and in Tel Aviv, Israel, that are named after the former Portuguese consul in Bordeaux. Confirmation of the current importance given by the Portuguese to Sousa Mendes came in 2007 in the form of Portuguese state broadcaster RTP, and their program *Os Grandes Portugueses*, which was based on the BBC series *The Greatest Briton*. Aristides de Sousa Mendes was voted the third greatest Portuguese person of all time.

CHAPTER 7

Retired, Outcast

WHATEVER THE FINAL NUMBER OF REFUGEES, Salazar was furious with Sousa Mendes for his insubordination. Salazar ordered the immediate recall of the consul back to Lisbon, where disciplinary procedures were soon instigated against him. Salazar's anger was based on two points: the insubordination itself and the timing of Sousa Mendes's actions. From Salazar's perspective, the first reason was not difficult to comprehend. Sousa Mendes had worked independently of the Portuguese Ministry of Foreign Affairs, where it should not be forgotten that Salazar was the serving minister. He had clearly not followed the rules for the granting of visas as outlined in Circular 14 and Sousa Mendes's actions had huge repercussions for Lisbon, which would have to house the refugees before their onward passage on the limited number of vessels that could be arranged.

By the time many of the refugees arrived in Lisbon, their limited finances had already been taken up in paying for transportation, hotels, and bureaucratic charges. In short, despite many of the refugees originating from middle-class families, by the time they reached the end of the line there was little or nothing left to support themselves and their families in Lisbon, a city already full of poor people it could barely afford to deal with.

The timing of the unilateral decision of Sousa Mendes to issue visas could not have been worse for Salazar and his carefully planned attempt to preserve Portuguese neutrality. Salazar believed that in order to achieve this key policy goal, he needed to personally retain sole control over all areas and aspects of foreign policy.[1] Indeed, the consul's actions led directly to a major increase in diplomatic tensions between Lisbon and Madrid at a key juncture in the war. With the German army on the French-Spanish border there was increased pressure on General Franco to join the war on the Axis side.

The actions of Sousa Mendes led to the Spanish closing the border with France. One Spanish official suggested that the Germans could go after the refugees and enter Spain and Portugal. The careful strategy of Salazar and the British of trying to induce Franco economically and politically to stay out of the war was, in the eyes of Salazar, jeopardized by the actions of one lone wolf diplomat. The Portuguese ambassador to Spain, Pedro Teotónio Pereira, reported to Salazar that the situation on the border was truly distressing, and that there was uncertainty whether the Germans would force Spain to join the war. The ambassador also talked of the extreme sense of nervousness of Sir Samuel Hoare, the British ambassador in Madrid.[2] In truth, the scene on the border was chaotic.

In his account of the fall of France, Arthur Koestler dramatically chronicled the confusion, fear, and rumors, and counterrumors that were circulating at the time of the final collapse of the country.[3] Many of the Jewish refugees who did manage to get into Spain were subsequently held at the Portuguese-Spanish border at Vilar Formoso by the PVDE. Eventually, with the intervention of rescue groups and the head of Lisbon's small permanent Jewish community, Moses Amzalak, most were let into Portugal and made their way to Lisbon. Amzalak was a friend and political ally of Salazar and his intervention was extremely important.

On June 2, 1940, Salazar ordered that Sousa Mendes return immediately to Lisbon[4] and on July 4, 1940, he formally ordered the start of a disciplinary process against Sousa Mendes.[5] The inquiry was led by the Ministry of Foreign Affairs.

The evidence against Sousa Mendes was complex, and based on a number of factors. In January 1940 while serving in Bordeaux, Sousa Mendes had been warned about his conduct in issuing visas to foreigners against the regulations issued by Lisbon, but the final straw for Salazar possibly came in the form of a written protest from the British embassy in Lisbon, which complained about an alleged special tax being charged by the Portuguese consul in Bordeaux in the name of charity. More specifically, Walford Selby was instructed by the Foreign Office in London to formally complain to the Portuguese about the extended opening hours of the Portuguese consulate in Bordeaux and that applications for visas were being charged at a special rate. Selby went on to suggest that on at least one occasion an applicant had been asked to contribute to a Portuguese charitable fund before a visa application had been signed.[6]

On top of these allegations, other historical examples of Sousa Mendes getting into trouble have been chronicled elsewhere, notably over a case involving a contribution to a charity while he was serving in San Francisco in 1923.[7] The fact that Sousa Mendes had a large family to support was a factor in some of the suspicions raised against him. With fourteen children, many of whom were still living at home in 1940, making ends meet could not have been easy on his relatively low level diplomatic salary.

Sousa Mendes's disciplinary hearing took place from the start of August 1940 and lasted until the middle of October. There were fifteen allegations against him. Two other diplomats, the Count of Tovar and Paulo Brito, led the formal disciplinary council. During the hearing, Sousa Mendes defended himself, rejecting the charges. He argued that the British accusations were groundless.

In terms of the charge of extra fees, he suggested that this might have originated from the testimony of an informer at the British embassy. Sousa Mendes recalled that he was allowed to receive a "personal indemnity" for each service rendered outside office hours, but never asked for one, except on one occasion. He admitted to asking Robert Rothschild for such an indemnity only because it was a Sunday and Rothschild refused to wait until the Monday to get his visa.[8] Regarding the fees, he speculated that the charge might have originated from an English-speaking woman who had to wait for her visa at the consulate and got fed up, argued with the staff, and subsequently stated that she would be lodging a complaint,[9]

Sousa Mendes explained that he acted out of humanitarian concern for the refugees who, if they had fallen into the hands of the Germans, would have been placed in mortal danger. He also cited historical context, arguing that he was trying to repair the damage to Portugal's image caused by the Inquisition. Most cleverly of all, he pointed out that Portugal was benefiting in political terms from his actions.[10] In other words, the images of the refugees in Lisbon and the news stories surrounding their plight cast Portugal, and Salazar, in a very favorable light.

In the end, the chairman, Paulo Brito, ruled that, due to the extreme situation in Bordeaux at the time, Sousa Mendes should be suspended from the diplomatic service for between 30 and 180 days with loss of pay. The Count of Tovar wanted Sousa Mendes to be demoted to the next lower rank within the diplomatic service. The key to the ruling, however, was that the chair, Paulo Brito, decided to send the final judgment on the case to Salazar.[11] After due consideration, Salazar ruled on October 30, stating, "I sentence Consul First Class, Aristides de Sousa Mendes to a penalty of one year of inactivity with the right to fifty percent of his rank's pay and after that he is obliged to subsequently retire from the service."[12] With these words, Aristides de Sousa Mendes's diplomatic career was terminated.

Despite a series of legal appeals from Sousa Mendes the ruling was not overturned. In the end, Sousa Mendes resorted to making a personal appeal to Salazar. In a letter to Salazar dated April 2, 1941, he pleaded poverty. His consul first-class salary was 600 escudos and he had a wife and fourteen children to support. He went on to remind Salazar that the refugees in Portugal had been treated with warmth and affection, and that had led to many compliments at both national and foreign level. People, he added, had seen the attitude of the Portuguese people as a great example of Christian virtues. He appealed to Salazar in the spirit of Christianity, and for his thirty-year service. Finally, he pleaded with Salazar not to ruin his family.[13] Salazar, however, was unmoved.

There was no further formal correspondence between Salazar and the Sousa Mendes family until two days after Sousa Mendes's death on April 3, 1954, when Salazar sent a visiting card to the family with only two words written on it, "my condolences."[14] The final years of Sousa Mendes's life had been very difficult. Living in poverty and with failing health, his relatives claim that he never regretted his actions in issuing the visas.[15] Much of his time was spent unsuccessfully trying to clear his name. He had hoped that with the end of the war in 1945 his case would be reconsidered, but Salazar resisted any calls for a pardon or to reduce the sentence.

In Portugal there are two major theories as to why his punishment was so harsh and was not subsequently reduced or dropped altogether. The first centers upon internal power struggles and intrigues in the Ministry of Foreign Affairs that involved Aristides's twin brother and the secretary-general of the Ministry, Luís Teixeira de Sampaio (the effective second most influential person on foreign affairs behind Salazar). This theory argues that Aristides Sousa Mendes's treatment was, at least, down to factors beyond his control.[16] The second theory, and the most widely accepted, is that he was treated harshly as the result of his actions in granting visas to Jewish refugees after the fall of France.

As a result of his treatment of Sousa Mendes, it appears that Salazar's attitude towards the Jews fits with that of the leaders of other nondemocratic European countries. On the surface, this charge appears to be largely confirmed by the treatment of other Portuguese consuls who attempted, on a smaller scale, to disobey him over this question. The fate of the Portuguese ambassador to Berlin, Alberto da Veiga Simões, who was recalled from Berlin and replaced by the more pro-German Count of Tovar following the fall of France, adds further fuel to the fire.

Veiga Simões had a long history of anti-Nazism. More specifically, he argued that Nazi policies could create a situation for Portugal if it had to suddenly accommodate a wave of Jews trying to get into the country for lack of choice of alternative destinations. Moreover, these refugees might try to stay in Portugal on a permanent basis due to a lack of funds to go elsewhere. He argued to Salazar that this should be prevented and proposed a series of measures to try to control this, at the center of which were consuls retaining the sole power to issue visas (contrary to the instructions of Circular 14). The ambassador went further and attempted to help groups of Jews, whom he determined as important, and helped them enter Portugal against the wishes of the PVDE. Despite being warned about his actions he continued to intervene when "special cases" arose. [17]

Veiga Simões's letters and reports to Salazar from 1938 onwards clarify two important points.[18] The ambassador was aware from a relatively early stage about the Nazis' methods for dealing with the Jews and what this meant in practical terms. More importantly, Salazar, who in all aspects of foreign policy spent time reading and studying such dispatches, also understood from an early stage the dangers and perils to which the Jews of Europe living under Nazi rule were exposed.

Indeed, Salazar was kept informed by the Portuguese embassy in Berlin about the Nazi methods for dealing with Jews throughout the war. In 1941, the embassy produced a detailed analysis of this question under the framework of differences between Portugal and Germany on the treatment of religions.[19] Despite this, Salazar was unyielding both in his determination that Circular 14 should be enforced, and in his utterances on the fate of Germany's Jews: For Salazar the Jewish question was an internal German issue and this was as far as he would publicly comment.

CHAPTER 8

The Jewish Question

SITTING IN HIS COLD OFFICE, AND OFTEN WORKING alone, Salazar's treatment of the dissenting Portuguese consuls and ambassadors was very much in keeping with his attitude of nonacceptance of any form of dissent from within his regime. To some extent, he believed that the diplomatic service had not been properly purged of lingering republican loyalties. Certainly some of its staff did not owe their original position to Salazar. At the heart of the matter, however, was Salazar's macro policy of preserving Portugal's neutrality. The ruthless pursuit of this central policy goal at the expense of everything else obscured several important points regarding Salazar and his treatment of the Jews.

Salazar's seeming indifference to the plight of the Jews living under the control of the Third Reich, and his active policy of trying to prevent Jewish refugees from entering Portugal, would appear to place him alongside General Franco of Spain in hostile anti-Semitism.[1] On top of this, his persecution of those individual Portuguese who acted on humanitarian grounds to help Jews escape the horrors of Europe is difficult to comprehend. The British, however, noted that there was no violent anti-Semitic feeling in Lisbon, although they acknowledged that the Jews had never been popular in Portugal.[2] But in general, Jews who made it to Lisbon were not treated badly by the regime.

Salazar allowed Jewish relief agencies to set up offices in Lisbon, and operate with generally little interference from the Portuguese authorities. Initially, this was done against the wishes of the British embassy in Lisbon, which argued that the Germans would exploit such a move as an opportunity to help alienate the sympathies of the local population from the Allied cause.[3] Once Salazar took the decision to allow Jewish relief groups to work in Lisbon, generally speaking his officials cooperated with these groups and local embassies on how best to deal with the humanitarian crisis.

Even at times of high pressure during the war when the Germans were threatening Portugal, Salazar did not introduce new draconian measures against Lisbon's Jews. When it became clear that many of the Jews would not be able to depart Lisbon for some time due to a lack of finance or the relatively small number of places on ships, he ordered that they be sent to camps in tourist areas. These towns, such as Ericeira to the northwest of Lisbon, had spare capacity due to the decline in the number of holiday makers. Conditions there were far from perfect, but this was generally due to economic reasons rather than any ideological hostility towards the Jewish refugees.

To many people these positive actions are not enough to absolve Salazar from strong criticism for his policies towards the Jews. But the reality is that even if he had made strong public proclamations during the war against the treatment of the Jews by the Nazis there is little evidence to suggest that it would have made any or much difference to their plight. Salazar's argument against such a course of action was simple: Portugal must protect its independence first and foremost, nothing was more important. This detachment from suffering and the horror of war irritated and enraged many, including the British foreign secretary Anthony Eden. He somewhat pointedly opined that Salazar was becoming much too detached from the war and its realities.

Yet for the Jewish refugees sitting in the cafés around Rossio, making their seemingly daily trips to respective consulates, and the offices of locally based Jewish rescue groups, Lisbon was a relatively safe place. There were a very small number of cases of well-known Jewish activists disappearing from the streets. In one notorious case a well-known anti-Nazi journalist and opposition figure of Jewish origin was arrested on a street in Lisbon by agents of the PVDE and handed over to the Gestapo.[4] This example was exceptional, however. What caused equal fear for the refugees were the rumor mills that went around Lisbon at the time. These rumors centered upon the alleged pro-German sentiment of the Portuguese secret police, and the potential of a German military operation against Portugal. On top of this there was a marked increase in the presence of German intelligence agents operating in the city, who were busy recruiting, usually through financial means, locals to spy on the activities of the refugees.

———————

The Portuguese secret police, the PVDE, were responsible for the refugees (Jewish and non-Jewish), from their arrival in the country until their departure. They were much feared by both the local population and the refugees. Comparisons were made between the PVDE and the German Gestapo, and in many official reports and accounts of the war they are viewed as being institutionally more predominantly pro-Axis than pro-Allied.[5] Both of these statements remain wide of the mark. Indeed, the PVDE during World War II actually bore a strong resemblance to the British MI5 in terms of organization.[6]

In October 1940, the British embassy in Lisbon formally complained about the PVDE, stating that there was no doubt whatsoever that the organization was in the hands of the Germans and that a great deal of discrimination was shown against the British. They went on to suggest that the Germans had been very clever and that many of the PVDE officers had received training in Berlin and Rome.[7] The Foreign Office subsequently raised the issue with the Portuguese ambassador in London, Armindo Monteiro, who argued that the commander of the PVDE had no pro-German tendencies, but did admit that some minor officials were indeed pro-German.[8] The issue at hand was the question of the difficulties that British subjects were reporting in obtaining visas to travel to Lisbon. The Portuguese Ministry of Foreign Affairs noted that the PVDE had taken over some of the responsibility for visas and the police were somewhat swamped by the large number of refugees entering the country due to the debacle in France.[9] There was a certain amount of political posturing about the British claims.

In late 1940, the British embassy staff in Lisbon had developed something of a reputation of being "chronic complainers" when it came to such matters as whether local organizations were pro-British or pro-German. What the complaints did reveal was the lack of reliable, good-quality intelligence the British had about the PVDE. This was to be rectified soon after, as more British agents arrived in Lisbon and helped develop a much more detailed and clearer understanding of the organization and where the political sympathies of each of its senior officers really lay. For the refugees wandering around Lisbon, often being tailed by PVDE agents or watched by local informants, the secret police were extremely intimidating.

The British did not give up on the PVDE. They simply changed tactics. Instead of making complaints, which the Foreign Office felt always fell on deaf ears, they decided to offer counterinducements to PVDE officers to match or better the Germans.[10] In January 1941, an attempt was made by British agents to bribe three leading officers in the PVDE with £10,000.[11] The belief was that many of the PVDE's officers were on the German payroll. Confirmation of this point appeared to come from the large number of Germans being granted visas to enter Lisbon with the assent of the PVDE. The Foreign Office hoped to limit the number of visas issued to Germans and use the PVDE to hinder the movements of the Germans while they were in the city. This they felt would be an effective way of blocking German influence. The attempt failed, but the British continued with the scheme.[12] It was decided that £10,000 was not a big enough inducement. On April 26, 1941, a request was made for an additional £90,000, which was felt to be a more realistic figure for the "inducement pot."[13]

The scheme was eventually scuppered by the British ambassador in Lisbon who felt that his unilateral charm offensive was having some success in their relations with the PVDE.[14] The embassy argued that the head of the PVDE was not to be bought, that any attempt to incriminate him with fake evidence would be foolhardy, and that it would be a disaster if they were found out. As the ambassador summed it up, the game was simply not worth the candle.[15]

Eventually, despite differences between the embassy in Lisbon and Special Operations Executive (SOE), it was agreed that an invitation should be issued to Captain Lourenço to visit London where the relevant people could make a fuss of him.[16] This was finally issued on October 29, 1941.[17] The Portuguese accepted the invitation in principle, but no date was set for the visit due to Lourenço's commitments in Lisbon. The ambassador felt that the invitation had flattered Salazar and that it had already achieved its purpose.[18]

———

The Germans had lures of their own: They decided that if some of the senior PVDE officers could not be tempted solely by financial inducements they would offer medals as part of a German charm offensive with the PVDE. The German ambassador in Lisbon recommended that three senior PVDE officers receive the "Adler" decoration in recognition of their services in helping with the repatriation of 320 German Consular officials from the United States back to Germany. The three officers were named as Paulo Cumano, José Ernesto, and Agostinho Lourenço.[19]

Showing his true motives, the ambassador went on to recommend to the Foreign Ministry in Berlin that these decorations should be granted quickly, as he had heard that the British were contemplating an award to these men as well. He argued that the British award would not be for services rendered, but rather to prepare the way for services to be rendered in the future. A case could be made that this was exactly the German motive as well. On February 14, 1942, after a delay of six months, the Portuguese responded through the Ministry of Foreign Affairs. The ministry consented to the three officers accepting the award, but asked that no fuss be made about it, and that the matter should above all not be reported in the press.[20]

So were the PVDE won over by the Germans or the British? Or neither? Captain Agostinho Lourenço, the head of the PVDE, offers a clue to the answer. Lourenço had fought on the British side during World War I in France and he was Salazar's righthand man in the field of security. The loyalty of the PVDE was very much devoted to the Estado Novo and Salazar, whom they worked to keep in power.[21] His subordinates always addressed Captain Lourenço as the Director.[22]

Like his good friend Salazar, Lourenço was a very strict disciplinarian and a hard worker. He agreed to take over and remodel the secret police on the condition that he should be given a free hand without any interference whatsoever from any other Portuguese authority. Salazar agreed to his demand and allowed Lourenço to develop the organization from the position of having virtually no funds into a well-funded and efficient secret police force.[23] The dispute between the PVDE and the Ministry of Foreign Affairs over the issue of who had the final say in visa approvals during 1940 was very much part of the attempt of Lourenço to secure total control over the movement of foreigners into Portugal.

In terms of his political preferences, Captain Lourenço was considered to reflect Salazar's own view. This could be defined in basic terms as being characteristically more pro-Allied and anti-Axis. In the sphere of secret police work, statistics need to be taken with a large pinch of salt as they often only partially reveal what really happened. That said, two groups of statistics are interesting in providing some evidence of where Lourenço's political preferences lay. Between 1931 and 1938 some seventy-three Germans were expelled from Portugal by the PVDE and only seventeen British.[24] During World War II, estimates suggest that some fourteen German agents were expelled or deported from Portugal against only four British.[25]

Lourenço's loyalty, however, was first and foremost to Salazar and naturally he despised communism and communists, whom he viewed, correctly, as the single biggest oppositional threat to Salazar and the Estado Novo. Britain's eventual alliance with the Soviet Union did not sit well with his own views. By the end of the war the British had come to view him more as an intelligent British police officer than a Gestapo chief.[26]

Despite giving the impression of a well-drilled and mild-mannered British detective, Captain Lourenço could be ruthless if ordered to do so, or crossed, as Walter Edward Lucas, the local correspondent of the London *Times* discovered to his cost in December 1940. Lucas's crime was to have published articles in which he talked about the Portuguese people as being Anglophiles, but that the government and the PVDE were pro-German.[27] Other quips included that the head of the Gestapo had sneaked into the country through Estoril Airport.[28] In the series of articles that appeared in the U.S.-based magazine *P.M.*, Lucas claimed that the Portuguese admiralty was based in Whitehall, and that Portugal did nothing to counter German espionage activity in the country.[29]

Lucas was hauled in by the PVDE on Christmas Eve and was given a six-hour grilling by Captain Lourenço and other PVDE officers. Lourenço was far from impressed by the answers he got from Lucas who spent his Christmas day writing grovelling letters of apology to both Lourenço and António Ferro (who was in charge of Salazar's message and propaganda department). The letters failed to do the trick and Captain Lourenço handwrote on Lucas's file that he was a danger and must leave Portugal within forty-eight hours. Lucas's sentence was eventually modified slightly—he was given until January 10 to leave the country. Lucas's *Anglo-Portugal News* was suspended by the PVDE.[30]

The expulsion was widely reported in both the British and German press. Naturally German papers such as *Königsberger Allgemeine Zeitung* welcomed the news when it reported the events in its January 7 edition.[31] Keen to show that the expulsion was not the start of a new anti-British drive, Captain Lourenço expelled Dr. Cezare Rivelli, an Italian journalist, as well for good measure.[32]

For the British the timing of the action against Lucas could not have been worse as it coincided with the arrival of the new British ambassador to Portugal, Sir Ronald Campbell.[33] Prior to arriving in Lisbon, Sir Ronald had served as ambassador to France. In Bordeaux, Campbell had witnessed the refugee crisis as France fell. He would now be faced with having to help deal with the refugees at the other end of the line in Lisbon. Campbell's appointment and arrival in Lisbon had been eagerly talked up by the British as representing a heightened sense of importance being given to Anglo-Portuguese relations by London.[34] The events surrounding Lucas ensured that Campbell was not off to a running start.

The handling of Lucas was clearly determined by Salazar, who was keen to act against the slightest excesses of exaggeration that he judged were dangerous for Portugal. The local Portuguese press in Lisbon was heavily censored with articles regularly cut, modified, or dropped out altogether on the orders of the government. Censorship had not been introduced as a result of World War II; its main aim was to stop internal opposition groups to the Estado Novo from being able to disseminate their message and use the media as a means for stirring up the people to rebel against the state.

The war, however, and Portugal's policy of neutrality, meant that wherever possible Salazar tried to control the news agenda in order not to alienate one of the warring sides. It was very much a carrot-and-stick approach. Censorship was also used to punish one of the warring parties if they were believed to have committed sins against Salazar. In this respect, the Estado Novo mirrored a fairly typical authoritarian state. Captain Lourenço made it clear that he would not tolerate insults from journalists like Lucas. The message was not lost on most foreign stringers in Lisbon, and with the exception of Reuters, they did not have the rather dubious pleasure of an extended interview with the captain during their stay in Lisbon.

One key event in the life of Captain Lourenço did come to take on a greater significance than even this top-level detective could have foreseen. In 1921 he was awarded a British medal for his service in charge of the security for the Prince of Wales (later King Edward VIII) during his visit to Lisbon.[35] In the summer of 1940, word reached Salazar that the former king, who since his abdication was known as the Duke of Windsor, and his wife the Duchess of Windsor, were in Spain and wished to come to Lisbon before returning to Britain. Salazar agreed to this request and ensured that Captain Lourenço was once again placed in personal charge of guarding the Duke of Windsor. This, as it turned out, proved to be no easy task.

CHAPTER 9

On the Run

IN FLEEING THE ADVANCING GERMAN FORCES AFTER
their entry into Paris, the Duke and Duchess of Windsor had
first stayed on the French Riviera, where the British Consul suggested that they should go to Lisbon and from there back to
England.[1] In a show of incredible self-importance, which wasn't
completely out of character, early in the morning of June 17, the
duke had telephoned Major-General Edward Spears and had asked
him to arrange a Royal Navy warship to pick him up from Nice.[2] An
irritated Spears had told the duke that no warship could be made
available and that the road to Spain was open to motorcars.[3] The
duke, as a result, somewhat sulkily, had left France by car on June
19, 1940, and arrived in Barcelona on June 21.[4] The duke and
duchess traveled on to Madrid, arriving in the evening of Sunday
June 23, where they stayed at the Ritz.

Spain at this time was not an ideal location for the duke.[5]
Madrid was a major centre of German intelligence activity. In addition to the usual espionage and counterespionage activities, it was
also a major listening post and decoding station for the Germans.
According to Walter Schellenberg, later the head of German Military Intelligence (the Abwehr), in all some 70 to 100 people were
employed in such activities and were based in an annex of the German embassy.[6]

At the same time as the duke was passing through Madrid, the Portuguese authorities were made aware of an Axis plot in the Spanish capital to stop "the playboy king" Carol II of Romania, from fleeing Europe.[7] The king claimed his own safety was at risk in Madrid, and Salazar allowed him to come to Lisbon.[8] He then left Portugal for a period of exile in Mexico, before returning to Estoril after the war. Here the king joined other royal exiles living in Estoril, a town that *Life Magazine* dubbed "the Royal Morgue of Europe."[9] After his death in 1953, King Carol II was buried in Estoril until his remains were allowed to return to Romania for reburial in 2003.

While British and German intelligence competed for influence in Lisbon, the situation in Madrid was much more difficult for the Allies.[10] Not only were there a higher number of German secret agents operating in the city, but the attitude of the Spanish authorities in general favored the Germans over the British. Madrid in the summer of 1940 was not a comfortable place for the Duke and Duchess of Windsor to linger.[11]

General Franco appeared at times on the verge of taking Spain into the war on the Axis side: The Portuguese noted a great deal of apprehension in the British embassy in Madrid over Spain's intentions towards the war.[12] David Eccles, who served in the British embassies in both Lisbon and Madrid in the summer of 1940, wrote simply that Madrid was hot and that tension was running high. The Germans, he added, were increasing their efforts to get Spain into the war.[13]

Samuel Hoare had arrived in Madrid only three weeks before the duke to take up his post as the British ambassador to Spain, and only on the previous day had his first meeting with General Franco. Hoare was also staying at the Ritz Hotel,[14] which he described as being full of aggressive Germans.[15] He was convinced that Gestapo agents were listening in to his phone conversations. The atmosphere, he concluded, was one of enemy espionage.[16] He himself couldn't wait to get out of the hotel, and had, at once, started the search for alternative accommodation. Writing to the parliamentary undersecretary for Foreign Affairs, R. A. Butler, on June 12, 1940, Hoare summarized that the conditions of work in Madrid were very difficult and that the conditions of living even harder.[17] Writing to Lord Beaverbrook on June 21, Hoare noted the worsening conditions in Madrid, suggesting that there was a depressing feeling of impending catastrophe in the air.[18] With regard to accommodation, Hoare, despite his misgivings about the Ritz, soon came to conclusion that there were no suitable rented rooms in Madrid for the duke and duchess.[19]

Winston Churchill, as a result, hoped to get the duke and duchess out of Spain and on to Lisbon as quickly as possible. When the duke arrived at the Ritz in Madrid and dined with Hoare on his first night, there was a telegram waiting for him from Churchill, with words to this effect. Once in Lisbon a flying boat would take the duke and his party back to England, where arrangements had been made to provide him with an official residence.[20] It was thought that he would spend a limited amount of time in Lisbon and the aircraft would be waiting upon his arrival in the Portuguese capital. Hoare strongly supported Churchill's policy of getting the Windsors out of Madrid as quickly as possible, and entertained the couple endlessly to help keep them out of harm's way.[21] The fact that Churchill and Hoare were working together, having been so opposed on the conduct of the war, strengthened the message of the British government to the duke.

The Duke of Windsor, however, was far from pleased with the prospect of returning to England in such circumstances, and preferred instead to serve the British Empire somewhere else. The duke clearly felt that it would be embarrassing to have to return to England and deal with the royal family, from whom he was still estranged after the abdication. Churchill argued that all this could be discussed when the duke was back in England, but the duke was not impressed by this response and held out for a posting somewhere else.[22]

Churchill's fears about Madrid proved to be well founded. Involved in a complex internal Spanish power struggle for influence over the country's foreign policy, the Spanish foreign minister, Colonel Juan Beigbeber, offered on June 23 to detain the duke and duchess in Madrid so that the Germans could make contact with the duke.[23] The foreign minister, who had a reputation as being a womanizer, was competing for influence with Ramón Serrano Suñer. In a sign of the diminishing power of Beigbeber, the Germans preferred to deal with Suñer over the question of the Duke and Duchess of Windsor. Suñer, as a result, came to play the major Spanish diplomatic role in the plot. After consulting with Franco, Suñer agreed that there was enough evidence from the duke's private criticism of the war that the duke could act as a potential peacemaker. They believed, in essence, that the duke could be persuaded to do a Rudolf Hess (without the parachute jump) and possibly be used against Churchill in potential peace talks with England.[24] Throughout the summer of 1940, as a result, both Franco and Suñer cooperated with the Germans in their plot to prevent the duke from leaving Europe. A Spanish diplomat, Javier "Tiger" Bermejillo was assigned to accompany and watch the duke, and report back on the duke's views on the war and future hopes. Bermejillo would also follow the duke onto Lisbon.

Under strong British pressure from both Hoare and Churchill, the duke finally agreed to move on to Lisbon. Edward, however, saw the negotiations over his final destination as far from over. Moody, self-absorbed, and with a terrible sense of self-importance, his behavior—at a time when Churchill was dealing with the imminent threat of a German invasion of England—was highly reprehensible. In his defense, it should be noted that he genuinely, if erroneously, felt deeply that the war was an unnecessary disaster for England. He was desperate to play a meaningful role in bringing the death and destruction to an end. In London, hostility towards the duke and duchess was growing. The king suggested that she (the Duchess of Windsor) did not want to return to London and be bombed.[25] In consultation with the king, Churchill decided to stiffen his tone with the duke. For his part, Churchill was clearly loyal to Edward until the last, but regarded him as to blame for the abdication crisis. Later in the war, Lord Moran recounted that when Churchill was visiting America, every time he was informed that the Duke of Windsor had asked for an appointment, the prime minister sighed before arranging the day and time.[26]

While the duke and duchess had been staying in Barcelona, Salazar was informed that they were being urged to come to Lisbon. The duke's potential arrival posed a number of problems for the Portuguese leader: With German military successes in the low countries and France, Salazar was deeply concerned not to antagonize Germany at this key moment. His ruthless punishment of the Portuguese consul in Bordeaux, Aristides de Sousa Mendes, showed, in part, how sensitive he was to displeasing the Germans, and also the Spanish. Salazar was aware that the British would expect a successful outcome for the duke's visit to Lisbon—he would have to be allowed to leave for England without incident. He also understood, however, that the Germans would not see such an outcome in the same manner.[27]

The timing could hardly have been more sensitive: Thousands of refugees were arriving in the city, and the official visit of the Duke of Windsor's younger brother, the Duke of Kent, to Lisbon was about to take place. Salazar was acutely aware that the abdication crisis had produced an irreconcilable Windsor family feud: It would be awkward to have both dukes in the city at the same time, especially since both brothers had made it known that they did not wish to meet.[28] The Duke of Windsor, as a result, remained in Madrid until his younger brother departed Lisbon on July 2. The Duke and Duchess of Windsor then traveled on to Lisbon, arriving the next day. As in the case of the Duke of Kent's visit to Lisbon, Salazar personally oversaw the arrangements for what was presumed to be a short stay.

By July 1940, Lisbon had become a city full of refugees, many of whom had to extend their stay in the city and the surrounding coastline until they could obtain the necessary paperwork to book a berth on one of the limited number of ships leaving the city. As a result, there was a desperate shortage of available hotel rooms. In the center of the city the Hotel Aviz and the Hotel Tivoli were both fully booked, and indeed looking to acquire more space by opening new annexes.

Portuguese hoteliers keen to maximize their profits had also levied substantial increases in the price of a room. The Hotel Aviz charged $6 a day for its best suites (more than most Portuguese earned in a month).[29] This hike in prices put a further strain on the limited financial resources of the refugees, many of whom were selling everything they owned (and in some cases themselves as well) in order to finance a one-way ticket on a boat out of Lisbon. The price of diamonds on local markets steadily fell between 1940 and 1943, as the refugees were forced to sell whatever they could to fund their prolonged stay.

Along the Lisbon coast, the most glamorous hotel, the Hotel Palácio in Estoril, saw a huge increase in the number of foreigners taking rooms. In 1940, 889 foreigners stayed in the luxury hotel, of which 238 were North American, 132 Spanish, 139 British, and 74 French.[30] This figure increased in 1941 to 1,981 foreigners, of which 779 alone came from North America as the United States entered the war and beefed up its presence in Lisbon.[31] The hotel was a favored haunt of spies and exiled businessmen, as well local and international aristocrats. One of the major attractions of the hotel was its proximity to Estoril Casino, whose round building was located at the top end of the gardens. The casino was the largest in Portugal and each night its tables were full of the Riviera set, as well as spies, smugglers, and diamond traders. The interior of the casino bore a resemblance to the gambling room in Rick's Café in the film *Casablanca,* but on a grander scale. Among those who played at its tables during the war was a young British intelligence officer, Ian Fleming, who took inspiration from both the casino and the hotel for his future James Bond books.

This shortage of hotel rooms became more acute as it became clear that the Allies and Axis powers considered certain hotels to be desirable and others not so. For example, the Hotel Palácio and Hotel Inglaterra, both in Estoril, were considered hotels for the Allies, and the Hotel Atlântico, also located in Estoril, became a favorite haunt of the Germans.[32] Hotel records confirm this to be the case, although they also show that the hotels were not exclusively used by one side or the other.[33] Sitting down for breakfast with the enemy at the next table was a common occurrence.

In the center of Lisbon the hotel situation was less clear. The Hotel Tivoli was rumored to be the place where the Germans stayed. However, hotel records do not confirm these rumors: Of the total number of Germans occupying the city's hotel beds, just fewer than 10 percent were based there.[34] The Hotel Metrópole at Rossio accommodated around 30 percent of the total number of Germans staying in the city. Groups of foreign nonresidents toured the various hotel bars in the evening. At the Tivoli, the bar was extended into the corridor that linked it to the dining room. It was a popular location as drinkers could sit and watch the goings-on in the Avenida from the low windows that were at street level. Others sat in the winter garden complete with art deco glass skylight.[35] Here you could find German spies next to Allied spooks, and all manner of refugees. The atmosphere was relaxed and typical of the other hotel bars in Lisbon as people came and went. There was little in the way of fraternization, with each table sticking to its own. It was a classic case of watching you, watching us.

Rumor, counterrumor, and tales of fantasy dominated the conversations in these bars. British and German spies told tales to enlist or frighten the clientele. Among the hotel and bar staff there were agents from both sides in the war, as well as paid informants of the PVDE. Information often bore little relation to reality, as tales were spun and plots hatched in order to achieve some short-term advantage over the enemy. Both the British and the Germans wanted to develop closer ties with the local Lisboetas, but more often than not their actions ended up alienating them further. The hotels in Lisbon, with all the intrigue and mixing of warring sides, were clearly not the place for the Duke and Duchess of Windsor to spend their time in the city.

CHAPTER 10

Operation Willi

Walford Selby, the British Ambassador to
Lisbon in June 1940, was an old friend of the Windsors from
his days in Vienna, and he attempted to organize accommodation
for the duke's party in Lisbon for what was originally thought to be
two nights. Two Sunderland military flying boats were readied to
pick up the royal party in Lisbon. The British embassy had taken
what appeared to be a sensible course of action and booked the
duke and his party into the Hotel Palácio in Estoril.

Just before they were due to arrive in Portugal, however, the
hotel manager called the embassy to inform them that owing to a
shortage of rooms, and security concerns, the hotel could no longer
host the Windsors.[1] It was at this stage that the embassy was offered the possibility of hosting the party at the home of Ricardo
Espírito Santo in Cascais (located just along the coast from Estoril).
The suggestion came from the hotel manager, but Salazar was
clearly behind making the arrangements.

As ever, Salazar wanted to ensure that he would control a key
event such as the duke's visit as much as possible. While mention of
the visit was made in the Portuguese press, Salazar used his powers to ensure that the press coverage would be of a general rather
than an inquisitive nature. The choice of the house of Ricardo Espírito Santo to host the duke was very clever. There the duke would

be relatively easier to guard than at a hotel that housed guests from the Axis powers. Indeed, the head of British intelligence, Stewart Menzies, asked that the Portuguese police take responsibility for guarding the duke.

Soon after the decision was taken that the duke would stay in Cascais, concerns were raised by a number of British officials at the embassy in Lisbon regarding the suitability of Espírito Santo to host the duke. Officials suggested that Espírito Santo (or "the Holy Ghost" as he was known by the British) was a close friend of the German ambassador to Portugal, Baron von Hoyningen-Huene, with whom he regularly dined in Cascais, Estoril, and Lisbon.[2]

The second charge against the Holy Ghost was that the bank he headed, Banco Espírito Santo, one of the biggest private banks in Lisbon, was trading heavily with the Germans. Putting two and two together, the officials concluded that Espírito Santo must have developed German sympathies. As a result, there was a certain amount of internal criticism of Selby as to how he had allowed such a development to happen. Selby argued that given the number of refugees arriving in Lisbon and the resulting lack of rooms, he had little choice but to accept the suggestion that the duke stay in Cascais, especially since he had been assured that Espírito Santo would not be staying in the house for the day or two of the visit.[3]

In truth, Salazar had cleverly outwitted the British ambassador.[4] Confirmation of this fact came when Ricardo Espírito Santo was on the doorstep of his villa to greet the duke and duchess upon their arrival at his weekend house in the aptly named Boca do Inferno (Mouth of Hell) area of Cascais. Selby was said to have been extremely surprised and pained by this apparent double cross.[5]

The Windsors' host was a man of considerable charm, who was well connected with diplomats from various countries. He would keep Salazar directly informed of the private conversations that took place. This point, along with the detailed written reports of the PVDE, would ensure that Salazar knew and understood the development of events, and the plans of the duke. Salazar's diary contains several references to meetings with Espírito Santo at which he states that the banker informed him of the duke's point of view on the war and his hopes for the future. Indeed, Espírito Santo discussed the duke with Salazar even after the duke had departed the country.[6]

The Duke and Duchess of Windsor had arrived in Lisbon on July 3, 1940. They headed straight for Cascais, where they arrived at 6 PM and remained indoors, settling in and recovering from the car journey from Madrid. On the surface, there wasn't much activity, as the report of the PVDE captain in charge of protecting the duke chronicled.[7] In the background, however, a German plot known as Operation Willi was already well underway.

Boca do Inferno sat on the edge of Cascais, a small sleepy fishing town that marked the end of the twenty-five-mile Lisbon coastline and the start of the Atlantic Ocean. A single white flashing light situated on top of the lighthouse warned ships of the perils of the rocks along the edge of the rugged coastline.

In the summer of 1940 the area around Boca do Inferno was a quiet and remote location, with only a cluster of large houses about one hundred meters apart, all with high walls and hedges to ensure the utmost privacy. Most of the houses faced directly towards the ocean. Their owners could watch the Atlantic waves break with great power and noise against the jagged black rocks below. From time to time, the spray and white foam would splash the unlit road that ran along the cliff tops. In one direction the road headed into the center of Cascais, and the opposite way towards the open green wilderness and sand dunes of Quinta da Marinha, before eventually winding out to the most westerly point in mainland Europe, Cabo do Roca. It was an idyllic location, and coupled with a good climate— mild in winter, cooling ocean winds in summer—made it a popular retreat for some of Lisbon's most prominent business and aristocratic families.

Espirito Santo's house was located on the very edge of the town. The two-story house, with additional rooms in the attic, was not overlooked. Its outdoor swimming pool and large enclosed terraced garden were not visible from either the coastal road or from the small side street that ran along the eastern edge of the garden.

The essence of the German plot known as Operation Willi, which was ordered by Hitler and planned by the German foreign minister, Joachim von Ribbentrop, was to kidnap and convince the ex-king to be of use for their policy and propaganda. The plot first came to public attention in the mid 1950s with the publication of captured German papers, which included cables between the German embassy in Lisbon and the Foreign Ministry in Berlin.[8] At the center of the coverage in the media was the attitude of the Duke of Windsor towards the British government and its conduct of the war. It raised the question of whether the duke, still deeply hurt and frustrated by his abdication, might have been tempted to aid the German cause.

In all the German attempts to persuade the duke to essentially cross sides in the war, it was never exactly clear what the Germans envisaged he might contribute to their cause. Various roles are mentioned in accounts of Operation Willi ranging from a so-called honest broker to negotiate a peace with England to avoid its total destruction, to the duke returning to the throne as a German puppet in the event of England being overrun in the autumn of 1940.

Whatever the Germans' plans for the duke, Ribbentrop believed that he had enough evidence to suggest that the duke would, at the very least, give serious consideration to overtures from Germany. Ribbentrop cited the fact that the duke was friendly towards Germany and saw the war as unnecessary. Furthermore, the duke made it clear that he did not wish to see the destruction of England. In conversations that had taken place on social occasions in Madrid, the duke had talked of his dislike of the policies of the present British government, which he felt were not going to succeed.

Finally, on top of this was the question of the duke's personal bitterness towards the British royal family for what he perceived as their harsh treatment of himself and the Duchess of Windsor. It was well known in Spanish and German diplomatic circles that the duke was unhappy with his role, and wanted the duchess to become an official member of the royal family and be addressed as "Her Royal Highness." All of these factors appeared to point to a deeply disappointed duke who was concerned about the future direction of his country, and was not hugely loyal to either the royal family or the government of England.

In order to try to achieve his aim, Ribbentrop had asked the Spanish authorities to find a means to detain the duke while he was staying in Madrid. On July 2, just as Ribbentrop was considering more drastic measures to persuade the duke to play ball, he had left Madrid bound for Lisbon, and with his departure it appeared that the German foreign minister's best opportunity to convince the duke had passed.[9] It was widely presumed that Churchill and British Intelligence in Lisbon, who were aware of the duke's apparent views, would persuade him to return to England or take up a post somewhere else in the British empire very quickly.

However, Ribbentrop was far from ready to give up, and dispatched Walter Schellenberg to Lisbon. In Schellenberg's account of his time in Lisbon he suggests that he wasn't particularly optimistic about the prospects of persuading the duke to voluntarily return with him to Spain, where he would then be used by the Germans. The more Schellenberg claimed to think about the whole plot, the more it became apparent that the German plot was largely based on impulsive remarks made by the duke about the British government during his stay in Madrid, which was the result of a temporary state of mind. In short, he felt that the Germans had attributed too much importance to the remarks in the hope that they reflected a more profound change in the duke.[10]

Schellenberg claimed to be further confused by Ribbentrop's call to use force, if required, to get the duke back across the border to Spain. He argued that surely the whole plot was dependent on the duke willingly returning to Spain—otherwise he would certainly not cooperate with the Germans once he got there.[11] Ribbentrop responded that force, in the first instance, be used against the British secret service in Lisbon. It should be used against the duke insofar as he might be fearful of returning to Spain, and a forceful German action would help get over this state. The notion was that if he felt he was a "free man" in Spain, away from the surveillance of the British secret service, he would be grateful to the Germans. To further sweeten the duke, some 50 million Swiss francs were to be put at his disposal.[12]

Critics of the duke's motives and loyalties largely support, at least part of, Schellenberg's account. The force that was planned, and indeed being prepared, was aimed directly at those who would try to prevent the duke's return to Spain.[13] In accounts that are critical of the duke's loyalties, he would not have proved a problem, and would have been willing to return to Spain rather than return to England. In other words, the duke was considering committing treason and the Germans were merely the facilitators in getting him away from the clutches of the British.

The German ambassador to Lisbon, Baron von Hoyningen-Huene, was not an enthusiastic supporter of the plot, rightly fearing that any attempt to move the duke by force would damage relations between Berlin and Lisbon. The ambassador had been on a major charm offensive with Salazar in the summer of 1940, hoping to translate the spectacular German military successes into greater German influence in Lisbon. After hearing the basis of the plot, the duke's loose conversation, and criticism of the British government, the ambassador was even less convinced about the chances for success. Nevertheless, according to Schellenberg, Hoyningen-Huene promised to give him whatever logistical support he could.[14]

Schellenberg's attempts to intimidate the duke into leaving Portugal were limited to such activities as having some yobs throw stones at the window of the villa in Cascais. He also arranged to have a bouquet of flowers delivered to the house that bore a note warning the couple to beware of the British secret service, and that a Portuguese friend had their interests at heart.[15] Schellenberg, however, was well connected in Lisbon, and used his influence to gather a great deal of evidence about the duke and his moods. The more evidence he gathered, however, the less he claimed to believe in the plot.

———·•·———

Upon the duke's arrival in Cascais, his mood was considerably darkened by the arrival of a harsh telegram from Winston Churchill. Both the king and the prime minister believed that the duke needed to return home first, before any decision about his future could be taken. Churchill's telegram reminded a reluctant duke that he was a soldier and that disobeying orders would create a serious situation. Churchill concluded with typical aplomb recommending that the duke immediately comply with the wishes of His Majesty's Government (HMG).[16] A furious duke was said to gone to the trouble of drafting a reply in which he resigned all military rank, but before he could send it an offer of a job arrived, which would mean not having to return to England.

Churchill's offer of the governorship of the Bahamas was not arrived at lightly. It was more a case of getting the duke and duchess out of Europe and giving the duke an official, but minor, role to play in the empire. David Eccles added that it would be easier to keep an eye on the duke in the Bahamas than in Europe. There is evidence that Churchill was acutely aware of the details of the German plot through the intercepts of German cables.[17] If this was the case, the prime minister needed to act fast if the duke, as appeared to be the case, was digging his heels in over the negotiations of his possible return to England.

The duke did not respond to the job offer, which he considered to be far beneath him. Instead, he decided to wait in Cascais and see how events developed with London. In other words, he would not be imminently returning to England by plane. The duke and duchess's arrangements for accommodation needed to be made as a result of this now potentially open-ended stay in Lisbon.[18]

The duke's host, Ricardo Espírito Santo discussed the issue with Salazar. Both felt that the location and the arrangements were satisfactory. With the extension of the duke's stay, Espírito Santo effectively moved back into the house, which was now shared between his family and the Duke and Duchess of Windsor. These arrangements caused alarm among some British embassy staff, who now saw that the banker had virtual free access to the increasingly disgruntled duke almost 24/7.

CHAPTER 11

The Portuguese Banker

M OST OF THE THEORIES THAT SURROUND OPERATION
Willi focus on the role of the Portuguese banker and host of the
Windsors, Ricardo Espírito Santo. A German cable between Berlin
and Lisbon talks of making use of a local German "confidant"—a
term that the German lawyer, Michael Bloch, translated as "agent."[1]
In this scenario, Espírito Santo was the man on the inside acting as
messenger between Berlin and the duke and who was helping to
convince, or pressure, the duke into returning to Spain.[2] A more
careful examination of the background of Espírito Santo and his
actions reveals that it was wide of the mark to suggest that Espírito
Santo was a German agent, or was indeed particularly sympathetic
towards the German cause.

In 1941, the British ambassador to Lisbon, Ronald Campbell,
stated that he would eat his hat if Espírito Santo were pro-German.[3]
In reality, Espírito Santo was pro-money and pro-entrepreneurship.
His background also does not fit with any pro-Nazi sympathies. He
married a Jew, Maria de Morais Sarmento Cohen (as did one of his
brothers), and was also responsible for helping the prominent Jewish family, the Rothschilds, financially during the war. It was true
that he was on good terms with the German ambassador, and did

regularly dine with him. He was also, however, on good terms with most of the diplomatic circle and dined with both Selby and his successor as British ambassador.

There remains no evidence that Espírito Santo preferred the Germans to the Allies. He would continue to deal with both sides until ordered otherwise by Salazar. Naturally, this did not please the British Ministry of Economic Warfare (MEW), who wanted to stop all trade between the neutral powers and Germany. Many of the rumors of the alleged pro-German bias of Espírito Santo had its origins from this department. As the trade between Portugal and Germany developed further from 1941 onwards, Espírito Santo, and the bank he headed, became a major target of the Ministry of Economic Warfare, and at the end of the war the French authorities as well.

The next most important relationship in Espírito Santo's life after his family was Salazar. Espírito Santo was always keen to please the Portuguese leader, both out of his personal friendship with Salazar and also for business reasons. The business reach of Espírito Santo went well beyond the world of banking and he wanted to stay on good terms with Salazar in order to help develop his family's rapidly expanding business empire.

In many ways, Espírito Santo viewed the political world as a massive networking opportunity. He was honored to have been asked by Salazar to be the guide for the Duke of Kent during his visit to the exhibition in Lisbon. He was equally thrilled to have the Duke of Windsor staying in his house, and organized dinner parties in his honor with the elite of Cascais and Estoril society. He also enjoyed playing golf with the duke at Estoril golf club, the construction of the course of which he had helped finance.

The German foreign ministry might very well have considered Espírito Santo a confidant, but many other diplomats from different countries would have made the same comment. As the war developed, the role of Espírito Santo became a central part of the trade between Portugal and Germany. The trading was undertaken under the direct orders of Salazar, who believed it to be an important part of helping maintain Portugal's neutrality.

———·•·———

During their stay in Cascais, the duke and duchess made the most of their time. The PVDE, who were responsible for their safety, produced detailed reports for Captain Lourenço, the important parts of which were passed on to Salazar.[4] Initially, much of the duke's time was spent visiting the British embassy, which held the duke's passport. On August 5, after visiting the embassy, the duke returned to Cascais and played golf at Estoril. When asked to pose for photographs and to be filmed he refused, stating that he did not want to be seen playing golf when England was at war.[5] He did arrange to pose for the cameras back at the residence in Cascais.[6]

The following day, a more relaxed duke consented to be photographed during his round of golf providing the photos would not appear in the newspapers and were only for a propaganda campaign for the local Lisbon coast.[7] Golf formed a regular part of the duke's routine and included at least two rounds with Ricardo Espírito Santo, who, as well as being the main sponsor of the course, was also a former Portuguese national golf champion. The golf club with its large clubhouse and outdoor swimming pool was a magnet for local society and foreigners. The duke and his party did not mix much with the membership, preferring instead to return to Cascais for their postgame drinks.[8]

Dinner was the key social event of the day for the duke and duchess. Espírito Santo was naturally well connected among both Portuguese and international society, and arranged a number of guests for each of the dinner parties he hosted or arranged in honor of his visitors. The foreign guests included the American ambassador and the Baron and Baroness de Rothschild.[9] Espírito Santo was keen to show his guests off to the elite in Portuguese society. He took the duke for lunch at the Turf Club in central Lisbon, the most prestigious and conservative gentlemen's club in Portugal.

Here the walls were covered with photographs of the old kings and queens of Portugal. The dining room had an intimate atmosphere, with the tables close together. The membership of the club was drawn from land-owning Portuguese aristocracy, and the leaders of big business. The duke was very much among his own and happily posed for a photograph with his luncheon party.

The PVDE reported that on the evening of July 8, the Spanish diplomat, Javier "Tiger" Bermejillo, assigned by Franco to shadow the duke, arrived at Sintra Airport, situated some fifteen miles northeast of Cascais.[10] Bermejillo arrived on the scheduled flight from Madrid to Lisbon and was met by the duke's assigned chauffeur. The duke had asked the Spanish authorities if they could intervene to make sure that the Duchess of Windsor's two houses in France were protected by the Germans, and if it would be possible to dispatch someone to pick up some personal possessions.[11] The duke was very pleased when the Spanish emissary who was dispatched to Cascais turned out to be Tiger Bermejillo, who had been with the duke the previous week in Madrid.[12]

The secret police noted that he appeared very close to the duke and the two often talked at length. In the subsequent days, Bermejillo accompanied the duke to Lisbon, separating only when the duke went to the British embassy. At this time, Bermejillo visited the German embassy in Lisbon to try to help arrange the necessary visas for a member of the duchess's staff to be able to retrieve their possessions from France.[13] Using the duke's chauffeur, the Spanish diplomat was a frequent visitor to the Spanish embassy in Lisbon.[14] The duke's chauffeur was dispatched to Lisbon on August 11 to collect an envelope containing documents related to the terms of the armistice conditions between France and Germany. The envelope contained other documents, but the PVDE did not discover their subject matter.[15]

On July 12, Bermejillo returned to the house in Cascais after visiting both embassies carrying four large files from the Spanish Foreign Ministry.[16] The next morning, he departed Sintra Airport at

6 AM to return to Madrid to report on the state of negotiations with the duke.[17] Once back in Madrid, Bermejillo's reports on the duke's views on the war, and his deep concern over his luggage and possessions appears to have created a new German and Spanish subplot to delay the duke's departure from Lisbon.[18]

The plot revolved around delaying the arrival of the couple's luggage and possessions, as well as detaining the maid who had gone to collect them, in the belief that the duke and duchess would not leave Europe without them.[19] On August 23, the duke tried to telephone Bermejillo, but the Spanish diplomat was not at home. He left a message for Bermejillo to return his call as soon as he returned, as he wished to discuss an urgent matter with him.[20] The duke was clearly worried about the ongoing saga involving the couple's luggage and possessions and their attempt to retrieve them.

During the duke and duchess's stay in Portugal, the British ambassador, Walford Selby, hosted them on a number of occasions for lunches and dinners. Opinions of the couple were mixed in British circles. David Eccles, from the Ministry of Economic Warfare, took an instant dislike to the couple. After lunch with the Windsors on July 4, he wrote in a letter to his wife that he wouldn't give ten shillings for Wallis (Duchess of Windsor), she was a poor creature. He considered the duke to be pretty fifth column.[21]

On July 8, after seeing the Windsors again, he wrote to his wife that he really didn't like the Windsors, and that they had no charm. He described the duchess as a battered warhorse in a halo hat, which was most unattractive.[22] Eccles was to keep a close eye on the couple during their stay in Portugal and was acutely aware of the duke's views on the war. By July 17, however, Eccles appeared to have been won over by the couple. He dined with them twice that week and had got to know them much better. Eccles felt he'd been seduced by the Windsors and that when they turned the charm on, they were hard to resist. He now felt that the duchess was incredible and that the duke had a confiding manner of talking that was dangerous to a degree. They were, as Eccles put it, the arch-beachcombers of the world.[23]

While all the intrigue and negotiations were going on behind the scenes, in public the duke was keen to carry on as normally as possible. On July 20, after dinner, the duke's party visited the Estoril Casino, where he was shown around and played bridge until 4 AM.[24] He also visited the palaces and castle in nearby Sintra, and made a trip to visit patients in the British Hospital in Lisbon.[25] All of his days were full and he gave the impression of being rather active. In Cascais, he spent time between his appointments swimming in the outdoor pool and sitting outside on the terrace.[26]

On July 26, the duke had a two-hour meeting with the Spanish ambassador to Lisbon, Nicolas Franco (the brother of General Franco), but by this stage the duke's mind appeared to have been made up to proceed to the Bahamas.[27] Despite the attempts of Nicolas Franco to persuade the duke to remain in Portugal, the ambassador reported that his efforts to persuade him to try to resist Churchill's pressure appeared to have failed.[28] Nicolas Franco's judgment was correct.

The duke wrote to Winston Churchill on July 31, stating that he viewed the appointment to the Bahamas as not being one of first-class importance, but that it at least brought a temporary solution to the question of his employment.[29] That evening during a dinner with friends at the Hotel Aviz in Lisbon, the duke publicly announced his decision to accept the post in the Bahamas and confirmed his departure for the Bahamas the next day.

The Duke and Duchess of Windsor sailed from Lisbon at 3 PM on August 1, 1940, on the SS *Excalibur* without their retrieved possessions or their maid. At least one man, Captain Agostinho Lourenço, head of the PVDE, was pleased to see the duke safely depart the shores of Lisbon. For the second time in his police career the Captain had delivered on his promise to protect the duke. On this occasion, with the duke threatened both indirectly and directly by various security services, this had proven to be no easy task. The duke and duchess would sit out the war in the relative safety of their tropical exile.

In a piece of amazing understatement Walford Selby recorded the events in a brief passage in his memoirs. He simply stated that the duke and duchess had made a relatively prolonged stay in Estoril (Cascais) before they had proceeded on to the Bahamas, and that they had met numerous Portuguese who had been very happy to welcome them. He concluded by stating that he had the impression that both the duke and duchess had enjoyed their stay in Portugal, and that they had lots of friends.[30] Before the end of the year, the visibly aging and tiring Selby was replaced by Ronald Campbell, an appointment that marked a significant increase in the attention that London was paying Lisbon.

The German plot to scare, induce, and persuade the duke to return to Spain was in reality a far-fetched one, which had been based on the belief that a disgruntled Duke of Windsor would be willing to turn his back on the British government. In retrospect, it was also a plot that few even on the German side felt had any real chance of success. The German, and even some of the Spanish, participants appeared to half-heartedly play out their roles in the belief that the plot would not succeed. Cables written by Germans at the time were devised to please their superiors rather than reflect the reality of the lack of possibility of success. In the end, the plot became enveloped in internal Nazi politics that did little to increase its already very limited chance of success.[31] When Schellenberg returned to Berlin, he was warmly greeted by his superior, Reinhard Heydrich, who felt that the young intelligence officer had handled his brief from the much-hated Ribbentrop with the correct amount of apparent enthusiasm and practical incompetence.[32]

Churchill, with the king's support, acted decisively using the carrot-and-stick approach to get the duke out of Spain, and subsequently Portugal, as quickly as possible. The duke's extended stay in Lisbon did not alter the course or direction of the war, but it did create more difficulties for Salazar, who was coming under increasing German pressure to be more favorable to them.

The duke's departure closed one problematic file on Salazar's desk, but plenty of new and potentially even more serious files were set to arrive in its place. Of all the challenges he faced, the most pressing was the need to preserve peace in the whole of the Iberian continent. In order to achieve this goal, Salazar needed to draw General Franco towards a deal, which to some extent drew Spain away from the orbit of Germany. Given the pro-German sentiment of parts of the Spanish government, and the fact that the German army after its occupation of France was camped on the Spanish border, this would be no easy task. The job had suddenly got much harder: Italy, long sympathetic to Germany, had decisively entered the war on the German side at last, making it harder for Spain and Portugal to resist.

Central Lisbon, where the street lights continued to burn brightly at night throughout World War II; but they cast deep shadows.

António de Oliveira Salazar (right), with two of his most important supporters, taken at the opening of the Exposição do Mundo Português (Portuguese World Exhibition) in the summer of 1940. Duarte Pacheco is on the left in his bowler hat with António Ferro looking on from the far left. Salazar, a dictator, never wore a military uniform.

Officials and dignitaries in top hats and morning tails at the opening ceremony of the *Exposição do Mundo Português* in 1940, at a time when British troops were being evacuated from the beaches of France.

The Duke of Palmela (left), who would be appointed Portuguese ambassador to Britain in 1943, hosts tea in honor of the Duke of Kent's visit to Portugal in 1940.

The British ambassador, Sir Walford Selby (second from the right, facing camera), dining in Lisbon with local business leaders while being closely shadowed by the German ambassador, Baron Oswald von Hoyningen-Huene (fifth from the right, facing camera).

The lavish interior of the Hotel Aviz in Lisbon. The hotel was a temporary home to the wealthiest of refugees and celebrity visitors to Lisbon during the war.

View of the Estoril beach where Jewish refugees sunbathed under the watchful eyes of bronzed Gestapo agents.

Salazar addressing a huge crowd in Lisbon in 1941. The event was organized by the regime to highlight support for national unity and for Salazar's policy of neutrality in the war. Salazar hated giving speeches to large crowds.

Rossio Square looking toward Chave d'Ouro café, where refugees spoke in hushed tones and were closely watched by agents of the Portuguese Secret Police (PVDE).

Aristides de Sousa Mendes, the Portuguese consul in Bordeaux, and Rabbi Kruger, who helped him issue exit visas to Jews, on their way to Lisbon after Sousa Mendes had been recalled by a furious Salazar.

The lucky ones. Two Lisbon-bound buses packed full of Jewish refugee children who had been helped out of German Occupied Europe by Jewish rescue groups based in Lisbon. Many similar attempts to get Jewish children out of Europe failed due to bureaucratic delays and visa mix ups.

Wealthy, well-dressed Jewish refugees patiently waiting to board a passenger ship in Lisbon bound for the United States.

Varian Fry, the American journalist, ran a rescue operation that helped thousands of anti-Nazi and Jewish refugees. Here, Fry is looking out over the French-Spanish frontier. Many of the less wealthy refugees who fled France had to go over the mountains on foot to reach Spain.

Café Chave d'Ouro in Rossio. The largest café in the city, crowded at night with locals and refugees, in 1941

Rossio station: the first glimpse of Lisbon for many refugees arriving at night.

Salazar and the Portuguese banker, Ricardo Espírito Santo, relaxing together. Espírito Santo did not do anything during the war without the approval of Salazar.

Ricardo Espírito Santo and the Duke of Windsor discussing the latest developments at the banker's house at Boca do Inferno in Cascais.

Ricardo and his wife relaxing in his garden in Cascais with the Duke and Duchess of Windsor.

A German propaganda shop in the Chiado shopping district of Lisbon. The display in the window portrayed Hitler as the best defense against Bolshevism. Many Portuguese shared this sentiment.

Senior officers of Portuguese Secret Police (PVDE) on a rare night off, attending a dinner function at the Spanish Embassy in Lisbon. The Spanish ambassador to Portugal, Nicolas Franco (the brother of General Franco), sits in the middle of the front row. To the ambassador's left is the head of the PVDE, Captain Agostinho Lourenço. Captain Paulo Cumano, the PVDE officer who the Allies considered to be the most pro-German is standing on the far left of the picture.

The German ambassador to Lisbon, Baron Oswald von Hoyningen-Huene, in his study. Clever and calculating, the ambassador built up a formidable network of social connections in Lisbon.

The British diplomat in Lisbon from the Ministry of Economic Warfare, David Eccles, intellectually bright, persuasive, and vain. He oversaw the complex wolfram negotiations with Salazar.

BOLETIM DE ALOJAMENTO DE ESTRANGEIRO

Para os efeitos do art.º 6.º do Decreto N.º 15.884 de 24 de Agosto de 1928, declaro que forneci alojamento ao estrangeiro cuja identidade consta do verso deste boletim.

PALACIO HOTEL

ESTORIL

data 20 de *Maio* de 194*1*

Nota: O nome e endereço podem ser substituídos pelo carimbo aposto nesse lugar.

Este espaço só será preenchido na polícia

E — .... em ..../...../ 19
S — .... em ..../...../ 19

BOLETIM INDIVIDUAL

Para os efeitos do art.º 1.º do Decreto N.º 16.386 de 18 de Janeiro de 1929
(Aprovado pelo Decreto-lei N.º 20.327)

Nome completo / Nom et prénom	*Ian Lancaster Fleming*
Nacionalidade / Nationalité	*Inglesa*
Nascimento / Naissance — local / lieu	*Londres*
data / date	*28 de Maio de 1908*
Profissão / Profession	*Government Official*
Domicílio habitual / Domicile habituel	*England*
Documentos de viagem / Documents de voyage — Passaporte / Passeport (a)	*Passaporte N.º 193543*
Expedido em / Delivré à	*Foreign Office*
Data / Date	*23 de Fevereiro de 1*
Auto.	N.º

Data–Date *20 / 5 / 19 41*   Assignatura–Signature

Ian Fleming's registration document at the Hotel Palácio. Fleming was kept busy in Estoril devising "Operation Golden Eye" and playing blackjack at the largest casino in Europe.

The Hotel Palácio in Estoril was full of spies from all the belligerents in the war. The hotel was the most glamorous place to stay, or be seen at, along the Lisbon coast.

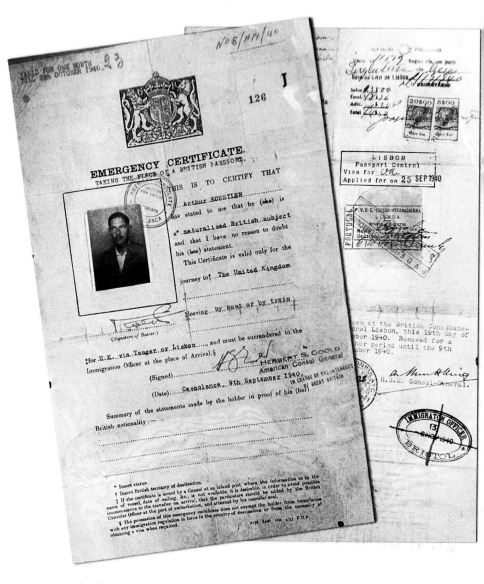

The film *Casablanca* hinges on who possesses the signed exit visa, permitting onward travel to Lisbon. Here is Arthur Koestler's letter of transit with the stamps showing his passage from Casablanca to Lisbon and then to Bristol, England.

Monte Estoril Hotel where Peggy Guggenheim and her entourage stayed after finding central Lisbon too claustrophobic. The children enjoyed playing in the park next to the hotel.

Peggy Guggenheim's registration document at the Monte Estoril Hotel. All foreigners had to complete this document.

BOLETIM INDIVIDUAL

Para os efeitos do art.º 1.º do Decreto N.º 16.386 de 18 de Janeiro de 1929
(Aprovado pelo Decreto lei N.º 26.327)

Nome completo Nom et prénom	*Marguerite S. Guggenheim*	
Nacionalidade Nationalité	*6. U. America*	
Nascimento Naissance	local lieu	*New York City*
	data date	*26 de Agosto de 1898*
Profissão Profession		
Domicilio habitual Domicile habituel	*Marselha*	
Passaporte Passaporte	*Passaporte N.º 245*	
Expedido em Delivré à	*Marselha*	
Data Date	*22 de Março de 1941*	
Auto.	N.º	
Data Date 9/6/19 41	Assignatura Signature *Marguerite Guggenheim*	

Peggy Guggenheim and Max Ernst (center) arriving in New York from Lisbon. Ernst, a German citizen, was given an extended grilling by the U.S. immigration authorities.

Jack Beevor, one of the brightest recruits to the SOE. Salazar expelled him from Lisbon, but the dossier which Beevor wrote on German espionage activities in Lisbon helped persuade Salazar to close down much of the German operation in the city.

The port area of Lisbon was always busy in World War II. If Portugal was invaded, the British planned to blow up the cranes into the river to try to prevent Axis shipping and submarines from using the port.

The Portuguese ship, the *Serpa Pinto*, departing for the United States with its human cargo of refugees.

Lisbon Portela Airport where, during World War II, Allied and German planes were parked next to each other on the tarmac.

Hollywood matinee idol Leslie Howard's (left) last supper in Lisbon before his ill-fated flight to England. The resemblance of Howard's agent, Arthur Chenhalls (right), to Sir Winston Churchill is striking.

The suave British ambassador to Portugal, Sir Ronald Campbell (right), discussing the international situation with U.S. Minister Bert Fish (left) at the British embassy in Lisbon in 1942.

Armindo Monteiro (third from the right) was the Portuguese ambassador to Britain who was widely considered to be an overt Anglophile. His relationship with Salazar soured in 1943 and he was recalled to Lisbon in virtual disgrace.

The Pan Am Clipper arrives in Lisbon. The clipper was used by only the wealthiest of refugees. In February 1943, it crashed on landing in Lisbon into the River Tagus.

Avenida da Liberdade at night—the Champs-Élysées of Lisbon. The Hotel Tivoli was located along its wide, tree-lined boulevards.

Lisbon's taxis screeching over tram rails. The city's taxi drivers continued to do good business throughout the war.

Rossio Square at night. This square was full of refugees, spies, and the Portuguese police watching everything and everyone.

Rossio Square at night. The lights show the silhouette of the medieval castle of São Jorge, which has overlooked Lisbon since the era of the Crusades.

CHAPTER 12

Spanish Connections

I N JUNE 10, 1940, WHEN ITALY DECLARED WAR ON
Britain and France, a disappointed Salazar merely responded by
replacing the old black-and-white picture of Mussolini on his desk
with a photograph of the pope. Like most wars, events moved fast
and old allegiances and alliances changed in previously unforeseen
ways. Salazar believed that Italy could have been kept out of the
war, but his priority in the second half of 1940, and throughout
1941, was to ensure that Spain did not follow the same path as Italy.

The diary of Salazar reveals that achieving this goal was sometimes a very lonely effort, and required all his considerable political and diplomatic skills. As the number of government files
continued to grow on his well-ordered desk, even somebody with
his famed ability to work long hours was starting to feel the
strain. He still believed that a small autocratic government was
the most effective means of governing, but he was already visibly
starting to age.[1] His hair turned gray and his face appeared drawn
with large black bags under his increasingly distant looking eyes.
Foreign diplomats noted his mood was darkening, and his fits of
bad temper were increasing. He had been prime minister for nearly
twenty years, minister of finance since 1928, and in 1941 there
was no end in sight for the war or Portugal's predicament. By
1942, Salazar's state of mind and outbursts would lead the British

ambassador to warn his superiors in London that he was becoming mentally unbalanced.

Salazar's mood reflected that of the city of Lisbon. The anxiety level of the city had gradually increased since the summer of 1940, and it wasn't just the refugees who were showing outward signs of nervous exhaustion and stress. The volume in the cafés and bars increased, as Lisboetas debated the latest news and the threat of being dragged into the war. Even the poorly educated locals understood that the key to the war was the attitude of the Spanish, and in particular General Franco.

Like all good neighbors, the Portuguese had a very limited understanding of Spain and Spanish politics, and vice versa; there was also a lack of Spanish understanding of Portugal, its people and politics. David Eccles was critical of the British ambassador to Spain's tone with the Portuguese, which he compared to how the Australians referred to the New Zealanders. Among most Lisboetas, the belief was that Spain and Franco were pro-Nazi, and would use any excuse to end Portugal's independence. There was also a general understanding that if Spain, or Germany, did launch an attack on the country, the Portuguese military could not do much to repel it. The British had already made it clear that in the event of an attack there was little the UK could do to help.[2]

Among the more educated chattering classes in Lisbon there was a lot of speculation as to what Salazar and the Portuguese government would do if the country were invaded. People recalled that when France had invaded the country during the Peninsular Wars, the royal family, the government, and leading economic figures sailed out of Lisbon to Brazil, where they remained in exile until well after the French had departed.[3] It was generally presumed that on this occasion Salazar and the government would depart Lisbon for one of the Portuguese Islands (the Azores as the choice turned out to be). From there they would continue to mount what resistance they could offer with probable British support, and run a government in exile.

Given the long-term damage that the last Portuguese exodus had done to the country, the prospect of Salazar trying to rule the country from the middle of the Atlantic Ocean in the middle of a global conflict was difficult to envisage. To make matters worse, part of the plan for an orderly withdrawal from Lisbon included sabotaging key installations along the banks of the River Tagus as well parts of the transport system.[4] If the Spanish or Germans had entered Lisbon they would have found a partially destroyed city whose key personalities were already on a boat headed for the Azores. For Salazar, this was the nightmare scenario.

Salazar's interests were aligned with Britain, whom he worked closely with in a frequently coordinated approach to dealing with Spain.[5] The maintenance of Spanish neutrality was of great importance to the British in order for it to retain control over the Straits of Gibraltar, to prevent the establishment of German air and submarine bases in northern Spain, Spanish Morocco, and the Canary Islands. In addition, the British wanted to secure essential minerals, particularly iron ore, of which Spain was a major supplier.[6]

Salazar's concern about a Spanish or German invasion proved accurate on both counts: Germany planned an invasion of the Iberian continent for 1941, and detailed Spanish plans for the invasion of Portugal also emerged.[7] The culmination of Salazar's diplomatic efforts to secure the continued formal neutrality of Spain was the signing of the additional protocol to the existing Treaty of Friendship and Non-Aggression Pact between Portugal and Spain on July 29, 1940.[8] The new protocol, in essence, linked the security of the two countries and created the impression of a relatively unified policy of neutrality in the Iberian Peninsula. Like most such protocols, the exact language was open to wide interpretation by both sides. The Falangist elements in Spain saw it as a means of bringing Lisbon more into the political orbit of Madrid. In other words, it fitted their nationalistic agenda of eventually bringing Portugal back under Spanish control.

In Lisbon, though, the protocol was conversely viewed as the best means of ensuring Spanish neutrality, and consequently, of reducing the threat of invasion to Portugal. Ironically, both Britain and Germany, at least partially, welcomed the protocol, arguing that it indicated that their respective Iberian allies were showing signs of protecting themselves against their enemies. Given the internal political instability in Madrid, and the ever-changing plans of Hitler, the protocol did not ensure the end of the Spanish threat, but to misuse a quote from Winston Churchill, it did mark the start of the end of it.

There would be more crises involving Spain, particularly in the economic sphere, and Salazar's attention to diplomatic detail and ability to get on well with General Franco would be required. Salazar's role in the successful managing of Franco from an Allied perspective would be highly debated by politicians, diplomats, and historians, but the broad consensus was that it was absolutely vital.[9]

The British felt that the role Salazar played in keeping Spain out of the war in 1940–1941 was central. David Eccles argued that Salazar and the MFA played a huge role in keeping Spain from joining the Axis powers. As a result, in order to bolster Salazar, and to reflect the heightened importance of Anglo-Portuguese relations to London, the British arranged three offerings for the second part of 1940 and the start of 1941. On September 24, 1940, Winston Churchill wrote to Salazar to thank him for his efforts with Spain, and to encourage him to keep them up:

> I have followed with the greatest sympathy and admiration the efforts you have made to prevent war spreading to the Iberian Peninsula. As so often during the many centuries of the Anglo-Portuguese Alliance, British and Portuguese interests are identical on this vital question.[10]

The second British offering was the decision of Oxford University to confer an honorary degree upon Salazar. In writing to

Salazar, the committee made it clear that they understood that Salazar would, due to work commitments, be unable to travel to Oxford to pick up the award. Instead, the awarding committee would travel to Coimbra University, where they would confer the degree upon him.

The award of the degree represented a superb opportunity for British propaganda purposes. Salazar understood this point, and hesitated in accepting the award for fear of offending the Germans. His academic background, and the fact that he considered himself to be a scholar, however, meant that he was reluctant to turn down the award from one of the world's most prestigious universities.

In the end he agreed to accept and travelled to Coimbra to have the degree conferred upon him. The ceremony was conducted with a great deal of formality that was part of the deeply held culture of both universities (two of the oldest in the world). The ceremony and Salazar's comments following it were filmed by Pathe News and shown back in England. All in all, the event represented a top-class British propaganda exercise, helping to impress upon the Portuguese their historic alliance with England.

The final part of the British jigsaw was the appointment of Ronald Campbell to succeed Walford Selby as British ambassador to Portugal. Bert Fish, head of the American delegation in Lisbon, thought the appointment of Campbell highly significant.[11] Fish argued that Campbell's appointment was meant to send a signal to Salazar that the British were upping their game in Lisbon, and was also intended to check the growing influence of the Germans in the city.[12] Fish also pointed out the increase in the number, and quality, of staff that worked in the new embassy building as a sign that the British were serious about making a stronger diplomatic impact in Lisbon.[13]

The major problem facing Campbell was the impact of the British economic blockade on Portugal. Fish argued that while both Salazar and the Portuguese were pro-British, they could not be expected to sit back and suffer from the impact of the economic blockade. The system was damaging to Portuguese trade, and according to the Americans, was being poorly managed by the British.[14]

Salazar viewed the question of trade in a very different light from the British. For him, there was no issue in trading with both the Allies and Axis powers. At this stage, it wasn't clear who was going to win the war, or indeed if either side would secure a total victory over the other. Even among the strongest Anglophiles in Lisbon, there was a feeling at this stage of the war that things were not going well for the Allies. Salazar viewed neutrality not as a rigid concept, but rather as a shifting one. At this stage of the war, it made sense for Portugal to openly trade with both sides. He also believed that if Portugal did not conduct trade with Germany, then this would lead to an increase in the threat of German military action against the country.

It was only much later in the war, when the outcome was assured for the Allies, that Salazar quietly gave the order to some of his close economic confidants to stop trading with the Germans. All of this might have appeared very logical to a poor country like Portugal, but to the British, and in particular the MEW, it was a major source of annoyance.

In response, the MEW started drawing up a blacklist of names and individuals who they claimed had traded with Germany, and after the war, action would be taken against them. The first problem that the MEW came across in Portugal was how to gather such information. Much of it needed locally based knowledge, so the MEW engaged a number of locally recruited employees to aid this task, as well as people who had directly been in business in Portugal.[15]

The problem of doing this in a small, centralized country like Portugal was that it was open to abuse in terms of placing a name or company on a blacklist, which was rival to somebody the local employee of the MEW knew. There were instances too of people not getting contracts and subsequently threatening to get the name of the company that didn't award them the contract placed on the blacklist.[16] Ricardo Espírito Santo, and the bank he headed, was thought to have been targeted in this way.

Economic life in Lisbon was not like London, and the MEW seemed to fail to understand the cultural factors that led the system to become open to abuse by dissatisfied or opportunistic individuals. The use of the blacklist, if at times a little unfairly targeted, was considered by the British, and subsequently, the United States as an effective weapon against Germany and those companies and individuals that traded with it. As the war dragged on, it became clear that the Americans were keener about the idea of a strict implementation of the blacklist, and it was made clear that Allied discrimination against blacklisted companies would continue in the postwar period.[17]

What the British and, to a lesser degree, the Americans failed to fully understand, was that all sectors of Portuguese society wanted to make something out of the war. It was not just the Portuguese state, the big banks, companies, the hotels and bed and breakfast owners and police informers, but also individuals who saw an opportunity to reap some rewards. New skills were learned, such as trading in rare stones and unofficial currency exchange.

Prostitution, which had always been a secret part of Lisbon life in the docks areas, became rife. Desperately poor local girls, many of them underage and living in terrible housing conditions, maximized their returns from trade with locals, as well as with the influx of foreigners that arrived in Lisbon between 1940 and 1943. Wealthy looking refugees staying in the city were often followed by prostitutes in the hope of getting some business at the end of the day. The hotel bars in Lisbon were notorious for allowing prostitutes to mingle with guests, after they had tipped the doormen.

It was not unknown for some of the refugees to turn to prostitution as well, in order to help finance travel tickets out of Lisbon.

There were stories of desperate refugees, whose stay in Lisbon had turned out to be longer than expected, due to the wait for their onward visa, turning to prostitution to fund their extended stay in the city. Reports and accounts of refugee prostitution were a little exaggerated in terms of numbers. Most of the activity took place involving local girls. The report of the records of the major dermato-venereological center in Lisbon showed there was an epidemic level of sexually transmitted diseases in the city during World War II.[18] Needless to say, the report was not given any coverage in the tightly controlled Portuguese press.

Back in London at the MEW, there appeared to be a lack of understanding of the overall economic activity that was taking place in Lisbon. The major Portuguese companies traded with whom Salazar advised them to deal with, and this included Germany. Most of the major companies, and banks in Portugal, were controlled by the elite families, many of whom owed Salazar a lot for allowing them to develop their business empires and would not have traded with the Germans without his direct blessing. The Germans were keen to trade with the Portuguese for a number of reasons, not least the fact that such trade links brought, in their view, the two countries closer together, and as a result, damaged Anglo-Portuguese relations.

On April 28, 1941, there had been a massive demonstration in Lisbon in honor of Salazar, national unity, and his policy of neutrality. Foreign observers of the demonstration had initially been skeptical of it, regarding it as being officially organized and therefore not a purely spontaneous display of national sentiment.[19] On the day of the demonstration the center of Lisbon was bedecked in flags flying from government buildings.

The day's celebrations started at 1 PM at the Ministry of Finance, where a bust of Salazar was unveiled in front of him and leading officials of the government.[20] All public offices closed an hour later and the demonstration started to form soon after. People traveled from all over the country to attend. They came on buses, in specially organized trains and some even on bicycles. They were entertained as they arrived in the Lisbon's main square, known as Black Horse Square, by fourteen Portuguese military bands.[21]

At 6 PM, Salazar appeared from one of the windows of the Ministry of Finance that faced the square, which had a huge Portuguese flag draped from it. After a prolonged and enthusiastic reception, Salazar delivered his speech to an impressively silent crowd below.[22] At the end of the speech there was prolonged applause and shouts of long live Portugal, and long live Salazar. After giving the fascist salute, Salazar withdrew, leaving the huge crowd to disperse quietly.[23]

The rally had been brilliant political theater and served its real purpose of reminding everyone that Salazar's policies towards the war were saving Lisbon from the horrors of war. Like all of Salazar's speeches there was little in the way of fiery rhetoric or promises of great things to come. It was, in reality, a carefully worded call for national unity and support for the policy of neutrality.[24] It was vaguely worded and said nothing new.

The event itself was of a greater importance than the speech delivered by Salazar. The British ambassador best summed the impact of the speech on the Allied side when he remarked that the event and speech had showed that Salazar's heart was in the right place, but he would like to know a little bit more what was in Salazar's head.[25] Nearly all of the Portuguese press covered the rally in great detail, and Salazar's speech was published in the inside pages of the dailies. Lisbon would not witness a political rally on this scale throughout the rest of the war. Salazar preferred to sit quietly behind his desk and work his way through the problem of keeping Portugal out of the war, and to consider the economic opportunities that the war offered the country.

CHAPTER 13

Secret Jewish
Rescue Lists

A**S SALAZAR WAS ADDRESSING THE CROWD, THE**
refugee crisis in Lisbon was still at its height. One mile west of
the window from where Salazar had made the address was the
main part of Lisbon's docks, situated in the area from Santos to Alcântara. Here the contrast could not have been greater, as ships
carrying the refugees slowly loaded their human cargoes and sailed
up the river towards the Atlantic Ocean, and usually to the United
States. Many of the refugees slept up against their luggage as they
waited the seemingly endless hours to board a ship. The offices of
shipping companies were scenes of great chaos and noise as people
tried to secure their onward passage. From time to time fights
broke out, but the Portuguese police assigned to guard the offices
of the various shipping companies soon broke these up.

For the wealthy, the Pan Am Clipper flying boat service offered
a quicker and more exclusive route out of Lisbon. These large flying hotels could reach New York in a single day with a refueling
stop in the Azores. They took off and landed from a specially designed port along the river. The Clippers were luxurious, and the
ticket prices reflected this. Inside there was a dining room and a
bar. Each passenger berth resembled a five-star hotel room com-

plete with turn-down bed service. However, despite all the luxury and service, many of the Clipper's passengers, particularly the children, suffered from terrible air sickness on the way to New York and as a result drank or ate very little.[1] Most of the tickets for refugees fleeing Lisbon were reserved in New York by wealthy relatives, friends, or donors of the refugees.

During the war, Lisbon hosted many famous celebrity refugees. Many of the Jewish refugees owed their presence in Lisbon to the work of an American, Varian Fry, who (like Aristides de Sousa Mendes) has been honored at Yad Vashem Holocaust Memorial Museum as one of the "Righteous Among the Nations." Varian Fry traveled to Marseilles in the summer of 1940 as a representative of the Emergency Rescue Committee (a private American relief organization). Here, using funds supplied by wealthy American Jews, he organized an escape line to Lisbon for a number of specially selected artists and public figures who were on the list he carried. Fry was more than a little uncomfortable with the nature of the list, which effectively selected the refugees that he could try to help.[2] His work was often very dangerous, Gestapo agents were closing in on him, but he continued his work until he himself had to flee France as well. Upon his return to the United States, Fry tried to warn the government about the plight of the Jews in Europe. Curiously, his work in France led him to be investigated by the FBI, who put him on their watch list. Fry died in 1967 while reediting his memoirs. His name often appears in biographies of the famous, many of whom owe their lives to him and his small dedicated team of helpers.

One of the groups of refugees whom Varian Fry helped out of France through Spain and into Lisbon were the art collector Peggy Guggenheim, her ex-husband Laurence Vail, and the artist Max Ernst, along with their extended party of family and friends. Their story, like many other tales of similar escapes, was a mixture of the extraordinary and the mundane. Peggy had been fleeing the

Germans since Paris, where she had been busy building up one of
the world's most significant modern art collections. While on the
run, canvases were often simply rolled up or pushed into suitcases.[3]
She had something of a reputation for collecting art that was not
particularly to the taste of the Nazis. As a result, the Germans were
very keen to catch her, although, in retrospect, the extent of the
German interest in her and the art appeared a little exaggerated in
her account of events. The biggest threat to her life was not the
art, rather the simple fact that she was Jewish, and Jews were already being singled out in France. Peggy was advised that if she
were questioned by the police to deny that she was Jewish and say
simply that she was an American.[4]

Fry had discovered in January 1941 that many of the refugees
could suddenly get exit visas from France.[5] This dramatic change in
policy, he believed, had been caused by the Gestapo, and other secret police organizations, completing their task of going through
the lists of political and intellectual refugees in France and deciding which they wanted to detain and which they would let slip
through their net.[6] A decision was made that not all Jews had to be
eliminated, as long as they were removed from France. The
Guggenheim-Ernst party appeared to be on the list of names that
were allowed to slip through the official net. This didn't mean that
the party was not in danger, but simply indicated that the Gestapo
was not actively looking for them nor would pursue them.

Peggy Guggenheim and her party arrived at Rossio station in
Lisbon in the spring of 1941. She still had on the distinctive ear-
rings she had worn since the south of France—long crescents,
hung with tiny framed pictures by Max Ernst.[7] Ernst, strikingly
handsome with powerful eyes and white hair, was there to meet
her at the station. He had arrived a few days before, carrying a
large roll of his own paintings, which he had brought with him from
France. In France, he had tacked up his pictures in the drawing
room of the house he stayed to show them off to Varian Fry and the
other refugees waiting to go to Lisbon.[8]

Lisbon in the spring of 1941, however, was not the place for impromptu art galleries, and Ernst clung tightly to his art. Peggy Guggenheim was equally nervous. Before setting out for Lisbon she had asked Fry a series of quickfire questions about travel arrangements and what to say if stopped by the police.[9] Fry had given her party, like all the refugees he helped, packs of cigarettes to bribe the border guards.[10] Peggy recounted a story of how, before her departure, she had tried to borrow fifty dollars from Marc Chagall, to help Ernst with some money for when he arrived in Lisbon before Peggy. Chagall, at this time, was trying to transfer some $8,000 to the United States. When asked, Chagall hesitated and said that he knew nothing about money and told Peggy to return to the hotel in the afternoon to talk with his daughter, who dealt with his financial affairs. Needless to say that when Peggy came back to the hotel, Chagall's daughter was nowhere to be found.[11]

Having been issued with mainly genuine papers and visas, the Guggenheim party's journey through Spain was largely uneventful. Although the papers were genuine in origin, Peggy's travel permit had a forged date to extend its time limit for travel.[12] It was standard for refugees to be prepared by Fry to try to bribe the border guards if their papers were found not to be in order. The fact that visa stamps were out of date was a particularly common problem among the refugees fleeing through Spain at the time.[13]

Peggy seemed oblivious to the fact that there were severe food shortages in Spain at the time. She ate well in Spain and put on some of the weight she had lost in France.[14] She claimed the markets overflowed with food.[15] In reality, Spain at the time was extremely expensive and exhausted the majority of the resources of refugees that were less well off than the Guggenheims.[16]

As the train wound its way through the orange-colored plains under a deep blue sky heading towards the Portuguese border, Peggy started to unwind for the first time in months. The PVDE had examined their papers at the border and after some delay had allowed the party to proceed onto Lisbon, where she arrived at the start of May 1941.[17] Peggy had messed up the recital of the script to use if questioned by police, which Fry had given her and all the refugees he sent down the line. Luckily, the Portuguese police officer had appeared remarkably disinterested in her presence on the border and let her go on her way.

As the Guggenheim party descended from the central station at the northern edge of Rossio, the first building they saw directly in front of them was the western side of beautiful Teatro Nacional D. Maria II. It was a spectacular neoclassical building featuring six Ionic columns on its façade. Lit up at night it dominated the north side of the Rossio.

The site of the theater, however, had a dark history. Before the theater was built, the north side of Rossio was dominated by the Palácio dos Estaus, which had served as the headquarters of the Inquisition in Lisbon. During this time, officials of the Catholic Church tried Jews in the building. If the accused were found guilty, they were handed over to the Portuguese state for punishment. In most cases, this meant the parading of the Jews into the main square of Rossio, where the punishment was first read out and then immediately carried out. The punishments ranged from beatings to torture and death, usually by burning, in front of large crowds of local inhabitants.

The Palácio dos Estaus survived the Lisbon earthquake of 1755, but was later destroyed by fire in 1836. The site was still known by locals as the place where the Jews were burnt. It was probably just as well that Guggenheim and her traveling companions had little idea of this grisly tale. Instead, she focused on finding help to take their luggage to a nearby hotel. The Guggenheims, like all the refugees Varian Fry noted, had far too much luggage with them for a group that was fleeing the Germans. For her part, Peggy simply wanted to get to a hotel and rest after the long train journey.

Once in Lisbon, Peggy Guggenheim was reunited with the members of her extended party who had arrived earlier.[18] Almost immediately tension and anxiety exploded into huge rows in the party about their complex relationships. In truth, the whole party was either physically or emotionally drained, or simply at the end of their tether.[19]

With her flamboyant dress sense and colorful jewelry, Peggy stood out from the local women who frequented the Café Leão D'Ouro, next to Rossio station. She found the Rossio area of Lisbon very claustrophobic and ventured out for long walks up to the Chiado shopping district and down to Baixa, the main shopping area that Marques de Pombal had rebuilt after the devastating earthquake of 1755. Both she and her extended party of friends, lover, and ex-husband visited several of Lisbon's *Miradouros* (viewing areas), where they admired the stunning evening views with the lights of Lisbon burning brightly as a reminder of the vague normality of life in the city.

The Guggenheim-Ernst party were, in part, financially supported by a group of leading Jews in New York. Solomon Guggenheim had contributed to this fund and he was essentially bankrolling his niece and her party in Lisbon, and paying for some of the tickets to New York. Peggy soon grew tired of the intensity of Lisbon and the party moved out to Estoril along the Lisbon coast. Here they checked into a modest hotel in Monte Estoril, with views to the sea below.[20]

Although the better air and the feeling of space appeared to reduce some of the internal wrangling within the party, there were still eruptions of temper and fits of jealousy as the group tried to relax. Peggy ventured back into Lisbon to check on visas and travel arrangements, taking the electric train that wound its way along the rocky coastline and into Lisbon. While the party was in little direct danger in Lisbon, there were awkward encounters with German spies and the PVDE agents who shadowed foreigners in the city. Wherever Peggy went she turned heads and attracted remarks—not always favorable—from local women. As she spoke no Portuguese, she was largely indifferent to all but the most obscene comments, usually accompanied by a corresponding gesture.

Peggy and her party, when not engaged in various feuds and relationship trouble, tried to treat their time in Estoril as a type of forced vacation. Like all good tourists they visited the town of Sintra with its beautiful colorful palaces and Moorish castle set at the top of the mountain.[21] Peggy noted the clearness of the air in Sintra, which was located up in the mountains and had been, in previous times, host to the poet Byron. Many members of the royal families of Europe used to spend their summers in the various palaces, enjoying the cool clear air and spectacular views. The light, as Max Ernst noted, was amazing, and he admitted that it influenced some of his subsequent works. Sintra proved to be a calming, restful break, and the couple visited it several times during their months in Portugal.

On one summer's evening, Peggy and Max threw caution to the wind and went nighttime skinny-dipping in Cascais, very close to Boca do Inferno where the previous summer the duke and duchess had stayed in Ricardo Espírito Santo's house.[22] On this occasion, there were no spies or PVDE agents hanging around the area, only a few bemused fishermen who sat mending nets. Afterwards, Peggy made love with Ernst among the black rocks that the Windsors had looked out onto the previous year. Their only problem that night was that the area of the rocks that they had made love in was used as the unofficial local toilet.[23]

Peggy recalled being trailed by a strange young local girl who followed them back to the hotel, where the doorman tried to send her away.[24] The girl started following them every time they went out until she suddenly disappeared. It was unlikely that she was a paid PVDE informer; she was more likely either plying another ancient trade or simply fascinated by the style and mannerisms of Peggy and Max.

Eventually, their day of departure arrived. There was last minute drama as Peggy tried to no avail to get additional names added onto their travel party. She soon discovered that they were short one bed on the Clipper.[25] Tensions and concern about those not accompanying the party led to more tears and repercussions for life in New York. Peggy Guggenheim, Max Ernst, and the party of eleven finally departed Lisbon on July 13, 1941, on the Clipper bound for New York. Peggy's only recollection of the flight was flying over a ship, which she believed carried her friends. Like all passengers on the Clipper, British agents who were keen to gather information about France interviewed the party upon their arrival in Bermuda for a stopover.[26] Her party, she noted, all gave completely conflicting accounts of their journey.

Peggy Guggenheim and Max Ernst were in Lisbon only a month after of the demonstration of support for Salazar and his speech, but it is doubtful that they even knew of the event or understood anything as to the pressures that Portugal was facing at this time. The artistic refugees, like Peggy and Ernst, as well as the painter Marc Chagall, who stayed in Lisbon for just under a month in 1941 after he had arrived in the city on May 11, were very detached from the reality of everyday life in the city of light. It was as if there were two Lisbons: one for the poorer refugees and locals, and the other for those who viewed the city as something of an enforced holiday camp.

Chagall was in a world of his own. Having been arrested in France, Chagall was helped by Varian Fry, with Solomon Guggenheim financing a large part of his journey through France and his ticket from Lisbon to America. After being arrested, Chagall became deeply fearful, like other refugees who had been detained in France. He was afraid that every time the doorbell rang it might be the local police coming to take him to the Gestapo.[27] This fear became too much for him and he started to show signs of serious mental strain.

In Lisbon, Chagall was an isolated lonely figure, and irritated at having to spend additional time in a city where delays were routine. Chagall did eventually leave for New York, but made little reference to his time in Lisbon.

For political refugees such as Berthold Jacob and his wife, their flight to Lisbon was much more dangerous and was to end in tragedy. Berthold Jacob was a well-known German-Jewish journalist who had founded a pacifist group that was known as "No More War." He had been a critic of the Nazis for a long time and had spent much energy trying to warn Germany, and the world, that the Nazis were rearming and preparing for war. Jacob and his wife were hiding in France, but with the deportation of other key German opposition figures, Varian Fry took the decision to send him down the line to Lisbon.[28]

Fry managed to obtain visas for them, which was strange in retrospect given that the Gestapo were very much more interested in Jacob than the artists and celebrity Jews such as Peggy Guggenheim. Jacob and his wife were sent down the line by Fry, but before they reached the Portuguese border, Fry had discovered that their papers were crude forgeries,[29] so crude that you could see the pencil marks where the forgers had tried to trace the original. To make matters worse, both Jacobs were traveling under their real names. Fry dreaded what would happen and he was soon informed that they had been arrested at the Portuguese border and sent to a prison in Madrid.

Fry raced to free Jacob and used a source in the criminal world who wanted 50,000 francs to get the Jacobs released and provide them with visas to enter Portugal. A skeptical Fry discovered soon after that the Jacobs had persuaded the Spanish authorities that their visas were genuine—a coded way of saying that the underworld connection Fry had paid had succeeded.[30] He discovered that the Jacobs were out of jail and staying in a hotel in Madrid.

Eventually, they entered Portugal without visas in the limousine of an influential Spanish businessman.[31] The border crossings were some of the most nerve-racking aspects of the escape lines that Fry had to organize.[32] It was never clear what would happen. Sometimes the crossings were routine, but on other occasions they were fraught with difficulty even if the refugee had obtained the correct paperwork. On this occasion the crossing into Portugal took place without the car being stopped and searched.

In Lisbon, the Jacobs lived illegally, waiting and hoping for exit visas to arrive. They never did. One day, when Jacob had gone out to inquire about his visa, he did not return to his hotel room. His wife contacted Varian Fry's colleagues and eventually the horrible truth was uncovered. Jacob had been stopped by two Portuguese officers (presumably PVDE) and a third man, who spoke Portuguese with a foreign accent, and who identified Jacob to the policemen. Some days later, Fry discovered that Jacob was in jail in Madrid and hired a lawyer to try to get him released. The lawyer never got to see Jacob who disappeared to a concentration camp and was never heard of again.[33]

The finger of suspicion was pointed at the Portuguese PVDE for aiding the Gestapo in effectively kidnapping Berthold Jacob off the street in Lisbon. It appeared to confirm the fact that the pro-German sympathies of some of the members led them to cooperate with the Germans. While attempts by both the British and Germans to try to bribe some of the senior officers in the PVDE had failed, or met with very limited success, German attempts at a lower level bore more fruit. There were at least three cases of lower-level agents being in the pay of the Germans.[34]

One of these cases was Agent José Correia de Almeida who worked in Captain Lourenço's office and was also linked to the counterespionage section. Correia de Almeida was being paid by the Germans to hand over information related to refugee passports and visas, which the Germans then used to identify refugees such as Jews and French agents passing through Lisbon and have them arrested by the PVDE.[35] Something of a fanatic, Correia de Almeida, employed ruthless methods to further his cause. It is widely believed, although not documented, that Correia de Almeida was the PVDE agent responsible for the arrest of Berthold Jacob.[36]

In 1940, another Jewish political activist and writer, Arthur Koestler, had experienced a much easier time in Lisbon, where he was largely left alone by the PVDE and German agents operating in the city. Koestler had arrived in Lisbon by boat on September 17, 1940, and stayed in the city for seven weeks, leaving on November 6, 1940.[37] Unlike many of the refugees staying in Lisbon, Koestler did not have money worries, thanks to regular royalty payments from his U.S. publisher. Koestler's problem was of a different nature: convincing the British authorities to allow him to reenter Britain. With money to fund a simple but comfortable lifestyle, there was little else to do but make regular visits to the British consulate.[38]

Like Peggy Guggenheim the following year, Koestler stayed in the modest Hotel Frankfort in Rossio. Later, as the likely extent of his stay in Lisbon became more apparent to him, he checked in at the cheaper Pensão Leiriense.[39] The Pensão was rather run-down and dusty, and was full of refugees. With the price of beds in Lisbon's hotels at hugely inflated prices in 1940, the Pensão was the best option for Koester's budget.

Despite the apparent financial well-being, Koestler was deeply concerned that the Portuguese authorities would hand him over to the Spanish, and this fear hung over him for the entire period of his stay in Lisbon.[40] In a subsequent interrogation by British authorities he talked up this fear, threatening to commit suicide if he was sent back to Lisbon. His apparent fear of returning stemmed from a series of articles he had written, which he claimed exposed the pro-German elements in the Portuguese administration; he was afraid that the Portuguese authorities would extradite him to Spain, where he would be tortured, or shot, or both. Given what happened to Berthold Jacob the following year in Lisbon, Koestler's fears—although they were admittedly mainly self-serving—might well have come true.

With a keen writer's eye on observing events and personalities in Lisbon, he undertook the research for the book *Arrival and De-*

parture, which was eventually published in 1943. It was a novel based on Koestler's experiences in Lisbon, with the central character, Peter Slavek, a fictional version of Koestler himself.[41] The novel, which was critically well received, was the first one Koestler wrote in English.[42] The fictional *Arrival and Departure* contains many colorful characters, but in reality Koestler was something of a lone wolf in Lisbon. He had a brief affair with an American woman, Ellen Hill, but aside from this he was usually alone wandering through the streets in the center of Lisbon and taking coffee at the Café Chave D'Ouro in Rossio. He did meet fellow intellectual refugees in Lisbon, but like many so-called political refugees he was closely watched by the PVDE, just in case he tried to meet with local dissident groups.

Such shadowing of refugees like Koestler was a normal part of the PVDE remit, who were deeply concerned that the arrival of these refugees, whom they presumed to be Communist, should not destabilize the internal political situation in Lisbon. The PVDE needn't have worried. There is very little evidence to suggest that political refugees on the run from the Germans showed any appetite for meeting local political dissidents. Indeed, detailed PVDE reports of opposition activity in Portugal did not contain much in the way of information on the refugees encouraging or stoking unrest during their time in Lisbon. By the time most of the political refugees reached Lisbon they were far too weary, and often too scared, to do much agitating even if they had wanted to. What seemingly united all refugees was the desire to get out of Lisbon as soon as possible and on to their final destination.

When Ricardo Espírito Santo was asked by the British about why the PVDE, at the outset, appeared to treat the refugees so harshly, he argued that the secret police thought most of the refugees to be communists or communist sympathizers. He also pointed out that the U.S. Consulate in Lisbon had treated many refugees in a harsh manner for the same reason.[43] Until the arrival of the refugees, Portugal under Salazar had been a largely closed country, due in no small part to its geographical position, lack of an international airport, and rather poor infrastructure for overseas visitors. The vast majority of foreigners in Lisbon before the war were Spaniards who came to the coastal resorts, such as Estoril.

Once the initial shock of the arrival of thousands of refugees in Lisbon had passed, the PVDE came to the conclusion that for the most part the refugees posed little or no threat to the Estado Novo, and were simply in transit. Refugees, in short, were not allowed to remain in Portugal on a permanent basis unless Salazar gave his personal blessing, which he reserved for several members of Europe's royal families who remained in Lisbon, effectively in permanent exile.

The question of his final destination was Koestler's major concern during his stay in Lisbon.[44] Koestler wished to go to Britain, but MI5 and the British Home Office continued to insist that Koestler was an undesirable alien and his entry into Britain was barred for security reasons. Koestler pleaded with a number of influential friends in Britain and America. Senior newspapermen, publishers, and Harold Nicolson from the Ministry of Information were all lobbied, but to no avail.

An increasingly desperate Koestler, whose mental health was rapidly deteriorating in Lisbon, discovered that his name was on Varian Fry's list of outstanding Jewish intellectuals to be rescued.[45] Despite the efforts of Fry's team to lobby on Koestler's behalf, there was no change in British policy.[46] Finally, and with some unofficial help from Henry King, the British consul-general in Lisbon, Koestler boarded the BOAC plane at Lisbon without the correct documentation on November 6 bound for an uncertain future in England.[47]

Koestler arrived at Whitchurch Airport near Bristol at 11:40 AM on November 6 and, when questioned, announced that he was afraid that they would have to arrest him as he had no visa.[48]

Koestler was interrogated and recounted his story in detail and with great drama.[49] His interrogator concluded at the end of the interview that Koestler was one third genius, one third blackguard, and one third lunatic.[50] The report concluded with the comment that Koestler was almost certainly a Jew, but that the question had not been put to Koestler in case of possible legal repercussions from his powerful employers at the *News Chronicle*. Despite failing to impress the authorities, who were initially keen to return him to Lisbon, Koestler eventually settled in London after a stay in His Majesty's Prison in Pentonville.[51]

The cases of Peggy Guggenheim, Berthold Jacob, and Arthur Koestler were just three out of the thousands of people who arrived in Lisbon in the period from mid-1940 onwards. For the first wave of refugees there was little in the way of organized aid and relief groups to help them. As the war went on, and the importance of Lisbon as the last gateway out of Europe came into sharper focus, the organization of emergency rescue groups gathered pace.

The attitude of the PVDE was less frantic. Their tactics were based much more on moving the refugees through the city as quickly as possible, rather than on intimidation. Another major improvement for the refugees arriving later was the increase in staffing levels at the British and American consulates, which at least meant that the time needed to deal with the issues of entry visas became much shorter. Lisbon was still a difficult, often scary experience for refugees, but at least the initial shock had worn off on the Portuguese, who continued to offer the refugees a strange mixture of Christian hospitality tinged with a degree of financial exploitation wherever possible.

CHAPTER 14

Double Dealing

SALAZAR'S OFFICE IN SÃO BENTO WAS JUST FAR enough away from the docks not to hear all the commotion of the refugees boarding the ships, the shouts, and the crying. He could, however, hear the sounds of the sirens that warned of the movement of the overhead cranes, which were busy loading and unloading more traditional cargoes onto the ships. The smell of the sea reached the building along with that of sardines being cooked on nearby barbecues.[1] During the hours of twilight, when Salazar was busy going through the diplomatic cables, the neighborhood was very quiet except for the shouts of children being bathed in nearby apartments. In order to clear his head of the day's business, Salazar often paused and went for a stroll through the garden in which he had personally supervised the selection of the flowers and the planting of the flowerbeds.[2]

As the carefully stacked piles of files continued to grow on Salazar's already overcrowded desk, one subject came to dominate his attention more than any other: the economic war. It was in this area that Salazar faced his biggest challenges in having to play the dual roles of both a neutral power and an ally of Britain.[3] In navigating Portugal through the minefield of demands and counter-demands, Salazar attempted to maximize the Portuguese gain from the economic war without unduly exposing Portugal to an economic or military backlash from either one of the warring parties. If one man was ever qualified to deal with this challenge it was Salazar.

The Portuguese leader was willing and able to devote the extraordinary long working hours required to deal with these issues, and, equally importantly, was able to command his brief in a manner that both impressed and, at times, intimidated his fellow negotiators. The economic war, and its incredibly complex and detailed sets of negotiations, came to test Salazar's personal relationships with the key players in the war to the limit. It was also to provide him with his finest hour of the war, and perhaps of his entire thirty-eight-year period in office.

British and, after their entry into the war, American frustration and anger against Salazar for his conduct during the economic war did not disappear until long after the guns had fallen silent. They were sure that Salazar had conducted the negotiations with the purpose of trying to maximize the Portuguese economic gain rather than being motivated by attempts to shorten the duration of the war.[4] Despite threats from the Allies to cut all exports to Portugal including petroleum and gas, Salazar proved very difficult to intimidate.[5]

The British originally tried to employ two weapons against Portugal in the arena of economic warfare. Upon the entry of the United States into the war, these economic warfare activities were rapidly expanded and were conducted on a joint British and American basis.[6] The first of these weapons was the use of the economic blockade, which aimed to stop neutral countries from exporting to the enemy.[7] The blockade was usually undertaken through negotiation with the neutral country on the quantity of imports needed, which determined a subsequent promise not to import more than was essential.

In World War II, the British felt that the most effective method of managing the blockade was to set up a system called navicerts. Here overseas exporters would notify the MEW in London of their desire to export a quantity of goods to Portugal, and MEW officials would check that it was within the limits and issue it a navicert that would allow the goods to pass through the naval blockade.[8]

The second weapon employed by the British was preemption. This involved overbuying from the neutral power in order to prevent it selling to the enemy. This tactic naturally required the agreement of the neutral country to sell all their goods to one market. The British could not, however, completely buy up the most important commodity that Portugal possessed in terms of waging war: wolfram. Even if the British could have afforded to buy every last ounce, they dared not risk totally depriving the Germans access to the Portuguese market for wolfram, in case it provoked them into simply seizing the heavy metal by invading the country, tungsten mines and all.

Wolfram (tungsten) was mined in the center and the northeast of Portugal, and among its many uses was the armaments industry, where it was used to harden steel. The boiling point of wolfram, one of the hardest and heaviest metals, is the highest of any metal. It was used for armor, armor-piercing shells, bearings, and in the manufacture of high-speed cutting tools, among the many uses of wolfram related to the armaments industry. The armor-piercing shells were hugely successful in Germany's North African campaign.[9] In short, without an adequate supply of wolfram the German armaments industry would have slowly ground to halt, and the war would have been lost for Germany.

The stakes for securing wolfram were, as a result, huge from a German perspective, and throughout the war they employed a range of tactics in order to secure it. As the war developed, many supplies dried up and the German military became extremely reliant on the export of Portuguese wolfram, and to a lesser extent Spanish wolfram. The "wolfram wars" became a central feature in the relationship between Portugal and the Axis and Allied powers.

The British economic boycott was never popular in Portugal. Even among the mainly Anglophile Lisbon business elite there was widespread anger about the damage that it was causing the country. As one of Europe's poorest countries, Portugal could not absorb the cost of cutting its exports. Under Salazar, Portugal had been involved in a lucrative trade of importing goods and resources from its colonies, including coffee, maize, sugar, cocoa, oilseed, and cotton, and then exporting them to the Axis countries at rates that ensured a healthy profit.[10]

As part of the British tactics a blacklist was created with the threat of sanctions against individuals and companies continuing after the war ended. The blacklist did not win many friends in Portugal. Open to abuse, with hard evidence becoming polluted by rumor and petty jealousy, the blacklist, while a deterrent, did much to further alienate British interests in Lisbon throughout the war. Towards the end of the war, when its outcome was much clearer, the blacklist took on greater importance as the Portuguese companies and individuals did all they could to avoid being put on it, and those already on it used all their powers to get taken off.

The negotiations, which took place in Lisbon, were never easy and the agreements reached sometimes not fully implemented by one of the parties. Eccles, who represented the MEW in the Iberian Peninsula, led the British side. He enjoyed Salazar's company immensely and looked forward to their meetings—a meeting of great minds, he felt. As if to prove it, each of them spoke to the other in French, the diplomatic language of the nineteenth century.[11]

The British ambassador usually accompanied Eccles to the meetings with Salazar. Ronald Campbell was an impressive figure: Confident to the point of being egotistical, he knew and understood their brief. Much to Salazar's pleasure both Campbell and Eccles could also understand the economic detail and theory of the subject matter they were discussing. Salazar also understood that both men had been given a degree of freedom from London to negotiate within the preset guidelines.

On July 24, 1940, Britain signed the Tripartite Agreement between it, Spain, and Portugal. This aided the Allies' preemption campaign and Portugal agreed to make its currency (the escudo) available to Britain against the pound sterling for the period of the war. This was a major help to Britain as the other neutral countries allowed their currencies to be sold only against gold, which Britain was rapidly running out of. The debt that Britain ran up with Portugal during the war reached around £80 million, and when Portugal did draw on this balance, it spent it all in Britain.

Other aspects of economic warfare were not so neatly arranged. The British Cabinet had voted on July 13, 1940, to ration goods to Portugal, mainly to prevent the reexportation of goods from Portugal across land to Spain and into German-controlled territory. Meanwhile Britain continued to impose unilateral quotas on Portuguese imports, particularly oil, which had a damaging impact on Portugal's economy.

In January 1941, Ronald Campbell called for a new system to be introduced that was more structured and clear: an agreed quota system, with a total ban on exports to the Axis powers and no stockpiling of goods by Portugal. Salazar agreed to part of the deal, but refused to give written assurances about the issue of the export of produce from the colonies. In reality, Salazar did all he could to get around the agreement with Campbell. While sympathetic to the British aims of the blockade, Salazar was none too keen to see it fully implemented. The economic consequences to Portugal of the blockade were felt all over the country, and a weak economy increased the threat to Salazar's regime from internal opposition groups.

The sale of wolfram to the Germans became the most important aspect of the economic warfare involving Portugal. As the near constant references to wolfram in Salazar's diary confirm, it was the single biggest issue of the war for Portugal.[12] Over the years Salazar lost more sleep over wolfram than anything else.[13] The negotiations over wolfram also dominated the lives of British, German, and American diplomats based in Lisbon during the war.[14]

Like the British, the Germans used the carrot-and-stick approach to deal with the wolfram issue with Portugal. The stick was German attacks on Portuguese shipping, such as the sinking of the

Portuguese ship, *Corte Real,* in 1941. The carrot was an agreement with Germany, which included an offer to supply Portugal with German weapons and other vitally needed supplies at favorable rates to Lisbon.[15]

As demand rapidly grew for the limited stocks of wolfram, so the price increased as well. By the middle of 1941, the price stood at around £1,250 per ton and by the end of the same year the price had risen to an astounding £6,000 per ton. These newfound opportunities for making huge profits from wolfram mining created a strange atmosphere that was akin to the gold-rush era in the United States. There were stories of people abandoning their regular jobs, famers leaving their lands, and fishermen leaving their boats to join the lucrative mining trade. A week's wages could be earned in an hour if wolfram was found.[16]

There was, as a result, severe disruption to the local economy in parts of Portugal. For, as villages with wolfram mines witnessed, it was as if their inhabitants had collectively won the lottery. Like many lottery winners they didn't really know how to spend, or invest, their windfall. There were stories of villagers in wolfram mine areas lighting their cigarettes with escudo notes.[17] Agents from both sides in the war attempting to buy wolfram in the villages came across fraud and deceit, and the term "wolframista"—meaning war profiteer—entered the Portuguese dictionary.[18]

⁂

The repercussions of the wolfram trade stretched literally around the globe. Events in distant Timor, an island nearly 9,000 miles away, led to something of a crisis in Salazar's relationship with the Allies. The Timor crisis began at the start of November 1941, when the Portuguese ambassador in London, Armindo Monteiro, informed the British foreign secretary, Anthony Eden, on November 4 that Portugal would resist any Japanese attack on Timor.[19] He added that in the event of such an attack, Portugal would consider asking Britain for military assistance.[20]

With the onset of World War II, Portuguese Timor had suddenly become strategically important. With the expansion of Japan into the Pacific, Timor became a potentially important base for Japanese submarines and aircraft, which could be used for attacking Australian-Singapore communications. The proximity of Timor to the Australian coast also made it a hugely important point of defense for Australia.[21]

Allied military leaders had noted this importance to Japan and on December 11, following negotiations between the relevant parties, the Portuguese government was informed that in the event of an attack on Timor, Australian and Dutch forces would come to the assistance of the Portuguese. Salazar accepted this offer on December 12.[22] Four days later Ronald Campbell was instructed by the Foreign Office to seek an urgent meeting with Salazar in his office at São Bento. During the course of the short meeting, Campbell informed Salazar that Japanese submarines had been detected near Timor and that the Allies suspected a Japanese attack. As a result, the British had arranged with the Australian government for Australian and Dutch officers in Timor to seek a meeting with the Portuguese governor and ask him for permission to land around 350 Australian and Dutch troops in Timor some two hours after the request.[23]

Salazar was not impressed by this move and instructed the Portuguese governor not to accept any assistance unless Timor was actually attacked.[24] He felt that any move prior to a Japanese attack would mean the abandonment of Portugal's neutrality and lead to a potential Japanese invasion of Macau, a German takeover of the Azores, and perhaps also lead to an invasion of the Portuguese mainland as well.[25] He was also furious with the Allies for what he saw as their underhanded tactics in planning this operation without the prior consent of the Portuguese.[26]

The Axis powers were quick to seize on the arrival of the Allied troops in Timor as evidence of a Portuguese breach of neutrality.[27] The resulting pressure that was applied on the Portuguese government by the Germans had two aims: to intimidate Lisbon and to secure more concessions in its negotiations with Portugal over the supply of wolfram.

In spite of Salazar's reaction, the landing of troops on Timor went ahead, leading Salazar to protest that it was a violation of Portuguese sovereignty. Anthony Eden publicly stated his regret that the landings had taken place and agreed that the troops would be withdrawn when Portuguese reinforcements arrived in Timor.[28] Before this could happen, however, the Japanese attacked Dutch and Portuguese Timor on February 19 and 20, 1942.[29] Salazar protested against the violation of Portuguese sovereignty this time by the Japanese, but again to no effect.[30]

The small Allied force in Timor moved inland and started to conduct guerrilla-style operations against the Japanese. In June 1942, the Portuguese suggested that if this force surrendered then the Japanese might be persuaded to withdraw from Portuguese Timor. The British thought that any such reassurance would simply be a Japanese ploy. The Allies and the Portuguese continued negotiating plans to recapture the islands, including whether or not the Portuguese armed forces would be involved in any such operations. These negotiations were still on going towards the end of the war.[31]

The crisis over Timor had caused considerable short-term damage to the Allies' relations with Portugal. Anthony Eden had been quick to lessen the damage, trying to rebuild trust in case the Allies needed to request access to the facilities in the strategically vital Portuguese Atlantic Islands known as the Azores.

By 1942, Portugal had become the single biggest European supplier of wolfram. Since the launch of Germany's invasion of the Soviet Union, its supplies of wolfram from the east had been all but totally cut. Berlin looked to Portugal, and to a lesser degree Spain, to supply it with all its wolfram requirements. From 1941 onwards, Germany made as much effort as possible to secure wolfram stocks through legitimate and illegitimate means. The German military, diplomatic services, and intelligence agencies were all involved in this effort to secure additional wolfram.[32]

An unregulated wolfram sector was not tolerable for Salazar. For months, Salazar had been receiving complaints from the agricultural sector about the loss of farm labor to the wolfram sector.[33] This was having a largely negative impact on Portugal's ability to produce foodstuffs and wines. Salazar also wanted to make sure that he had control over the wolfram and was in charge of its distribution to the Allies and the Axis powers.

In February 1942, Salazar took the decision to set up a new system of restraints on the wolfram trade, which came into effect on March 1, 1942. Lisbon set strict limits of the amount of wolfram mined and set the price at 150 escudos per kilogram.[34] Naturally, the government took a tax out of this price, which was set at 70 escudos.[35] Crucially, all wolfram, including that from mines owned by British and German companies (or Portuguese fronts for these countries), was to be bought by the Portuguese government at a set price and the subsequently sold to foreign nations. The government also introduced heavy fines for anybody involved in the illegal mining and export of wolfram.[36] This effective nationalization of the wolfram sector ended the gold-rush era, and allowed Salazar to deliver wolfram to the Germans as part of an agreement he had struck with Berlin.

Germany was subsequently able to employ the carrot approach with Portugal by increasing trade with Lisbon. Berlin's share of Portuguese exports increased from 19.02 percent in 1941 to 24.36 percent in 1942. Additionally, Portuguese imports from Germany increased from 8.08 percent in 1941 to 12.62 percent in 1942.[37] This trade became extremely lucrative for Portugal, which had promised not to make any money out of the war. The British, and the Americans after they entered the war, were far from impressed with Salazar's attitude towards the wolfram trade. The Ministry of Economic Warfare in Whitehall wanted tough action taken against Lisbon for this incomprehensible trade with the enemy.

Salazar's defense was both simple and complicated at the same time. He argued that, given the German demand for Portuguese wolfram (especially after 1941), he had little choice but to strike a series of agreements to supply Berlin with the material that it needed to keep its war effort going. If Portugal refused to sell to the Germans then, given the importance of wolfram to Berlin, there was a strong possibility that the Germans would have invaded Portugal (and Spain) in order to secure the wolfram supplies.

Given that Portugal did not have a large well-equipped standing army, there was little that Lisbon could have done to prevent such an invasion. Britain remained unable to help the Portuguese repel such an invasion, instead focusing its efforts on dealing with a German-occupied Portugal. Portuguese neutrality would have been violated and the country would have found itself a battle-ground in a major European war. For Salazar, exporting wolfram to the Germans was a way of effectively buying Portugal's neutrality.[38] More subtly, Salazar was trying to play one of the warring parties off against the other by selling itself to both belligerents. If it stopped selling to one, it would no longer be of use and would be open to threat from that power.

The Portuguese justification for the sale of wolfram was best summed up by its ambassador to London, the Duke of Palmela, in a letter to Salazar in December 1943. The duke argued that it was not fair for Britain to have put pressure on Salazar over this.[39] If wolfram were considered as indispensable to the war as the British claimed in London, Germany would have searched for it violently, if Portugal had denied it to them. Neutrality of the Peninsula was considered to be of the greatest importance for England. There-fore, the exports of wolfram to Germany might well be considered the price you pay for the conservation of that neutrality.

CHAPTER 15

Under Pressure

THE ENTRY OF THE UNITED STATES INTO THE WAR in December 1941 greatly strengthened the Allies' financial capability in the arena of economic warfare, but even with American participation it was still not clear which side would ultimately win the wolfram wars. In June 1942, the British and Americans formed the Joint Wolfram Committee in Lisbon to buy up wolfram preemptively. This was an expensive war. It was estimated that the Allies spent around $170 million, evenly split between the British and the Americans, purchasing wolfram from Portugal.[1]

The Germans countered the Allied preemptive purchases by making constant demands for more wolfram themselves, above and beyond agreements with Lisbon. At times, this pressure became threatening, but the Portuguese politically tried to stick to the agreements. Illegal German efforts were stepped up to get wolfram out of the country to Spain and from there onto German-controlled territory. Many of Portuguese mines were near to the Spanish border and with quiet mountain roads it made smuggling a relatively easy task.

As the war developed, the question of wolfram supplies became intertwined with other issues. It was only when the overall tide of the war turned in the Allies' favor that the wolfram war appeared to be won. As the Allies gained the upper hand on the battlefront, so

Salazar came under enormous pressure from both London and Washington to place an embargo on further sales of wolfram to Germany. The Allies argued that such a move would shorten the war. Still Salazar disagreed, stating that a reduction in wolfram supplies to Germany was possible, but an embargo was not in Portugal's interest.[2]

In one desperate throw of the dice, the Germans had tried to pressure Salazar by holding a Portuguese liner, the *Serpa Pinto*, and its crew and passengers hostage on the high seas off the coast in Bermuda by a German U-boat.[3] The ship was on its regular Lisbon-New York route and was full of refugees traveling to America. Acting under direct orders from Berlin, the U-boat captain ordered the ship searched, arguing that there was an illegal cargo on board. Terrified passengers were questioned and evacuated from the ship into the lifeboats.

The 385 people on board were left floating around in the Atlantic Ocean for nine hours while the captain of the U-boat awaited orders from Berlin as to whether to sink the ship. Eventually, the passengers were allowed back on board and the ship was permitted to go on its way. During the process of reboarding the boat, however, one passenger died. The operation of seizing the boat was intended to send a clear message from Berlin to Salazar. There remains some doubt over the extent of the contacts between Berlin and Lisbon during these nine hours, but it is clear that Salazar did not back down. Following the incident the Portuguese government complained to Berlin in unusually strong terms.

Intense negotiations continued through the spring of 1944, with each side becoming increasingly irritated by the other. Salazar defended his position, arguing, at first, that Germany might still respond violently to such an embargo. The British pointed out that Germany was in no position to undertake any attack on Portugal. Salazar countered that there still hadn't been any Allied landings in Western Europe. Finally, Salazar resorted to the argument that he had an agreement with the Germans and had to deliver at least some wolfram to them in order to honor it.

The Allies increased the pressure on Salazar: Churchill and President Roosevelt wrote to Salazar personally.[4] The Brazilian ambassador to Lisbon used the argument that Portuguese wolfram was indirectly killing Brazilian soldiers who were fighting in bloody battles in Italy. For Salazar, becoming ever more weary in his office in São Bento, the question of the wolfram became the catalyst for a series of problematic developments, which both threatened Portugal's neutrality, but also offered it the possibility of huge financial gain.

With Lisbon's infrastructure crumbling, and increased grumblings from the opposition groups to Salazar, as noted by the PVDE, Salazar needed to conduct a difficult balancing act. For some British politicians and diplomats, Salazar had become too much. He was accused of ignoring moral points of view of right and wrong in the war.

At a dinner party the previous year at his house in Boca do Inferno, Ricardo Espírito Santo had reported to James Wood, the U.S. financial attaché in Lisbon, details of a conversation that he had recently enjoyed with Salazar at which he had asked him whether his bank should discontinue all business with the Germans. Salazar had replied that the outcome of the war was clear and that the Allies were definitely going to win. He added, however, that it would not be "gentlemanly" to suspend all business with the Germans. [5]

Woods concluded from the discussion that Salazar appeared keen to continue the highly profitable trade with Germany.[6] As the war headed towards a conclusion, Salazar's reasons for continuing to trade with Germany were stripped away one by one, until only profit maximization explained Portugal's not immediately giving in to Allied calls to stop.

Increasingly isolated, and in danger of becoming a pariah, Salazar eventually bowed to intense Allied pressure and did what

London and Washington had been demanding he do for months: declare a total embargo on wolfram mining. The decision to do so was announced June 4, 1944, on the eve of the Allied invasion of Western Europe.[7] It was to become effective on June 8, 1944.[8]

The Americans noted that the timing of Salazar's announcement—just as the invasion of Western Europe was about to commence—was no coincidence. The decision, they argued, marked the success of Salazar's policy of neutrality, which had allowed the Portuguese to exploit both belligerent sides for as long as possible. The Americans claimed that only through Washington's insistence had Salazar agreed to a total embargo on wolfram. The British, they argued, had put up with Salazar's compromises.[9] To the Americans, even the British were guilty of putting their national interest before that of the Allies.[10] Indeed, some American officials were far from impressed about the level of cooperation between the Allies on dealing with the wolfram wars from the outset.

The decision to introduce the embargo meant that around 90,000 Portuguese workers who were engaged either directly, or indirectly, in the mining industry would be thrown out of work. The Americans pointed out that the Portuguese government had taken no steps to absorb the wolfram miners, who came mainly from low-income agricultural jobs, into other employment. At the start of the wolfram wars, Salazar had been concerned about the dislocating impact of the mining on the job market in the areas of the mines. The wolfram industry had grown throughout the war as the demand for wolfram had increased from Germany, and the lack of alternate sources of supply to Berlin had all but dried up.

In reality, by the time Salazar made his decision to impose an embargo on wolfram exports there was little that Berlin could do in response. There was little military action Germany could take against Portugal at this stage of the war. The German ambassador in Lisbon, Baron von Hoyningen-Huene, claimed he viewed the decision as final and made no attempt to secure further wolfram exports to Germany.[11] The ambassador, who had been deeply involved in the German wolfram negotiations with Salazar, reflected on the reality of the situation and understood that the war was lost for Germany.[12]

The introduction of the United States into the war had changed the game plan for Salazar. As the war developed and the question of the export of wolfram became intertwined in a series of issues, the presence of the United States appeared to make him less inclined to be openly supportive of the Allies. In truth, throughout the war Portuguese-American relations were never particularly warm or close. American officials often felt that the British were too soft on Salazar and put too much faith in the ancient historic alliance between the two countries.[13] During the wolfram wars, the United States had taken a tougher line with Lisbon than the British had. It would be oversimplistic to suggest that the British and Americans coordinated a good-cop/bad-cop routine, but, at times, there was an element of this in the Allies' conduct of negotiations over the supply of wolfram.

Salazar's vision of the world was reflected in his handling of the wolfram wars. It would be wrong, however, to judge his supply of wolfram to the Germans, and his resistance of Allied pressure to end the supply until the very last minute, as an indication of his own support for the German cause. Salazar's own perspective on the war was largely governed by his changing perception of how he foresaw the postwar European and New World Order, and was detectable in his meetings with foreign diplomats in Lisbon during the war. At the center of his belief set was a deep fear of the threat from the Soviet Union and communism in general. For Salazar, the real conflict was not a war between the Western European powers, but rather the coming confrontation with the Soviet Union.

Initially during World War II, Salazar appeared to fear a total victory for either the Allies or Axis powers. He carefully studied what the implications for a German victory would mean for a new European economic order, and was concerned how Portugal would fit into that orbit. Once the United States entered the war, he considered that an Allied victory of sorts was inevitable, but was concerned about the future role of the United States in Europe after the war. He felt that America would try to dominate Europe economically and militarily. Salazar had little time for America.

In a meeting with Eccles and Campbell, he informed the British diplomats that the Americans were "a barbaric people illuminated not by God, but rather by electric light."[14] American positions towards Portugal, particularly in the arena of economic warfare, were less conciliatory than those of the British, and to some extent these exacerbated Salazar's unease with the emergence of American hegemony in Western Europe. During the wolfram wars, Salazar steered by his own sense of what was best for Portugal. When he finally chose to limit Portugal's relationship with Germany he did so reluctantly.

While Salazar was negotiating with the Allies and Germans over the supply of wolfram he always needed to keep one eye on the internal political situation in Portugal. Opposition groups, particularly the communists, stood to reap the political gain from any economic unrest. The introduction of rationing and the short supply of some raw materials were viewed as dangerous developments in an authoritarian regime whose rule was underpinned by the relatively passive nature of the Portuguese population, the vast majority of whom accepted the Estado Novo without ever really warmly embracing it. Around Lisbon there was a feeling that when the war ended there would be major political developments and a move towards a more democratic state.

Salazar conducted the negotiations over wolfram as if he were the village bookkeeper trying to balance the books and put a little bit in reserve for future needs. His detachment from the horrors of the war, or apparent lack of understanding on how cooperating with the Allies could shorten the war, risked having him classified by the Allies in the same manner in which they did General Franco of Spain. In being unwilling to take any risks, he came very close to putting the future of Portugal at risk in the long term. The British ambassador in Lisbon, Ronald Campbell, speculated during the war that Salazar was starting to become mentally unbalanced. Given his work schedule and his visible signs of aging it was clear, at the very least, that he was starting to feel the four years of continuous pressure.

CHAPTER 16

Shocked to Discover That Spying Is Going On

WITH SO MUCH CRUCIAL TRADE, A STRATEGIC European coastline, and an inscrutable leader whose policy decisions were hard to parse in advance, it was unsurprising that Portugal should have become home to a conclave of spies. In Lisbon, and along its coastline at Estoril, spies were to be found almost everywhere. Some were real spies, and some were not quite so real. The Hotel Palácio in Estoril, with its grand ballroom and casino nearby, were often full of spies from all the belligerents in the war. Dressed in black tie and playing at the card tables, there was an air of grandness to one of the oldest professions. Many colorful local personalities from big business, and foreign businessmen cashing in on Portugal's neutrality, as well as wealthy refugees, added to the eclectic mix of guests at the hotel and casino.

The hotel barman was reputed to mix the best Manhattan cocktails in Europe, and its chambermaids were on the payroll of one, or both, sides in the war.[1] An American who passed through the doors of the hotel said that it reminded him of the Mayo Clinic, because you could see on the faces of all its guests that something was troubling them.[2]

During the war, the hotel, and especially the casino, came to host many of the European royal families who were fleeing the Germans, or their own countrymen, or both. On weekends and during the holiday season the place was close to full, and brimmed with intrigue and rumor. Many of the rumors had been planted by one of the sides in the war, and were sometimes exaggerations of facts, or in many cases were outright lies. In between the Allied and German intelligence officers stood the PVDE and its network of local informers, who carefully recorded all the movements and conversations of the foreign spies in case they made contact with elements of the local opposition.[3] The police reports went directly to Captain Lourenço, who passed summaries of important developments on to Salazar to digest the goings-on between the spy set and its interaction with local society figures.

On May 20, 1941, Ian Fleming, the future author of the James Bond novels, checked into the Hotel Palácio in Estoril, describing his occupation simply as a government official.[4] In reality, Fleming was in Lisbon as part of his work in planning Operation Golden Eye for British naval intelligence. The plan was to be implemented in the event of a German invasion of Spain, and was a mixture of sabotage activities and maintenance of communications networks with London. As the plan involved several intelligence agencies, in multiple locations, it is not surprising that its creation was hindered by fierce internal departmental and service rivalries.[5] Fleming's time in Lisbon was spent dealing with the Portuguese end of the operation and making arrangements with the Lisbon station chiefs for its potential implementation. He also spent time with his old friend, David Eccles from the MEW. Fleming was in transit from England via Lisbon to the United States.

The Pan Am Clipper service from Lisbon was a popular service for British agents, who connected with the Clipper through BOAC flights from Bristol and Poole. Fleming arrived at New York's La Guardia Clipper dock on the afternoon of May 25,

1941. Fleming and his boss, Admiral John Godfrey, who was in part the inspiration for Fleming's fictional character M in the Bond novels, were in America to study and examine the levels of security at American ports.[6]

Fleming returned to Lisbon on his way back from America in late July to make a brief inspection of the local facilities and equipment for Operation Golden Eye.[7] On this occasion, however, he did not enjoy the splendor of the Hotel Palácio, but instead stayed in the room that had been vacated by David Eccles.[8] During a visit to Tangiers, Fleming displayed a bit of the Bond trait of drama, having to hire a private plane in order to get back to Lisbon as soon as possible. His duty report shows that he claimed £110 in expenses for the private use of the aircraft.[9]

Suave, cool, and enjoying his intelligence wars, Fleming passed his brief time in Lisbon not reveling in the closeness of the enemy or the thrill of the game, but trying to get often competing British intelligence departments to agree to do what was needed for Operation Golden Eye.[10] On his second night in Estoril, Fleming and Godfrey spent an evening in the unusually quiet casino where Fleming played the table for relatively modest amounts of money, and lost. As he was leaving he reportedly turned to Godfrey and said, what if those men at the table had been German agents and we had cleared them out of their money.[11] The event was thought to have inspired the scene in Fleming's first Bond novel, *Casino Royale*, in which Bond does just that to the evil communist spy, Le Chiffre.[12]

From Fleming's hotel room he could see the promenade that ran along the top of the beach from Estoril to Cascais. The beach below the promenade was littered with enemy agents. Beautiful suntanned German agents posed as Swiss neutrals in the hope of seducing Allied senior personnel who were lonely and a long way from home. Overall, Fleming was impressed by the intelligence setup in Lisbon, which compared favorably with many of the other stations he visited on his tour.[13]

The reality of the spy work however, was very different from the James Bond movies that Fleming would start to write after the war. In truth, much of the work in Portugal was not glamorous. Indeed, on the contrary, the majority of the work of spies in the city was caked in seediness, and although some of the settings were grand, there was an air of desperation as both British and German spies failed to achieve their aims and risked offending their superiors. On top of this, interagency competition was rife, although sometimes the rivalries were exaggerated and used as convenient excuses for the failure of missions.[14]

The wolfram war was just one of a number of reasons why Lisbon was flooded with spies from both the Allies and Axis powers during World War II. Other reasons included the centrality of Lisbon in the naval wars, the fact that it represented the end of the line for refugees attempting to flee Nazi-controlled mainland Europe, and its role as a gateway to Africa and South America.

Both sides in the war, in addition to their own sets of spies, tried to recruit elements of the local population to work for them. This was often undertaken with only minimal research into the potential candidate or as the result of some half-useful piece of information that had been proffered. As the majority of the Portuguese population were illiterate, or had at best only elementary reading skills, much of the information passed on was done so by word of mouth. Rumor and counterrumor started in Lisbon's cafés and spread across the city like wild fire.

Often there might be an element of truth in the original piece of information or tidbit but by the time it had done the rounds across the city it bore little resemblance to any form of reality. To complicate matters, each side would start its own fictitious rumors and let the tale spin out of control, in the hope of doing as much damage to the other side as possible. At times, it appeared that almost everyone in Lisbon was either a spy or pretending to be one. Previously nondescript locals increased their social standing by hinting that they might be involved in such activities. The cafés and restaurants in Rossio were full of spies, both locally recruited and foreign, as were the bars of the city's most glamorous hotels. Nothing, as a result, remained secret in Lisbon for very long—unless Salazar wanted it that way.

On the official side of spying, each side in the war had a clear set of aims.[15] For the Germans, the priority was to smuggle as much wolfram as possible out of the country to Spain and on to occupied France. When Salazar moved to effectively nationalize wolfram production and export in 1942, this did not stop the black market in wolfram trading. Indeed, as the German sources of alternative supply dried up, so German agents became much more active in the smuggling of wolfram.

The other major aim of the Germans was to cause as much damage as possible to the pro-British sentiment in Lisbon. At official level this was done in a number of devious ways, but generally centered upon attempts at stoking Salazar's alleged paranoia of British plots to overthrow him, either by backing the internal opposition towards him and the regime, or by calling for the return of the monarchy.[16] From time to time the Germans encouraged the belief that the British were planning troop landings in the south of the country. It was within this framework of maximizing British-Portuguese suspicions that the Germans undertook a plot to expose the activities of the British Special Operations Executive in Portugal in late 1941 and the first half of 1942. The fallout from these revelations represented one of the most potentially difficult moments in the war for Anglo-Portuguese relations.

The SOE had been founded in secret during July 1940 as a small and strongly effective British fighting force to help deal with the seemingly ever-expanding Nazi empire.[17] Its remit was to work with the forces of resistance in countries that were occupied by the Germans and in the neutral European states such as Portugal. Parliament was to have no say in how it was run or what actions it took and didn't take. Its funding came from a secret vote, based on a longstanding parliamentary convention that the House of Commons did not inquire, and the House of Lords was not allowed to get involved.[18] A minister, as a result, nominally controlled the SOE. After some discussion, the Ministry of Defence was ruled out on the grounds that it didn't have the time. The Foreign Office was also rejected as nobody trusted it, and for fear of competing interdepartmental rivalries with existing Foreign Office–controlled security services.[19]

The eventual compromise was that it was handed to the MEW. The Ministry, however, did not run the SOE. The employees of the SOE used working for the MEW mainly as a cover story. The SOE did have a small office space in MEW headquarters in Berkeley Square House. The minister who became responsible for it was Hugh Dalton, an imposing politician who didn't care much for making friends on either side of the House of Commons. Key members of his staff included a rising diplomat, Gladwyn Jebb, who had been transferred from the Foreign Office.[20] They worked well together.

The British aims and intentions in the spying arena in Lisbon were relatively clear, but rather difficult to achieve. Actions to prevent wolfram smuggling by the Germans became a priority as the British embassy in Lisbon began to discover the extent of the German efforts to smuggle wolfram across the border to Spain.[21] This discovery led to an intensification of all types of action, from preventative measures, such as plans to effectively render the wolfram chemically unusable, through to physical attempts to disrupt the German network of supply routes.[22]

The SOE was eventually put in charge of planning and executing the final version of the plan for the destruction of key installations and resources in the event of a German invasion of Portugal. Other agents observed shipping activity in and out of Lisbon harbor, noting the materials that Portugal was importing and making sure that there was compliance with the blockade. Finally, the exposure of the German spy rings became more of a priority as the size of these networks increased and the penetration of them deepened into the Portuguese authorities.

Jack Beevor was one of the brightest recruits to the SOE. From the moment he walked through the door of their modest headquarters in Baker Street in central London, Beevor, with his education from Winchester, one of England's finest public schools, showed a strong appetite for leadership and improvization in times of difficult conditions. Upon arriving in Lisbon, Beevor had first to do battle with the embassy staff, most of whom saw the SOE and its leadership as a dangerous sideshow to the relationship between London and Lisbon.

Walford Selby, during his stint as British ambassador to Portugal, banned the SOE from undertaking any action. When Ronald Campbell succeeded Selby as ambassador, he too had reservations about letting the SOE loose in Portugal. Campbell feared the damage to Britain's standing in Lisbon, and to his personal relationship with Salazar, if SOE agents were ever caught by the Portuguese while undertaking an operation.[23] Sir Samuel Hoare, the ambassador to Spain, went further, in effect barring all covert activities that could damage relations with Franco or efforts to keep Spain out of the war.[24] Hoare's ban effectively meant that much of the covert activity in such areas as prevention of supply of wolfram to the Germans had to take place in Portugal. Once in Spain, SOE agents were severely limited as to what they could physically do to prevent the vital ore from reaching German-occupied Europe.

After only three weeks of training in Baker Street, Beevor arrived in Lisbon in January 1941 with no previous experience of covert activities and with no knowledge of the Portuguese language. His period of training had at least allowed him to familiarize himself with the SOE material on Western Europe and study the possibilities of a German invasion of the Iberian Peninsula.[25] He had also taken the opportunity to participate in a three-hour crash course on demolition techniques. In the embassy in Lisbon,

Beevor's cover was the position of assistant military attaché. He used this role to effectively develop the SOE networks in Portugal and to start his work.

An immediate problem, which Beevor became involved in dealing with, was the German naval intelligence section in Lisbon (Abwehr) that was tracking all the routes of the British convoys crossing the Atlantic.[26] The Abwehr had set up some brothels, and financed others, in the docks area of Lisbon in order to attract British seamen who came ashore in Lisbon. The girls had been trained to extract from the sailors the details of routes and dates of the convoys and memorize them.[27] This German tactic had proved productive at the start of the war, but eventually the British broke up this network. British sailors coming ashore were also given stern warnings about the brothels in Lisbon, and how enemy agents controlled them. Most of the work in exposing this ring was undertaken by MI5 and SIS, but nevertheless Beevor enjoyed taking a little bit of the credit in a world where competition between intelligence agencies on the same side was very strong.

Beevor's main objective, however, was to plan for the demolition of the River Tagus oil installations, in the event of a successful German invasion of Portugal. Beevor considered the threat of such an invasion to have passed by April 1941, and certainly by the German invasion of the Soviet Union in June 1941, but nevertheless had to have the relevant plans in place.[28] For a man whose knowledge of Portuguese ran to ordering a *bica* (coffee) or browsing the menu of the local restaurants, this proved to be no easy task.

Operation Panicle was devised, and subsequently amended, to respond to an invasion of Portugal in two stages: balloon operation (at the time of invasion) and postballoon operations (postinvasion activities). The major thrust of the recommendations for balloon activities was that resistance to an invasion would be counterproductive given the size of the Portuguese armed forces.[29] The size of the Portuguese army was estimated at around only 30,000, with very little in the way of air defense to help protect them.[30] The

British Chiefs of Staff produced a secret report on April 29, 1941, that argued that if Portugal were invaded there was very little that Britain could do to help try to repel the invaders.[31] Indeed, as the Operation Panicle memorandum argued, widespread resistance to the occupation would result in the exposure and elimination of the most valuable elements in the country.[32]

The SOE preferred to concentrate its plans on the postballoon stage, which would start about a month after the balloon had gone off. The center of these activities in Lisbon was to be the port area.[33] Here the plan called for the total destruction of the five major oil and gas installations of Sacor, Atlantic, Shell Banatica, Socony Vacuum, and SONAP,[34] either by dynamite or naval bombardment. At the docks the mobile cranes, mobile bridge, and other equipment was to be blown up to help block the entry to the docks.[35] The cranes were to be blown by simply targeting their front legs so they fell into the docks.

Road and railway exits to Spain were to be blown up, including Campolide Station near Lisbon. Communications lines were to be destroyed.[36] British agents considered the airports in the area to be so primitive that there wasn't much they could do except to block the drains in winter, which might cause the runway to flood.[37] Lisbon's first international airport at Portella was not yet finished. Across the country, electricity stations were to be attacked, and the SOE had drawn up detailed plans of the various types of power stations and how best to destroy them, while conserving as much dynamite as possible.[38]

The main aim of Operation Panicle was to prevent the Germans from using Portugal's Atlantic ports for its U-boats and naval vessels.[39] Although much of the planning for the balloon and postballoon activities had been undertaken after talks with the Portuguese, the scale of the British plans would have surprised the Portuguese military commanders and Salazar. If all the destruction had been carried out it would not have been easy for the Germans or the Spanish to operate freely in the country. SOE agents, working with local volunteers, could have put the port area of Lisbon out of action for extended periods of time. While these plans were open to discussion and negotiation with the Portuguese, Salazar discovered in 1942 evidence of a much more sinister unilateral SOE plot to demolish a far greater number of key installations in Portugal than he had been told about.

The implementation of Operation Panicle would have represented the nightmare scenario for Salazar. His policy of neutrality appeared to be working in the two areas that most worried him: the maintenance of Portuguese sovereignty, and preventing the war from being used as a catalyst by opposition groups in Portugal to overthrow the Estado Novo.

Jack Beevor, tasked with the demolitions, had to recruit a number of local Portuguese agents who could be relied upon to carry out the task if the need arose. Beevor had to also employ local British residents who were fluent in the language and who could communicate with the local demolition teams. All this was undertaken, according to Beevor, with the greatest discretion, but given the nature of the plans, and the number of local agents of varying quality involved, there was always the possibility of something going very badly wrong. And go very wrong it did.

According to Beevor, the crisis started with a seemingly innocuous event in February 1942. Beevor was asked by an agent of SIS for use of an apartment for a secret meeting with a local informant whom he didn't want to bring to the embassy. Beevor had just such an apartment, which he regularly used for similar purposes for the SOE. Beevor agreed to the request in the name of good relations. Some weeks later the man the SIS agent had interviewed at the apartment was picked up by the PVDE, and under interrogation stated that although he couldn't remember the name of the British official he had met he knew the address of where the meeting had taken place. Soon after, the police discovered Beevor's name on the lease and put two and two together. The discovery was part of a wider process of investigation undertaken by the

PVDE based on a tipoff, which had been planted by the Germans, about SOE activities in Lisbon.

The truth of the matter was rather more complicated than mere bad luck, and more sinister. The trail that led the PVDE to the apartment was part of a wider police operation that had started in the winter of 1941. The Germans had managed to convince elements within the PVDE that key members of the British business community were involved in the wave of communist antigovernment agitation that had spread throughout Portugal after the German attack on the Soviet Union.[40]

The PVDE response to the unrest continued as scores of local people were arrested who were alleged to be plotting against Salazar. Of those arrested, several were part of Beevor's network of Portuguese agents, including some of its leaders. The process of the discovery of the existence of the SOE and its members and plans was soon concluded, and Salazar was informed of the findings of the PVDE-led investigation.

Reading the file late at night in his office, Salazar viewed developments with a mixture of anger and opportunistic interest. The anger was based on the fact that the British had been running a secret network of agents who were given instructions in demolitions to act accordingly against targets in the Lisbon area in the event of the Germans overrunning Portugal. There had been an agreement with the British over help in demolition duties, should such an event occur, but this unilateral British plan to target key installations was new and unacceptable. To some extent, Salazar's anger was based on the local membership of the SOE, which included many people who were regarded as subversive enemies of the Estado Novo.

Once more Salazar's paranoia about the British aim of trying to replace his regime returned. From an early stage in his deliberations on the subject, however, Salazar, once he had calmed down, decided to take a more sober view of what he felt was a major crisis and exploit the situation to send a clear and direct warning to

both the British and the Germans that they should not try to interfere in internal Portuguese politics. Such interference was to be
regarded as a red line, which under no circumstances should be
crossed by either of the warring parties. This was, in effect,
Salazar's price for doing business in the spy trade. The British and
German intelligence agencies were free to continue their work
against each other's interests, but not against Portuguese interests.

Naturally, Salazar needed a sacrificial lamb in order to make his
point. Jack Beevor's head was offered on a plate to Salazar by
Ronald Campbell, the British ambassador. Salazar summoned
Campbell to his office on March 4, 1942.[41] He coolly informed him
that he had a very serious matter about which he must speak to the
ambassador.[42] Speaking slowly, and without passion, Salazar outlined the case. The police had discovered a considerable British
organization, which, according to the evidence provided by the
Portuguese nationals who had been arrested, was engaged in secret preparations for demolition and was spending large sums of
money on bribery and the like.[43]

Salazar went on to state his strong objection to such activities
and expressed his pain and surprise at learning of their existence,
especially as the very matter of demolitions was being openly and
frankly discussed between the two governments. Adding a touch
of indignation, Salazar said he thought the operation was stupid,
as London had agreed that any resistance in metropolitan Portugal
to an invasion should be only symbolic. In other words, it had been
agreed to remove the objects that would have been useful to the
enemy such as fuel stocks and dockyards. This covert unilateral
British operation was much more extensive, and included bridges
and roads, and their destruction would have merely added to the
suffering of the population.[44]

Before dismissing Campbell, from his chair Salazar issued a
clear warning to the British. The British must choose between
working with Lisbon through intergovernmental channels, or maintaining the secret organization (SOE) in the face of police opposi-

tion. He added coldly that he did not think that the latter would produce very good results for the British.[45]

In the days following the meeting between Salazar and Campbell, the police increased their campaign against British interests in order to show their bite. Further arrests by the PVDE brought the total number of suspects questioned to 300.[46] An increasingly worried Campbell noted to London that the police campaign against British activities was starting to amount to persecution.[47] Campbell attributed the campaign to a number of factors, of which the discovery of the activities of the SOE was a catalyst. Even at this early stage, he predicted that the incident would lead to British diplomats being effectively expelled from Lisbon.

London tried to stall Salazar by not directly responding to his question of how they wanted to pursue the SOE matter. On March 14, Campbell held what he felt was a much more positive meeting with Sampaio, the head of the Ministry of Foreign Affairs, at which Campbell believed he had taken the heat out of the issue by attacking the tactics of the PVDE. Sampaio merely indicated that Salazar was far from impressed that the British had not responded to his question on the future of the secret organization (SOE).[48]

After consultations with senior embassy staff in Lisbon and the Foreign Office in London, Campbell decided that offense was the best form of defense. In a stormy meeting with Salazar on March 16, 1942, Campbell accused the police of using Gestapo tactics, adding, that, in a country where the police had so much power, it was natural that there were those among the police who admired the Gestapo. Only the head of the PVDE, Captain Lourenço, was spared the wrath of Campbell.[49]

Building up something of a head of steam, the ambassador asked whether Salazar was aware that at the very moment of their meeting, honest Portuguese patriots, fervent partisans of the regime, were being beaten up in Portuguese prisons in the hope that they would disclose something incriminating on the British embassy. Salazar listened to what he considered to be something of a rant from Campbell and then casually moved the subject back to the links between the internal opposition in Lisbon and British agents.[50]

The verbal attack out of his system, Campbell tried to reassure Salazar that the SOE had been put into cold storage, and, at any rate, their plot was not at a very advanced stage. No equipment or radios had been distributed to local agents. The latter point wasn't strictly true, but Campbell moved on quickly to assert that the organization had not trawled the highways to look for communists to become its agents.[51]

Despite his strong defense of the SOE, Campbell had already made up his mind that the continuing presence of SOE personnel in Lisbon was highly problematic. He understood that the police already knew the identities of the SOE leaders and that their retention in Lisbon would sow the seeds of doubt about Britain's sincerity towards Portugal.[52] Campbell was becoming agitated and wrote to the Foreign Office reminding them that more than two weeks had gone by without an official response from London on whether they were going to put a stop to any further activity by the SOE.[53]

What followed within British circles was an effort to shore up the British position. The SOE in London was angry that Campbell had effectively given them up to Salazar by refusing to deny his charges, and wanted every effort made to dissuade the ambassador from insisting upon the expulsion of Beevor.[54] Permanent undersecretary of foreign affairs Andrew Cadogan, was consulted and met with the SOE in London. It was decided that as Campbell had made the confession, a sacrifice would have to be made and this would most likely take the form of a man overboard.[55]

Campbell, though, should be discouraged from offering up to Salazar the expulsion of Beevor.[56] On the key point, it was agreed that the SOE would suspend its activities such as the spread of propaganda, and the demolitions issue would be resolved by diplomatic negotiations between the British and Portuguese.[57] Cadogan pointed out that it was important that Campbell could look Salazar in the eye and give him a truthful assurance that the SOE was doing absolutely nothing in Portugal.[58]

Meanwhile, in Lisbon, the rumor mill was in full swing. The alleged British plot was the latest hot topic at society parties.[59] According to Campbell, even some of Britain's best friends were starting to believe it. Due to the highly effective work of German intelligence, the details of the plot were constantly exaggerated to cause maximum damage to the British. Campbell's hope that the issue would be left alone after Salazar's apparent emergence from his "black mood" proved to be false.[60] Salazar was not quite ready to intervene and the PVDE continued at pace with its operation, seemingly intent on cleaning up the whole organization.[61] From Salazar's perspective, he had not yet obtained his pound of flesh, nor had the British—or indeed the Germans—duly absorbed the lesson he was intent on teaching them.

For Campbell, developments went from bad to worse. In a classic British cock-up, Campbell met with Salazar on the evening of March 25, 1942.[62] During the course of the meeting the ambassador informed Salazar that Beevor was the "fountainhead" of the SOE in Portugal. Salazar nodded and added that he already knew this fact. Campbell tried to appease Salazar further, telling him that his first instinct had been to send Beevor home, but he felt that he couldn't because the Military Attaché needed Beevor's help, and more importantly that it would give the Germans the immense satisfaction of seeing him removed. Salazar intervened to suggest that it would be better if the British removed Beevor before they were formally asked to do so.[63]

The drive from Salazar's office in São Bento to the British embassy in Lapa takes only a couple of minutes. This was ample time for Campbell to contemplate whether he had done the right thing in essentially providing the leader of another country with the name of the senior SOE agent operating in that country. As Campbell mulled things over in his mind, he also prepared himself for a possible hostile reception back at the embassy. In a meeting the previous day, he had given no indication to Beevor that he was about to take this highly unorthodox step with Salazar.[64]

Immediately upon arriving back at the embassy, Campbell was handed an urgent cable from the Foreign Office, which had arrived less than an hour after he had departed for his meeting with Salazar.[65] As he read the cable, Campbell inhaled a deep breath, and the blood drained from his face. The cable read that while the Foreign Office sympathized with his difficulties with Salazar it would be a mistake to even mention the removal of Beevor at this stage.[66] Such an action would be interpreted by Salazar only as further evidence that Beevor was responsible for the plot. Not only should Beevor not be named but also no mention of his departure should be tolerated until adequate arrangements were in place for his replacement. If Beevor was forced to go at this stage it was likely to have a very serious effect upon SOE activities not only in Portugal but across Europe.

On the following day, Campbell produced a long account of his meeting with Salazar for the Foreign Office that highlighted the fact that the ambassador believed that he had taken the good fight to Salazar and had brought home to the Portuguese leader the apparent unfairness of the investigation and subsequent actions of the PVDE.[67] In truth, Salazar had politely listened to the ambassador and casually jotted down some notes. He had already got what he wanted from the whole sorry affair.

This wasn't the end of the affair by any means for Campbell. The SOE was furious with him for sacrificing Beevor without consultation.[68] To make matters worse for the SOE, in their eyes, Beevor had been abandoned without any tangible benefit to the British cause.[69] Campbell had emerged from his meeting with Salazar, they charged, having agreed that Beevor would go at a moment indicated by Salazar. Indeed, Salazar would give a private hint when he felt the time was right for Beevor to go.[70] To make matters worse, Salazar had failed to promise to halt the police drive that was now expanding to include the arrests of British subjects.[71] The SOE were not alone in questioning Campbell's judgment.[72]

The MEW also felt that the withdrawal of Beevor would be a mistake and would do little to allay the suspicions of Salazar regarding British activities. The Foreign Office in London soon came to the same conclusion and instructed Campbell that he wasn't to agree to Beevor's withdrawal without first consulting London.[73] He was also told in no uncertain terms to go on the offensive against Salazar and call for an end to the police campaign and the release of the British nationals held in connection with the affair.

CHAPTER 17

The Dossier

BEEVOR RESPONDED TO HIS IMPENDING WITHDRAWAL by undertaking two important tasks for the British. The first of these was to prepare a report for Campbell on activities that should take place in Portugal if the country was invaded.[1] This report needed to be written in a form that could be shown to Salazar. The second task involved writing, with the help of SIS, a dossier on illegal German activities in Portugal, which in Beevor's opinion were at a stage much more widespread and serious than those of the British. After being edited and cleared by the Foreign Office in London the latter report was to be delivered personally by Campbell to Salazar.[2] Beevor viewed it as vital that Salazar, who had given the British a good diplomatic beating over the first quarter of 1942, be taken down a peg and that his police be made to investigate the British claims of German foul play in Lisbon.[3]

Campbell duly delivered the dossier on German activities in Portugal not directly to Salazar, but rather to the director-general of the Ministry of Foreign Affairs, Sampaio, on April 1, 1942. Soon after, Campbell wrote to the Foreign Office that the dossier had an immediate impact on Sampaio, but that the real test of its worth would be seen in how Salazar reacted to its contents and whether he would order the police to investigate its multitude of allegations.[4]

British intelligence did not present quite such a flattering account of Sampaio's reaction. In this instance, it needs to be understood that the dossier was an attempt at a rerun of a similar operation that had been used on General Franco with some pretty instant positive results for the British.[5] When Sir Samuel Hoare had gone to make his protest to General Franco about German espionage activities, he had dressed the senior members of the embassy in full military uniform and they had gone as a body to see the Spanish leader. The style of Campbell in Lisbon was very different. Campbell preferred a quiet and intimate fireside chat with the director-general of the Portuguese Ministry of Foreign Affairs.

In truth, Sampaio's reaction to the presentation of the document was calm, rather dismissive, and, at times, quite amusing.[6] He questioned Campbell on a number of points. Most specifically, he accepted that if the dossier were true that it was wrong of Germany to engage in such activities.[7] He naturally inquired if the British were sure of their sources. He added that there were other countries whose espionage activities were not far behind Germany in Lisbon (a clear reference to Italy) and that a move against Germany would mean having to move against them as well. He finished with something of a verbal flourish of diplomatic logic, wondering why warring powers must indulge in espionage. If only they would concentrate their whole intelligence resources on counterespionage, and then there would be no objection from anywhere in Lisbon.[8]

It took some weeks for Salazar to respond officially to the report. Some of the German activities had shocked Salazar, particularly the extent to which they had penetrated official Portuguese circles and government departments. Beevor claimed that as a result of the dossier Salazar had seriously reconsidered his request that he be withdrawn.[9] In the end, however, Salazar had concluded that it was best that Beevor should leave, but he left the date of his departure to the discretion of Campbell. With plans for Beevor's replacement at an advanced stage, he left Lisbon during the second week of June to return to the SOE in London.

Salazar articulated his red lines on spying in a meeting with Campbell on April 20. He acknowledged that no country could be free of espionage in wartime and that a neutral country need not be too concerned as long as the belligerents confined themselves to spying on each other. They must not, however, involve Portuguese nationals or commit acts that were directly connected with military operations. In closing the topic he promised to investigate the British claims, but felt that many of the bold British statements lacked any supporting evidence.[10] In reality, gathering evidence of espionage activities was not always easy in the field, and especially in Lisbon where both the Allies and Axis powers went to great lengths to cover their tracks and not do anything strictly illegal, which could get their local agents and informers into trouble with the authorities.

A textbook example of how the Germans did business with the local Portuguese and avoided the attention of the Portuguese police was described by Jack Beevor. He described a notionally important Portuguese official who was viewed by the Germans as being sympathetic to the British and needed to be turned, at least temporarily, to become more pro-German.[11] The process would run as follows: A plan is put into action where a locally based German resident arrives in the official's office and says that unfortunately he has been recalled to Berlin at rather short notice. He owns a large Mercedes, which is in excellent condition with four good tires (an important feature during the war), and he has to find a buyer within the couple of days he has left in Lisbon. He is asking only a very reasonable price and the purchaser can pay him in installments over the coming year. Does the official know of any potential buyer for it? After some time the official comes back and suggests that he does, and the deal is struck to sell the car to the official.[12]

Around three days later a different German arrives in the official's office. He introduces himself as having just arrived from

Berlin and is in need of a Mercedes in good condition, with four new tires. Moreover, as he needs it urgently he is willing to pay a high price for it in cash. The official, after a short period of time, informs the German that he knows of just such a car. The deal is soon clinched and the official pockets the not insubstantial difference between the price he paid for the car and that at which he sold it. The Germans have not paid a bribe and the official has not accepted a bribe. As a result he could not be punished for what were two separate transactions.[13] But a debt has been established.

German espionage tactics in Lisbon were sophisticated, and went well beyond the red lines that Salazar outlined to the British. Lisbon was a poor city where the average salaries of even the most senior officials were not high. As a result, financial inducements often provided the best means of securing a favor, or information and action. The Mercedes car trick was one of many ways of getting money to local officials, but at lower levels, a simple envelope filled with escudo notes could do the trick just as easily.

According to the British, in 1942, Albert von Karsthof led German espionage activities in Lisbon. He was based in the German embassy in Lisbon and agents regularly crossed the border into Spain, both legally and illegally. Von Karsthof had a wide network of agents that reached as far as North and South America. His agents in the Portuguese colonies were in regular communication with Lisbon, and the British claimed (although they didn't provide a great deal of evidence) that he had recruited a number of Portuguese citizens to spy on Portuguese troop and naval movements.[14]

The most significant charge that the British warned Salazar about was the alleged presence of a German sabotage organization in Portugal. The British pointed out that Lieutenant-Colonel Hans Joachim Rudolph was the head of the German sabotage organization in the Iberian Peninsula, and was responsible for directing operations against British shipping.[15] The main aim of his work was to try to place bombs on Allied shipping and he had done this successfully using locally recruited agents. Rudolph was on the lookout to bribe locals to undertake this type of work.[16] This time the British did provide some more examples to support the charge, arguing that the loss of two boats could be attributed to the work of Rudolph and his agents, but still not a lot of specific supporting evidence.

The extent to which Salazar already knew of the growing German influence in the PVDE was difficult to measure. The British tried to leave him in no doubt about the specific individuals that they felt were in the pay of the Germans.[17] They noted that probably the most pro-German of the PVDE's leadership, Captain Paulo Cumano, held regular meetings with von Karsthof, and that there was evidence that Cumano recruited informers to obtain information requested by the Germans. Allegations were also made against specific other members of the PVDE who were in regular contact with leading German intelligence agents. In MI5 it was widely believed that, in the event of a German invasion and takeover of Portugal, Cumano would become the head of the PVDE.[18]

The rationale of the British efforts to expose German activities in Lisbon, and in the rest of the country, was naturally to inflict as much damage as possible on the German war effort. The result of the protracted police investigation, which Salazar had ordered, was eventually transmitted to Ronald Campbell in his meeting with Salazar on May 29, 1943.[19] The investigation confirmed most of the charges made by the British. The British were particularly pleased that some of the senior figures in German intelligence were exposed by the report, and in one instance expelled from the country. Salazar confirmed in the detailed report that the German activities were a serious breach of trust, but indicated that the investigation was now closed.[20]

The findings came as something of a surprise to the British intelligence since, in his meeting with Campbell on May 11, Salazar had indicated that the Portuguese police had reached conclusions that differed from the British ones.[21] Salazar had added during the meeting that the British had misclassified minor figures as major figures, and vice versa in the dossier.[22] This was a mistake that Kim Philby admitted the British actually made on many occasions.[23]

The Foreign Office was intent on keeping the pressure on Salazar to take more active action against German espionage activities in Lisbon and asked Campbell to continue with the counteroffensive against the German activity. Campbell eventually came to defend Salazar, arguing to London that the Portuguese leader was working with defective tools in having to use the PVDE to investigate the claims.[24] Since some of the British claims had been directed at key members of the police, there wasn't much appetite in the police for a full investigation.

The poor economic levels of the majority of Lisboetas, however, coupled with very poor levels of education, made many people very susceptible to approaches for the supply of information or action in return for money. There was little that Salazar could do to prevent this from taking place, especially as both the Germans and the British were investing such high levels of human and financial resources into their various operations. By the summer of 1942 Jack Beevor's war in Lisbon was over. He continued to work for the SOE, and indeed the organization continued to operate with a much-reduced remit in the city. Salazar had sent a carefully planned and perfectly executed signal to the warring parties that he would not tolerate any recruitment of opposition forces in Portugal for use as agents. The extent of both the British and German espionage activities in the city had surprised him, but he had used each to repress the other's influence in a classic example of outmaneuvering the belligerents when starting from a position of weakness.

CHAPTER 18

Agents and
Double Agents

AWAY FROM THE LARGE CAFÉS OF THE ROSSIO, IT was only a ten-minute walk to the riverfront. Down by the river, the city became something very different from the upmarket shopping districts in central Lisbon of Baixa and Chiado. From the docks area at Alcântara up the river to Cais do Sodré, narrow streets with tall, often poorly maintained buildings ran behind the main avenue, which formed the start of the Marginal road linking the city to the coastal towns of Estoril and Cascais to the west. In these densely populated backstreets near the river, in discretely marked brothels, the city's prostitutes did a roaring trade with sailors in port for a few days.[1]

Initially, the Germans largely controlled the seedy red-light district, but by 1942 the British and Americans had exposed the German spy ring that duped sailors into giving details of the movements of Allied convoys crossing the Atlantic.[2] The Germans paid the local prostitutes to entice the usually highly intoxicated sailors into providing detailed plans and maps of existing, and future, Allied shipping movements. The size of the convoys and the contents of the cargoes of the ships were also extracted from indiscreet sailors who were desperate to have a good time in Lisbon with the olive-skinned prostitutes from the city.

The breakup of this German "waterfront organization" was viewed as one of the initial few early British intelligence successes.[3] German intelligence complained that much of the information that they were fed by sailors turned out to be wildly inaccurate.[4] The Abwehr felt cheated. They discovered that a lot of their material had been faked by the British.[5] On top of this, as the impact of the war started to damage the Portuguese economy, a lucrative information network was established by local inhabitants with the aim of inventing naval information and selling it to the Germans in order to make money. Attempts were also made by the Germans to try to cultivate some of the sailors returning to England with financial inducements to become German agents spying on movements of ships out of England.[6]

Salazar kept a close eye on the activities of the intelligence gathering agencies through the work of the PVDE, but providing they did not threaten the interests of the Estado Novo, he tolerated much of the espionage activity in Lisbon.

SOE's colleagues, and sometimes rivals, in Lisbon were the Secret Intelligence Service (SIS), better known as MI6. On paper the two groups had very different functions and masters. SIS was an information gatherer, whilst SOE's role was much more sabotage oriented and therefore much more likely to provoke Salazar's wrath.[7]

SIS's role was to watch the Germans and their local agents, and gather as much information on them as possible. SIS was directly responsible to the Foreign Office (unlike SOE, who continued to report to the Ministry of Economic Warfare).[8] Relations between SOE and SIS officers in Lisbon were generally good, but relationships of senior officers in London were fraught, and cooperation between the two agencies was not always as good as it should have been.[9]

Prior to the outbreak of World War II, SIS had not regarded Lisbon as an important source of intelligence gathering. Indeed, as part of a cost-cutting exercise, the station in Lisbon had been closed down during the early 1920s. It was only reopened in September 1939, when it moved into a small room in the British consulate.

After the fall of France in 1940, the station took on a much greater importance and this was reflected in the increase in staff levels and the renting of new, more spacious accommodation.[10] The station reported to the Iberian subsection in England, headed by Kim Philby (later exposed as a Soviet agent), and included, at various times in the war, the writers Graham Greene and Malcolm Muggeridge.[11]

At the beginning of the war SIS suffered from staffing problems and poor security.[12] SIS's main aims in Lisbon, which were similar to those in Spain, were the monitoring of German fifth column activities, helping to establish a post-invasion stay-behind force, and developing intelligence links with Italy.[13] By 1942 it had notched up some notable successes, mainly in its part of the "Ship Observers Scheme" in which observers were planted on neutral shipping in order to report on movements and anything of a suspicious nature on board.[14] In terms of Italy, however, SIS in Lisbon had failed to obtain any important intelligence material.

Despite these successes, and the fact that SIS by 1942 was aware of almost all Axis espionage operations in Lisbon, London was never completely satisfied with the work of the SIS in Lisbon.[15] SIS station chiefs in Lisbon were told to stop activities related to the economic blockade, as well as counterespionage activities in order to concentrate on other issues of vital concern. An increasingly important part of the work of the SIS in Lisbon and Spain was as part of escape lines for POWs, who were being passed down newly established lines over the Pyrenees with Lisbon as the final stopping point. From Lisbon the successful escapees were flown back to England on the BOAC-run aircraft to Bristol and Poole. SIS officers were employed in Lisbon to control the end of the line and repatriation of personnel to England.

Lisbon provided the SIS with two very useful sources of information. The first of these were the thousands of refugees who entered the city. This eventually became the domain of MI9 acting under the cover of the Repatriation Office. MI9 agents interviewed recently arrived refugees to gather up-to-date intelligence on the situation in France and to help expose Abwehr agents posing as refugees.[16] The second lucrative source of intelligence material was the large British expatriate community in Lisbon. Here senior SIS personnel were quick to develop close ties with key members of the community whom it mobilized for intelligence work against the Germans. One advantage of using the local network of expatriates was that they were normally under less surveillance by the PVDE than SIS staff members.

Kim Philby described the intelligence and political situation in Lisbon as much more fuzzy and complicated than in Madrid.[17] Philby argued that the Foreign Office was nervous about taking action for fear of disturbing the wily doctor's balancing act. There was concern that if Salazar was forced down off his fence, he might too easily come down on the wrong side.[18] SIS was additionally cautious, Philby pointed out, because many of the Portuguese senior officials who were taking money from the Germans were also taking money from the British. The last thing SIS wanted was for those officials to come to the British and ask them to make good any lost extracurricular earnings if their German paymasters were expelled. Even espionage had to work to a budget.

At the end of 1941, the signal traffic between the SIS in Lisbon and England was greater than any other SIS station in the world.[19] During the war, the work of the station in Lisbon led to a number of major successes, including the exposure of British traitors, and the exposure of 1,900 enemy agents, 350 suspected enemy agents, and 200 Germans with known intelligence links.[20] SIS's work also led to the exposure of a number of businesses in Lisbon that were commercial covers for German espionage activities.

As elsewhere, there was a tendency among British intelligence operatives in Lisbon to overestimate the efficiency of German intelligence. It became clear only during postwar interviews just how fragmented and lacking in organization the German intelligence machine was during World War II.[21] This was also found to be true of German radio interception performance, which was not as efficient as the Allies had believed during the course of the war.[22] Precautions taken by the Allies for key operations, as a result, were often overelaborate, or altogether unnecessary.

Various Allied double agents either passed through, or were based in Lisbon at different stages of the war. Perhaps the most famous was the Spaniard, Juan Pujol, whose British code name was "GARBO." Pujol had developed a deep hatred of both Fascism and Communism as a result of the Spanish Civil War.[23] Initially, he offered his services to the British in Madrid in January 1941, but was turned down.[24] Acting alone, he then approached German intelligence and boldly informed them that he was traveling to London and wished to work for them. Pujol tried to convince the Germans by flaunting his apparent extreme right-wing views and offered to spy for them in either Lisbon or England.[25] He was turned down again, but did not give up.

The Germans had indicated that they might be interested if he could secure a way to get into England. Pujol then traveled to Lisbon, where he secured a forged Spanish diplomatic pass by tricking a slightly dim local printer into believing that he was a member of the Spanish delegation in Lisbon.[26] He then retuned to Madrid, where he showed his pass to the Germans. After some time, and several security checks, the Abwehr agreed to take him on and gave him the codename "ARABEL."[27] He was provided with $3,000, which he hid in a condom, and given a course in the use of writing in invisible ink.[28]

The Germans sent him on his way in July 1941, but Pujol still got only as far as Lisbon. Here he approached the British embassy again, but without luck. Still based in Lisbon, Pujol pretended to be in Britain by creating a fictitious set of characters and locations, and dispatched a mass of misinformation to his Abwehr handlers.[29] He spent much of his time in Lisbon in Baixa and Chiado, and in Rossio where he sat in the cafés watching and listening to refugees. He visited the many bookshops in Chiado and quickly read travel books on Britain as well as newspapers and journals.[30] He needed to familiarize himself with Britain quickly in order to make the false information he was sending back to German intelligence convincing.

Much of this misinformation centered upon false reports of Allied troop movements mixed with tales of drunken sexual orgies in whorehouses.[31] By February 1942, the counterintelligence branch of SIS had identified him as the author of these false reports, which they were receiving through decryption of German intelligence communications, and in March Pujol was finally recruited as a double agent. SIS had also acted on a tip-off about the work of Pujol from a Lisbon-based American diplomat.[32]

The running of GARBO caused a number of disputes between the intelligence chiefs. MI5, which dealt with intelligence issues on British soil, was in conflict with SIS, which dealt with the same issues on foreign soil.[33] Eventually Pujol was brought to London on April 24, 1942, where he was run by MI5. The resulting tensions from this episode took a long time to resolve among the senior personnel in both agencies.

From a German perspective, Pujol had seemingly become one of their most successful agents, running a network of some twenty-seven subagents, none of whom actually existed.[34] In the three years in which GARBO was operative he sent some 1,399 messages and 423 letters to his extremely satisfied German handlers back in Madrid.[35] His prose was never dull: He wrote with brio, always keen to seemingly praise the Germans and to attack the Jews wherever possible.

The success of Pujol's double life and value to the Allies is confirmed by the fact that he remains one of the few agents to be decorated by both sides in the war. On July 29, 1944, he was informed that Hitler had awarded him the Iron Cross for his contribution to the German war effort. In December of the same year he received the MBE from the British.

Not every German was enamored of Pujol or espionage in general: The German ambassador to Lisbon, Baron Oswald von Hoyningen-Huene, revealed during the alleged plot to kidnap the Duke of Windsor during the summer of 1940 his distaste for the darker side of such activities, and his fear that the conduct of such operations risked damaging his relationship, and influence, with Salazar.

As the war progressed, Hoyningen-Huene, while accepting the need for what he saw as legitimate espionage activities, constantly argued for a reduction in the number of Abwehr agents operating in Lisbon.[36] This naturally led to tensions between himself and the Abwehr senior agents in Lisbon and in Berlin. The ambassador also disapproved of German agents who worked for independent intelligence agencies and who were not therefore under direct control. Baron von Hoyningen-Huene greatly valued his relationship with Salazar and, like Ronald Campbell, saw many problems in conducting espionage activities in a neutral country, which encroached upon the interests of the hosts.

Both sides' intelligence agencies were from time to time reined in by their ambassadors or by their respective headquarters. Interviewed after the war, Baron von Hoyningen-Huene recalled the constant struggles to keep elements of German intelligence in check, and admitted to not being fully in the picture as to some of their activities.

CHAPTER 19

Death of a
Hollywood Star

THERE IS AN OLD SEPIA-TINGED PHOTOGRAPH OF
the British-born Hollywood actor Leslie Howard, enjoying
what would turn out to be one of his last suppers in the restaurant
of the Hotel Aviz in Lisbon. As on most nights, the hotel bar and
restaurant was full of a mixture of wealthy locals, prostitutes, spies,
and local informers. This photograph, however, creates an intimate
portrait of a single table with its four diners. The table is covered
with a simple large white tablecloth, and its contents of bottles and
glasses provide the evidence that the photograph was taken towards the end of a spirited evening of conversation.

In the center of the picture, looking down at his glass as a waiter
in formal white-tie dress tops it up, is Leslie Howard. He looks
tired, slightly melancholic, and a little reticent. In reality, he was
very probably simply suffering from the wearing effects of travel,
and from the strain of giving one-man performances to expectant
local audiences. Two fellow diners are smiling and laughing, on either side of his chair. They were obviously enjoying being in the
company of a Hollywood great, a little more than he was enjoying
being in theirs. Behind the table the headwaiter is beaming in the
knowledge that all appears well at the VIP's table. On the far side

of the table, looking away from it, is Howard's agent, Alfred Chen-halls, sitting relaxed with legs crossed. He was a well-dressed, bald and portly man, who looked to be in his sixties. He had the expression of someone who was enjoying puffing on his large cigar as he listened to the anecdotes and stories told by Howard, all of which he had heard many times before on this trip, and on previous ones.

Leslie Howard was visiting Lisbon and Madrid on a British Council–sponsored propaganda tour. Howard had cultivated something of a reputation as being a marketable instrument of British propaganda, both in making patriotic films and by undertaking performance and speaking tours to bolster the war effort. Howard was born in Forest Hill in southeast London into a Jewish family. His outstanding performance as Ashley Wilkes in the blockbuster movie *Gone with the Wind* helped make him one of the biggest movie stars of the era. An elegant gentleman who was always well dressed in Savile Row–cut double-breasted suits, complete with matching waistcoats, fedora hat, and club tie, he was a major draw on the lecture and solo performance circuit.

In public, the British Council was openly thrilled with his trip, and his performances were described as a resounding success.[1] In truth, Howard's visit had not been without difficulties. Howard was critical of the British Council and its chief representative in Madrid at the time.[2] His reading of Hamlet's soliloquies was described, however, as extraordinary and deeply moving.[3]

Part of the problem relating to Howard's lectures had been caused by the British Council having to use their own small lecture facilities. The local British Council representative in Madrid pointed out that if they had used a public theater or hall they would have run into all sorts of difficulties. The council would have had to provide copies of scripts to the censor, where many Axis agents operated. The local police might have broken up the performance anyway on the grounds that it was not legal. Public lectures in which the guest was not invited by the Spanish authorities were not tolerated. Worse still was the threat of local pro-Axis Falangist elements gaining entry to the lectures and demonstrating or starting a row. In trying to find a way around this problem the council had come up with the idea of requesting the already hard-pressed, overworked, and in poor health Howard to agree to give repeat performances of his lectures to smaller audiences.

The British Council claimed to have had no idea that Howard was not travelling alone.[4] This was curious, since correspondence had taken place months before his arrival with the Foreign Office who understood perfectly well that Howard would under no circumstances agree to travel alone.[5] The council also appeared to have no idea of the nature of Alfred Chenhalls's business relationship to Howard.[6] Again, the Foreign Office had detailed background information on Chenhalls and his motives for visiting Spain.[7] Chenhalls was the director of a number of film productions and also served as Howard's agent and accountant. In setting up Howard's visit for their own propaganda purposes, the Foreign Office used the British Council simply as a front and failed to communicate with its officials anything more than the rudimentary details of the trip. Howard's visit was of great importance to the Allied propaganda efforts in the Iberian Peninsula, and the Foreign Office didn't want the British Council to mess up it up.

When a weary Howard and Chenhalls arrived in Madrid after the long train journey from Lisbon they were greeted by the local director of the British Council.[8] Upon his arrival, Howard is said to have thrown something of a theatrical-style tantrum. He informed his host that he didn't wish to visit Madrid at all, and had only agreed to go to Lisbon. What followed was a blazing row in which both Howard and Chenhalls were reported to have demanded modifications to the program and that all repeat lectures be cancelled. Howard then informed the council that he wanted to get back to Lisbon much quicker than expected, to spend a week's holiday in Estoril. Only reluctantly he agreed to do the bare minimum of two lectures for the council. To make matters worse, Howard failed to show up for several of the big receptions and dinners that had been arranged in his honor.[9]

Once back in Lisbon, Howard was keen to get back to England and tried to take an earlier flight back. The BOAC flight from Lisbon to Whitchurch Airport on the outskirts of Bristol, however, was usually fully booked. It was the main route of transporting official personnel down to Lisbon from England. Howard and Chenhalls showed up at the airport on the morning of May 31, 1943, in the hope of persuading a couple of passengers to give up their seats, but they were out of luck.[10]

The camouflaged aircraft took off and headed up past Porto and over northwestern Spain and the Bay of Biscay. Flying over the Bay of Biscay the flight was at risk from Luftwaffe patrols flying out from their bases in Western France. On this occasion a German fighter spotted the flight, but the pilot of the BOAC plane dove into cloud cover and circled for a number of minutes, before making his escape through a storm.[11] There had been previous attacks on the aircraft by German fighters flying out of their bases in France. The BOAC pilots flying out of Lisbon used different tactics to avoid detection. The most popular one was to fly as low as possible.

On the morning of June 1, 1943, Howard and Chenhalls climbed the steps to Flight 777A. The plane left on time at 9:30 AM. During its crossing of the Bay of Biscay it too was spotted by a Luftwaffe patrol. The Dutch pilot, instead of diving for the cover of the clouds, chose to remain at a high altitude and the unarmed plane was first followed by a German fighter plane, and then attacked with deadly precision. The pilot of Flight 777A radioed Whitchurch, the destination of the plane, to say that he was being followed and then again to warn that he was under attack.[12] After this point, contact with the plane was lost. The pilot of the German fighter confirmed the "kill" after seeing the aircraft fall towards the sea. No survivors or wreckage was ever found.

Several theories have been put forward to explain why Flight 777A was attacked. The initial theory revolved around Howard and Chenhalls, and was quoted by Winston Churchill in his history of World War II, and argued that the plane was shot down in a case of mistaken identity. A German agent working at Lisbon Airport mistakenly took the portly, bald, cigar-smoking Alfred Chenhalls to be Winston Churchill. The agent radioed Berlin, who gave the order for the plane to be shot down. The British prime minister was visiting North Africa at the time for a summit meeting in Casablanca and was thought to be returning to England at around this time. To add a little spice to this story it was also suggested that Leslie Howard resembled Churchill's bodyguard, helping the agent in Lisbon to put two and two together and make five.

Churchill wrote that the tragedy much distressed him. He was amazed, not by the brutality of the Germans ordering one of their aircraft to shoot down the defenseless aircraft, but rather by the stupidity of the German agents in Lisbon. The prime minister wondered how the Germans could think that, with all the resources he had at his disposal, he would have booked a passage on an unarmed and unescorted plane from Lisbon that was due to fly home in broad daylight. (In reality, Churchill flew back from Casablanca making a wide loop by night from Gibraltar into the Atlantic Ocean.)[13]

On the surface, the explanation of mistaken identity appeared to hold some merit. It was true that the Germans knew that Churchill was in Casablanca and would be flying back to England at some point after the conclusion of the summit. German agents across North Africa and Iberia had been told to look out for a plane that could be carrying the British prime minister. British intelligence knew that German planes had orders to shoot down any aircraft flying between Lisbon and Portugal during the first few days of June 1943 in the hope of killing Churchill.[14]

In recent years, an additional line of inquiry into the tragedy has focused on the role of ULTRA intelligence in the crash.

ULTRA intelligence was the name given to intelligence gathered from the intercepts of German radio messages, which were produced by the ENIGMA code-breaking machine. Among the intelligence community of the era it was widely known that the British intercepted a German communication stating that the plane was going to be attacked. Intelligence bosses allowed the plane to take off to its doom, in order to protect the secrecy of the existence of ULTRA. If they had cancelled the flight they would have sent a signal to the Germans that their communications were intercepted. There was also a sense of acting to protect the life of Winston Churchill.[15]

The benefits of the information gathered as part of ULTRA were huge.[16] In Portugal, and in the other European neutral countries, it helped SIS gain a strong advantage over Axis intelligence and made a major contribution to the Allies' important operations of deception.[17] The Allies went to great lengths to try to keep its existence secret: SIS never shared ULTRA intelligence with the Soviet Union.[18]

The German agent accused of marking the plane in Lisbon was Baron von Weltzein, whose name became public knowledge in December 1943 when the British press published it.[19] Kim Philby and SIS had been watching Weltzein in Lisbon for some time, and two files had been opened on him.[20] Two spellings of his name, "Weltzein" and "Weltzen" had led to the two separate files being created before they were merged into one amid much office rancor in 1942.[21] Weltzein was in his mid-fifties, balding, with a red face and rather portly waist.[22] He was well dressed and spoke Portuguese with a strong German accent. Wherever he went in Lisbon, he stood out and wasn't difficult to shadow. Weltzein was the chief recruiter and contact of local Axis agents in Lisbon. The British knew of his work and by 1943 had compromised most of his ring of local agents.[23]

The timing of the shooting down of Flight 777A caused the Germans a great deal of further difficulties in Lisbon. Salazar had just informed the British of the result of the police investigation into the dossier on German espionage activities in Portugal. The British Foreign Office had instructed Campbell to increase the pressure on Salazar to take robust action against the German operations in Lisbon. The attack on Flight 777A shocked Salazar and he decided that Portugal had endured enough in the espionage wars.

On June 7, 1943, a new decree was introduced stating that spying both by foreigners and the Portuguese had become a criminal action and the PVDE was charged with enforcing the new law.[24] But giving power to the PVDE to investigate and enforce the ban on spying did not bring an end to spying activities in Lisbon. It merely deepened the plots and allowed officers in the PVDE to increase their extracurricular salaries by taking inducements from both sides in the war.

CHAPTER 20

Farewell to Friends

W HILE IT WAS NATURAL TO FOCUS ON THE DEATH
of Leslie Howard aboard Flight 777A, there were many
other important passengers on board that could have been potential targets for the Germans. Ivan Sharp was the top British
wolfram expert, whose work was vital to the Allies in Portugal.
Another British agent on board the doomed flight was Tyrrell
Shervington, a director of Shell Oil in Lisbon, as well as the Foreign Office–based head of British embassy inspections team, Gor-
don MacLean.[1] Any or all of these important British personnel
could have been targets. Moreover, it was well known to the Germans that the route from Lisbon to Whitchurch was used by a
number of British intelligence agencies to fly their personnel to
and from Portugal. Most of the flights contained Allied personnel
and also returning POWs, who had reached Lisbon at the end of
the well-established escape lines.

Also on board Flight 777A was Wilfrid Israel, a leading Zionist
activist and Jewish rescue worker, who was working in Lisbon aiding the escape of Jewish refugees out of Europe and helping to organize their onward passage out of the city. Israel's arrival in Lisbon
in 1943 was a sign of the growing frantic nature of the rescue mission in Lisbon given the worsening plight of the Jews in Europe,
and also a reflection of the increasing organizational divisions and

procedural problems that were damaging the rescue efforts in Lisbon. The situation was complicated by the perception that the policy of Spain was making it more difficult for Jews to transit through its borders, and by British reluctance to open up Jewish emigration to Palestine.

The last photograph of Wilfrid Israel shares some similarities with that of Leslie Howard's at one of his last meals in Lisbon. The photograph of Israel shows a handsome, slightly balding, well-dressed man wearing a dark suit with a white shirt and tie. He is sitting in a restaurant in Lisbon. Members of the Jewish community based in Lisbon flank Israel on either side of the long table decorated with several flower arrangements.[2] He is speaking with his hands interlinked in front of him. He looks calm and at peace. His hosts appear delighted with his company, grinning at the camera.

The reality in Spain was that Franco's policy had not changed—Spain still allowed Jews to pass through as long as they did not attempt to remain in the country.[3] What altered, depending on the state of the war, was the belief that Franco, under pressure from some quarters, was about to change this policy and ban the transit of Jews.

Wilfrid Israel had written to his wife in March 1943 to tell her that the Jewish agency wanted him to proceed to Lisbon without delay to help deal with the refugee situation.[4] He added that he could not, and dared not, say no to the request. During his stay in Lisbon, Israel had concentrated on trying to get refugees to Palestine, particularly children. This was often done against the wishes of the British, who had a policy of not accepting any additional adult Jewish refugees from enemy-occupied Europe into Palestine above strictly controlled limits. This policy formed part of a series of British attempts to limit Jewish immigration to Palestine in order to appease the Arab states.

In the Foreign Office, there was an understanding that the Arabs were more strategically important to the British during the war, as well as a fear that some of them could be tempted to support or join the Axis powers. The Arabs saw Jewish immigration to Palestine not as rescue missions but as an attempt by Jewish groups to alter the demographic balance of Palestine in favor of the Jews.

Wilfred Israel departed for Lisbon on March 26, 1943, for the most difficult mission of his career. The day before he left England he made out his will and made sure that his papers were in order.[5] He flew the route from Whitchurch to Lisbon on a BOAC flight similar to the one on the fateful June 1. His preparations had not been without incident. The respective authorities in Lisbon and Madrid had turned down both Israel's applications for visas to stay in Lisbon and to enter Spain.[6]

Ronald Campbell in Lisbon intervened, and the authorities issued the visa for Israel to visit Lisbon on March 16, 1943.[7] The Spanish took longer to approve a brief visit to the country in late April 1943. The initial aims of his mission were to distribute the 200 certificates to go to Palestine that the Jewish agency had secured from the British Mandate Authorities in Jerusalem.[8] His wider goal was to look at ways of improving and speeding up the movement of Jewish refugees out of Portugal and Spain.

Wilfrid Israel created something of a stir among the local permanent Portuguese Jewish community and the various relief agencies working in the city. In the first instance, they were hopeful that his arrival would lead to a reduction in the number of refugees who were dependent upon their funds.[9] The reality was very different. Israel's funds were limited, as were the number of certificates for entry into Palestine. For most of his stay in Lisbon, Israel chose to work alone. Jealousy and petty rivalries among the various rival groups, together with personality clashes, made it difficult, although not impossible, to work efficiently with these groups. The groups understood that Israel was carrying for them the much sought after certificates for refugees to enter Palestine, and the various groups complained about the choice of candidates to receive the certificates. SIS gave Israel a wide berth, as they believed that there were German agents among the refugees. MI9 spent much of the time interviewing the refugees to uncover these agents.

Almost immediately, Israel made the decision to issue the largest number of certificates to Jews stuck in Spain, as he believed they were in greatest danger.[10] There was also the question of whether to give the certificates to the old or to the young. The Jewish authorities in Palestine hoped that the certificates would be given to the younger refugees, who could do most to help in the coming conflict with the Arabs. Israel's work was not confined to Lisbon; he traveled up to the towns of Ericeira and Caldas da Rainha in order to visit the Jewish refugees housed in these holiday towns.

Israel had little time for bureaucracy and attempted to speed up processes in Lisbon. A brief visit to Madrid starting on April 29 left him in no doubt that conditions were much worse there and highlighted the need to get these refugees out through Lisbon as quickly as possible.[11] In truth, Israel was struggling against a worsening situation. The Bermuda Conference on refugees, which aimed to develop a coordinated Allied policy on refugees, had produced few tangible results.[12] The British authorities in Jerusalem were becoming increasingly nervous about taking even an agreed quota of refugees and were looking to further restrict future immigration certificates to Jewish immigrants. Nonetheless, Israel continued his efforts up until the last, and as he left Lisbon there was a sense that his presence on the ground had made some positive difference. He left no formal report of his work in Lisbon, and his death on Flight 777A left a large hole in the rescue operations in Lisbon.[13] Sir Samuel Hoare in a letter to foreign secretary, Anthony Eden, paid tribute to Israel as being enthusiastic and sensitive.[14]

The extent to which Wilfrid Israel was a priority target for the Germans remains questionable. Despite his important work in saving the lives of Jewish refugees, it is doubtful that his murder would have had the same impact and publicity as that of a Hollywood actor. Israel left Lisbon having largely achieved his goal of helping secure the onward passage to Palestine of a group of Jewish children. His time in the city also helped expose the difficulties, and mistakes, that the various rescue groups were encountering, and also inflicting upon themselves.

The shooting down of Flight 777A was not the only air crash that shook Lisbon in 1943. On February 22, 1943, the Pan Am Yankee Clipper arrived in the Lisbon area some fifteen minutes ahead of schedule.[15] On board were twenty-seven passengers and twelve crew members who had left the Azores earlier on the same day.[16] Everything appeared normal, with the plane in radio contact with the station in Lisbon, who gave it instructions to land from south to north and turned on the River Tagus's landing lights.[17]

Sunset was at 6:22 PM, and it had been dark for around twenty minutes when the plane commenced its descent. The sky was lit up from time to time by distant flashes of lightning. At 6:47 PM, while attempting to land on the river, the left wing of the plane hit the water and the plane broke up. Despite a rapidly mounted Portuguese rescue mission involving boats and divers, nineteen of the passengers and five crew perished either in the impact of the accident or as a result of drowning.[18] Most of the other passengers, some critically injured, were taken to a hospital in a fleet of nineteen ambulances.[19] Among the passengers was the actress Jane Froman, who was severely hurt but was pulled to safety by one of the pilots, whom she later married.[20]

The wreckage of the plane was difficult to retrieve as the strong current in the river at the time scattered parts in all directions. It took some days to find even the main parts of the wreckage. For weeks afterwards people continued to come across airmail letters that had been carried, as always, in the plane's wings. The American embassy in Lisbon sent personnel to trawl the riverbanks for secret documents that a member of the legation who was on board the flight was carrying.[21] Among the documents they successfully recovered and smuggled away before the Portuguese authorities came upon them were badly damaged air target maps of Yugoslavia and Bulgaria.

Crash investigators immediately ruled out foul play in the absence of any type of explosion or fire aboard.[22] The investigators rejected the testimony of the Clipper's captain, Robert Sullivan, who survived the crash, when he insisted that the control system had failed and that the plane had descended from 600 feet at a severe angle of 45 degrees before hitting the water. Other witnesses at the station suggested that the angle of descent was more like 20 degrees, and was normal. For reasons that were not clear, the pilot had tried to land on the river in the direction from east to west.

The crash illustrated the apparent dangers of trying to land on the river at night in winter. Some years later several of the passengers, including Jane Froman, sued Pan Am for $2.5 million in damages for injuries to her leg caused by the accident.[23] The Clipper service to New York, as a result, was suspended for a time after the accident, forcing wealthy refugees to try to secure passage on a ship instead.

The Azores was a vital bridge for the growing transatlantic service between Lisbon and New York, serving as a refuelling area for the Pan Am flying boats. During World War II, the islands became an important bridge for the Allied military and its efforts to bring equipment to Europe, and in the campaign against the German U-boats, which were causing heavy losses in both ships and manpower from the Atlantic conveys. Winston Churchill and President Roosevelt had discussed the importance of the islands to the Allied cause at their meeting at Casablanca in 1943, along with strategies of how to persuade Salazar to allow the Allies access to the military facilities on the islands.

Both Churchill and Roosevelt wanted to be able to put the islands to good use. The resulting efforts of the Allies to achieve their aims brought them up against a reluctant Salazar and revealed deep divisions between the Allies on the best method for achieving their goal. Before they undertook this difficult process, the Allies looked to score a major military victory in North Africa by launching Operation Torch. As this operation brought the military campaign close to Portugal, Salazar would need to be informed of its intent as soon as it was launched.

CHAPTER 21

Ancient Alliance

S UNDAY, NOVEMBER 7, 1943, HAD BEGUN AS SOMETHING of a quiet day for Salazar. He was in his office working on the introduction to a book that consisted of a collection of his most important speeches.[1] In the evening, as usual, he dined alone and was planning on getting to bed early. But at 9:30 PM he was informed that the British ambassador requested to speak with him on the phone. Ronald Campbell asked for an immediate interview. The ambassador's voice sounded grave, but Salazar decided that it would be better to try to put him off until the morning. Campbell nonetheless insisted upon seeing Salazar that evening.[2]

Eventually, Salazar agreed to see him at 1:00 AM. Some moments later, Salazar's phone rang again and this time it was Portugal's ceremonial head of state, President António Óscar Carmona, who had received a call at his weekend residence in Cascais from the American embassy; the American ambassador was also asking for an immediate interview. For a terrible minute, Salazar thought that the Allies had invaded the Azores.[3] Such an action, he believed, would have killed off the policy of neutrality and would have dragged Portugal into the war. Luckily for Salazar, the Allies merely wanted to inform him of their landings in North Africa.

Operation Torch, the successful Allied landings in North Africa at the end of 1942, meant that the Iberian Peninsula's importance to the overall conduct of the war started to fade[4]. Churchill was grateful to Franco for not opposing the landings. Churchill described his indebtedness to Salazar in a personal message passed on to the Portuguese leader by Ronald Campbell on November 7, 1942.[5] He promised that there would be no change to Anglo-Portuguese relations, despite fighting in lands next to Spain and Portugal. Churchill suggested, noting the close relations between Portugal and Spain, and the weight which would be attached to "your Excellency's" advice in Madrid, that Salazar might consider it useful to inform the Spanish government of this message.[6]

Churchill also asked Salazar to use his influence to reassure the Spanish regarding the intentions of His Majesty's government, and of the United States government, who both desired to spare the Iberian Peninsula the horrors of war, and to see that not only the Portuguese, but also the Spanish, took their place in the peace and prosperity of the postwar world.[7] Churchill's flattery was only mildly successful. In response, Salazar merely expressed his hope that the campaign would be brief. Later, he would become increasingly impatient for the conclusion of the North African campaign.[8]

To reinforce the Allied tactics, Salazar received a personal message from President Franklin D. Roosevelt the following day, on November 8, 1942.[9] President Roosevelt's letter was similar in tone to Churchill's, pointing out that he hoped that Salazar would accept his solemn assurance that Portugal should have no fear of the motives of the United States. Roosevelt promised no move against Portugal, or its island possessions.

The last part of the promise turned out to be almost impossible to keep. Within twelve months both Britain and the United States were ready to invade the Azores. The issue of the Azores came to dominate Salazar's agenda above all others in 1943. Sitting in his unheated office during the cold winter months of 1942/43, surveying his detailed maps of the islands, Salazar quickly learned an important point: While Operation Torch had led to a lessening in the value of the Iberian Peninsula to the Allies, it had not reduced the importance of the Azores.[10]

The nine islands that make up the Azores were located across a 500-mile radius around one third of the way across the Atlantic Ocean from Lisbon to New York. The islands form part of a volcanic range, and some of them still had active volcanoes. The largest island was São Miguel with its capital, Porta Delgada, which had a population of some 20,000. Hitler had originally wanted to invade in order to develop bases for his U-boats, but was persuaded not to by his naval commanders, who wanted instead to get on with attacking Allied shipping routes.[11]

For the British, and after its entry into the war, the United States, the islands were viewed as a vital link in the antisubmarine warfare of the Allies against the German U-boats,[12] and to the efforts of the Allies to open up a southern Atlantic route for the conveys crossing the ocean, bringing badly needed equipment and manpower to the European theater.[13] Despite their distance from Portugal, the fight for control over the islands took place in talks held in Lisbon.

The eventual outcome of the often bitter and bad-tempered negotiations was instrumental in helping to shorten the war. The conduct of the negotiations would also lead to the Portuguese ambassador to London and former minister of foreign affairs, Armindo Monteiro, being sacked—charged, in effect, with going native with the British. He was recalled to Lisbon in virtual disgrace, and would never hold a senior position within Salazar's regime again.

For a visibly tiring Salazar, the question of the Azores was yet another problematic issue in which he needed to balance Portugal's interests with the realities of the war, which appeared to be turning slowly, but decisively, in favor of the Allies. He was becoming weary, easily irritated, and, more problematic for the Allies, extremely obstinate.

During the first part of 1943 his workload had started to affect his health. He suffered from chronic eye infections, which slowed

him down, and from bouts of seasonal flu.[14] Given the centraliza-
tion of government power in his hands it was becoming ever more
difficult to get a quick decision out of him. During peacetime this
might not have proved such a problem, but in 1943, and with the
Allies on the offensive, they needed Portugal to move with rather
more haste in giving them what they wanted in order to help
shorten the war.

Salazar's ever-increasing workload, together with the winter del-
uges, made it difficult for him to escape Lisbon for any meaningful
rest and recuperation in the countryside. In spite of the increasing
number of official papers on his desk, correspondence, and meetings, he still continued with his personal correspondence in which
he speculated on what the various outcomes of the war would
mean for Portugal and Europe.

By early 1943, it looked as if there were only two realistic outcomes: a total Allied victory, or a negotiated surrender by Germany.
Salazar had a strong preference for the latter, believing that a total
Allied victory would lead to a situation in which the Americans and
the communists, in the form of the Soviet Union, would play dom-
inant roles within Europe. Ronald Campbell noted that any obligation that Salazar felt towards Britain as the champion of the small
powers was jaundiced by his fear that the complete defeat of Germany would let loose anarchy and chaos in Europe.[15]

Time and time again, Salazar, for all of his lack of his own world
vision, or notion of where Portugal fitted into global politics, got it
right in forecasting the postwar order in Europe. Total Allied victory over Germany would lead to a bipolar world system, run by
two nations, and two philosophies, in which he had little faith.
Salazar also expressed his doubts about the establishment of regional blocks, which Churchill had called for during a speech he
had made on March 22, 1943.[16]

Churchill's speech had been given a lot of coverage in the Portuguese press, and several articles had suggested similarities between the approaches of Churchill and Salazar in the problems of

small states.[17] Salazar noted to Campbell the seemingly chronic squabbles of the Balkan states.[18] He was also concerned about how Portugal and Spain would fit into Churchill's regional blocks. On this issue, he behaved like a typical Portuguese man who believed that Spain would have absorbed Portugal long ago if it were not for Portugal's alliance with Britain.

The decision of Salazar in 1941 to accept the British suggestion, that in the advent of a German invasion of mainland Portugal only token resistance would be offered with his government moving to the Azores, had led to the Portuguese starting to reinforce the islands. The British informed the Americans of these developments in May 1941. It was agreed between London and Washington, at this stage, that the discussion over the use of the islands should be left mainly to the British.

British policy towards the Azores had previously illustrated differences in London between the Foreign Office, which favored taking the islands by force only if it was absolutely clear that the Germans were going to seize them, and the prime minister, who favored seizing the islands by force in order to prevent any possibility of the Germans taking them over. As a result of these internal divisions nothing was done except to have a force on standby for any immediate landings on the islands. President Roosevelt had been informed of these military plans in September 1940.[19]

Washington preferred a more robust approach to the Azores even than Churchill: The Americans were willing to use a substantial military force to occupy the islands if need be. President Roosevelt had referred to the importance of the islands, and the dangers to the United States if they fell into German hands, in a key broadcast to the American people on May 27, 1941. The broadcast had angered the Portuguese, who feared that it might provoke the Germans into taking over the islands in order to frustrate a potential preventative occupation by the United States or Britain. The American red lines were clear: If Germany moved against the Azores, then it would move to seize them. The United States also asked the Brazilians if they would be willing to take part in a temporary occupation of the Azores.[20]

On February 12, 1942, without consulting the British, President Roosevelt suggested to the president of Brazil that it should take over the defense of the Azores. The Brazilians, believing that Salazar would not accept this offer, did not approach the Portuguese, and the Americans agreed to consult with the British before taking any further action.[21] On May 10, Churchill noted that the Chiefs of Staff had asked for his authorization to start discussions with the Americans on a combined approach to dealing with Salazar over the Azores. Churchill agreed, and he was willing to inform Lisbon, even at this stage, that if it did not agree to the Allied request then the islands would be taken over by force.

Both Ronald Campbell in Lisbon and Anthony Eden in the Foreign Office agreed that negotiations with Salazar were the best route to pursue.[22] In Campbell's estimation, Salazar would agree to a temporary British military presence on the islands for the duration of the war. It became apparent that the argument over the military or diplomatic strategy was a little premature, as Britain could not ready the correct military force before the end of August.[23] When this point was put to Churchill he erupted, arguing that an occupation would save a million tons of shipping and thousands of lives of Allied seamen. He went on to forcibly argue that the fate of all small nations depended on an Allied victory, and that Britain should not hesitate to take steps that would shorten the war and save lives.

Eventually, the War Cabinet overruled Churchill arguing that no military action could be taken for at least two months. The British military plan to occupy the Azores was known as Operation Lifebelt and the Chiefs of Staff (CoS) had been refining the plan throughout the late spring and early summer of 1943. The plan became subject to political interference when the government insisted that Salazar be given a few hours in the form of an ultimatum upon the commencement of the operation.[24] The CoS had originally planned for a Trojan horse operation with three Royal Navy destroyers asking for permission to land in the normal way. Inside the three destroyers would be commandoes who would emerge and then capture the key points in Porta Delgada.

An alternative plan of a full frontal assault was then considered, but the chiefs would not recommend it. The CoS wanted the warning element of the plan to be dropped by the War Cabinet. The overall judgment was that the aims could be achieved from a military perspective, but that it would be no pushover if Salazar ordered the well-dug-in Portuguese garrison on the key islands to resist.

Ronald Campbell had first formally introduced the topic of the use of facilities in the Azores in an indirect manner during his meeting with Salazar on May 31, 1943.[25] Campbell had given Salazar a general review of the war in which he underlined the Allied strength in every sphere except in that of antisubmarine warfare, which the ambassador suggested remained the Allies' weak spot. As ever, Salazar was careful in his response, merely indicating that he understood what Campbell was saying. The ambassador appeared to take this as an indication that when the time came to make the formal request to Salazar, it would be eventually met in the affirmative.

CHAPTER 22

Reluctant Participant

ON JUNE 18, 1943, RONALD CAMPBELL'S OFFICIAL car made its way from the embassy to Salazar's office in São Bento. Campbell felt he had been carefully preparing Salazar for this moment. Salazar also understood that it was most likely that at some point during the war an official request would come from the British to use the Azores. In arranging the appointment, Campbell had confessed that he had something to communicate from the British government of the highest political importance.[1]

For Salazar, the issue of the Azores could not be separated from one of the fundamental aims of his policy of neutrality, the maintenance of the physical integrity of the Portuguese empire. There was still resentment and deep suspicion of the Allies in Lisbon due to events in Timor in December 1941. On top of this was Salazar's reluctance to be seen to give in to Allied demands too readily, a move which could have inclined the Germans into making a military response of sorts against Portugal.[2] During the course of the meeting of June 18, a slightly nervous and very serious Campbell formally requested that Britain wished to use the facilities on the Azores.[3] Salazar did not respond, but promised to do so in due course.

Six days later, on June 23, came the reply. Salazar summoned Campbell to his office for a meeting that was scheduled to last for two hours. It was set to start at 5 PM, which was the normal time for

Salazar to host meetings, and given the extreme hot weather in Lisbon it was something of a relief for Campbell not to have to do it during the afternoon heat. Salazar noted that Campbell appeared very nervous.[4] The Portuguese leader then went through a French translation of the document and there were no interruptions or requests for clarification. Salazar agreed in principle to the request under the terms of the ancient alliance.[5] He also made it clear that he wished to provide the facilities without endangering Portugal's neutrality—Portuguese troops would not contribute directly to the Allied war effort.[6] Campbell confirmed to Salazar that London did not want Portugal to enter the war as a result of the negotiations over the Azores.[7]

Salazar then referred to a key Portuguese demand: If Britain was granted access to the Azores, adequate measures would need to be taken to make sure that Portugal's Atlantic coast did not fall into German hands.[8] He added that he was unwilling to allow any troops other than the British to use the facilities. At the end of the meeting Campbell said that he was very happy with the response of the Portuguese government and Salazar noted a smile of relief light up Campbell's face.[9]

At this stage, the British foreign secretary, Anthony Eden, advised Campbell that he thought it best not to discuss the potential use of the Azores by American troops.[10] This separate discussion could take place when Britain had secured a formal agreement with the Portuguese. Salazar warned the British that the discussions would be detailed and would take a long time to complete.[11] Campbell argued that the talks should be held in London where the Foreign Office had secret facilities for such meetings.[12] Salazar was having none of this and insisted that they had to take place in Lisbon.[13] He added that it would not be wise for the British foreign secretary, Anthony Eden, to travel to Lisbon for the talks. He was so well known a figure that his presence in Lisbon would endanger the secrecy of the negotiations.

While the British Foreign Office remained satisfied with Salazar's seemingly logical conditions, Churchill was not so content. Correctly fearing that Salazar aimed to drag the talks on for as long as possible, Churchill wanted to impose a deadline on the detailed discussions. Anthony Eden, however, argued that Salazar understood full well that Britain wanted a successful conclusion to the talks as soon as possible and that any deadline would be viewed as an ultimatum and would be counterproductive to British interests.[14]

In order to try to sweeten Salazar, the Foreign Office looked to make tangible concessions to him in other areas. The most obvious area was in the sphere of economic warfare. In this respect, the Foreign Office asked the MEW to come up with some ideas to offer Salazar. The MEW had no objection to the increase in the number of quotas for imports to Portugal and an extension of the period of the navicerts to make it easier for Portugal to receive goods. Conversely, they argued that Salazar should be told that the British government did not expect Portugal to break off commercial ties with the Axis powers altogether. They did insist that Portuguese exports to the Axis powers were related to the goods they received in return from the Axis.[15]

In terms of wolfram, the MEW argued that Salazar should be allowed to honor existing deals, but that he should end the alleged discrimination against sales to Britain. It was also thought to be wise that Salazar should be reminded of the German efforts to smuggle wolfram and shown evidence gathered by British intelligence of these operations. Wolfram smuggling by the Germans took many different forms. Some methods were basic, such as quite literally strapping the wolfram onto the backs of donkeys and taking it over the Portuguese-Spanish border, far away from the main roads and border crossing points. Other smuggling efforts involved disguising the wolfram inside other products. Central to most smuggling operations were the German "ghost trains" that ran from the Portuguese-Spanish border through Spain and into German-occupied France. British intelligence believed that there was a high degree of Portuguese involvement in these German operations. They claimed that brown paper bags stashed with escudo notes were given on a routine basis to Portuguese smugglers who would assist the Germans. Salazar denied any official Portuguese involvement in the smuggling.[16]

In terms of the Azores, the stick came in the form of the American policy of tightening up the amount, and range, of goods that Portugal was permitted to import. The British promised to use their influence to try to prevent this from happening. All Salazar had to do was to sign an agreement over the Azores and the Allies would respond favorably to Portuguese efforts to loosen the restrictions imposed on what it could import.[17]

Campbell paid a prenegotiation visit to Salazar on June 26, 1943, in the hope of getting his agreement for a timetable and format for the talks.[18] With Churchill pressing for a more active approach towards the Azores, the Foreign Office wanted to gain the agreement of Salazar to start the negotiations as soon as possible. Salazar, however, was in low spirits and did not share the British senses of urgency. Portugal was going through an unprecedented heat wave with daily temperatures reaching 40 degrees Celsius.[19] This drained the energies of even the most robust Portuguese, including Salazar, who wanted to get out to the coast at Estoril and Cascais in order to enjoy the cooling winds from the sea.

While Campbell pitched for a rapid conclusion to the negotiations, Salazar continued to stall.[20] He informed Campbell that he had not yet selected the Portuguese "party of experts" that would form its delegation. He also tried to lobby the British to make sure that its delegation was small in number.[21] Ever patient, Campbell understood that for Salazar the concept of inviting foreign forces onto part of the Portuguese Empire was not easy for him to digest. The ambassador pointed out to the Foreign Office that Salazar was not yet fully broken in to the idea, which had come upon him abruptly, and was still rather shy about the process.

On June 28, 1943, a Foreign Office official took the Portuguese ambassador, Armindo Monteiro, for lunch in London. In retrospect, the conversation at lunch that day proved to be rather extraordinary. Monteiro spoke English with an accent that was closer to Oxford or Cambridge, than to Lisbon. This point was important: The preferred language of most Portuguese diplomats was French. Partly as a result of his perfect "King's English," as well as his carefully honed diplomatic skills and his moderately aristocratic background, Monteiro had proved to be something of a hit in London.

The Foreign Office viewed Monteiro as a strong Anglophile, and a man who could influence Salazar. Monteiro's status was also boosted by the importance that the British government attached to relations with Portugal. There appeared, however, to be a strong level of ignorance among the British officials about the growing differences between Salazar and Monteiro. These differences were starting to become too deep to cover up entirely and could be seen in the increasingly detailed and terse correspondence between the two men.

In a letter dated May 31, 1943, Monteiro had written to Salazar arguing that with the victory in Tunisia, and other Allied successes, the moment had arrived where Portugal should choose to openly back the Allies.[22] He argued that there was a growing sense of a "bad atmosphere in London" towards the regime. The government in Lisbon was coming to be seen as being sympathetic to the Germans; many British people considered it to be fascist. Downing Street was preparing for the final offensive against the Germans and was noting who was and was not contributing to this effort. The time for neutrality had passed. Lisbon should come off the fence. The passion and articulation of the letter surprised Salazar, if not the actual contents of it.

From a Portuguese perspective, the conduct of Armindo Monteiro during a routine lunch with an official from the Foreign Office in June 1943 was hugely questionable. During the course of the lunch, Monteiro overstepped his role as ambassador and started to speak as a "citizen of Portugal and a friend of Britain," whose views apparently ran contrary to his boss back in Lisbon. He advised his somewhat surprised host that on the question of the negotiations over the Azores, that while it was better not to try to fix a timetable from the outset, Britain should continuously insist on the urgency of the matter. The British negotiators should also argue that the Allies were the victim of the pressure of events and could not therefore afford to delay establishing a presence on the islands.[23]

The Portuguese ambassador's wife was also present at the lunch and she added a little piece of useful information. She recounted how her son had just arrived from Lisbon that morning and had confirmed that the country was going through a terrible heat wave. The crops were all dried up and that, as a result, there would be a very bad harvest later in the year.[24] The ambassador talked about how the economic questions would play a major role in the negotiations. The Foreign Office duly noted this information and cabled it to Campbell in Lisbon for use in future negotiations.

Three days later, on July 1, 1943, Monteiro wrote to Salazar.[25] This twenty-page letter could be regarded as one of the longest political suicide notes in modern diplomatic history. Monteiro, in a tone that was mildly condescending, attempted to dismantle large sections of Salazar's World War II foreign policy. In overall terms, he argued that only an alliance with the Allies could guarantee the independence of Portugal and its colonies.[26] On the question of the Azores, Monteiro wrote that they were in a position of strategic importance of the first order. Portugal should invite the Allies to use the facilities they needed.[27] This would create a feeling of gratitude from the Allies, which was better in the long run.[28] The Portuguese flag would continue to fly in the Azores, which would help secure the country's long-term role as an Atlantic power.

In his diary of July 1, Salazar simply wrote that he had received a letter from Monteiro that was critical of the foreign policy of the government and especially the attitude of the prime minister towards the Allies.[29] Needless to say, Salazar was furious with both the content and the tone of the correspondence. After reading the extended critique of his foreign policy, Salazar picked up his favored black fountain pen and handwrote a response to the letter next to the typed text of Monteiro.

Salazar opened his devastating analysis of Monteiro's position by simply arguing that the ambassador in London was writing for history.[30] Salazar charged Monteiro with trying to create a narrative in which he should have tried to move Portugal towards an alliance with Britain. What followed was vintage Salazar. Realizing that the letter would be a key document in future research by historians on Portugal's role in World War II, he wrote his rebuttal over the top of the original letter to make sure that people would see his rationale for his policies at the same time as they read Monteiro's. In a rare show of emotion, which illustrated the anger and deep hurt he felt at Monteiro's insubordination, Salazar wrote that Monteiro's letter was written in the tone of superiority. As Salazar put it, "This letter expresses the air of a great lord who lives in London, is related to the leaders of the world, and speaks of all that is superior to a poor man of Santa Comba Dão."[31]

From the moment that Salazar picked up his pen, Monteiro's career in the diplomatic service was finished—all that remained was to determine the timing of his departure. In this respect, Salazar understood very well that Monteiro's recall would not be viewed positively in London. Indeed, Salazar sensed that the British Foreign Office, and Winston Churchill, would lobby Salazar to try to persuade him to change his mind and allow Monteiro to remain in his post. It was certainly true that both Churchill and the foreign secretary, Anthony Eden, were very sorry to see Monteiro recalled.[32] Salazar understood that he would have to quickly find a new ambassador whom the British would not be able to refuse, and who would follow and implement the foreign policy of Portugal without diverting from the script.

CHAPTER 23

A Painful Set of
Negotiations

O N JULY 2, 1943, SALAZAR LEFT LISBON.[1] WHILE THE
majority of the inhabitants of Lisbon headed out to the beach
in order to gain some relief from the stifling heat of the city, Salazar
headed home to Santa Comba Dão in the interior of the country to
spend the weekend. The talks with the British delegation over access to the Azores were due to start on the following Monday
morning and Salazar wanted to clear his head and tend to the vegetable patch in his modest garden.

The drive from Lisbon to Santa Comba Dão took around four
and a half hours in 1943. Salazar's car made its way northwards to
Santarém, where the road was a single lane in each direction, and
headed north towards the old capital city of Coimbra. The country was at peace, with the biggest danger being the habitually impatient Portuguese motorist attempting to overtake heavily
loaded, slow-moving lorries, which appeared to go backwards on
step inclines.

Out of Lisbon the roads were not in good condition. Deep pot-
holes added to the discomfort of motorists already struggling with
the heat, which remained stifling even at night. Traveling through

the villages of the interior with their whitewashed houses, it was possible to see the extent of the poverty, which continued to blight the rural parts of the country. It remained a peasant-based agricultural sector, where donkeys pulling plows were the norm, and tractors were few and far between.

Salazar had much on his mind. His anger towards Monteiro remained. In truth he did not trust part of the Portuguese diplomatic service, which he believed had not been purged of their pre–Estado Novo republican tendencies. Salazar also wanted to go through what he wanted from the British as a result of the negotiations over the Azores.[2] He still believed that his carefully crafted policy of neutrality was the correct one for Portugal. Salazar believed Monteiro was wrong to suggest that if Portugal did not throw in its lot with the Allies it would not receive a postwar advantage, and that its colonial possessions would be under threat. With the war shifting clearly in favor of the Allies, however, Salazar understood that he needed to be careful not to antagonize the likely victors as they increased the tempo of the offensive against Germany.

Salazar's car reached Coimbra. The ancient university was built on top of the hill, with a clock tower that was visible for miles. It was in this city that Salazar had studied and started his professional career as an academic. From Coimbra his car headed northeast, in the direction of Viseu, on a road that wound its way up past the Bussaco forest where the forces of the Duke of Wellington had defeated the French during the Peninsular Wars. Finally, he entered the small village of Santa Comba Dão where, in a small hamlet called Vimieiro, he kept a modest house for use at the weekends. Salazar spent his weekends working on his vegetable garden and catching up on his paperwork and writing.[3] The one luxury in the house was a black phone that kept the prime minister in touch with events in Lisbon.

The formal negotiations between the British and the Portuguese over the use of facilities on the Azores opened in Lisbon on Monday, July 5, 1943. Salazar made it clear at the outset that Portugal wished to agree to the use of the facilities, but they wanted it done in a manner that would attract as little attention as possible, to allow Portugal to remain outside of the hostilities.[4] Salazar suggested that the British should initially use as small a force as possible, and that once on the islands it would be possible for the British to develop its forces. While the German army was still situated in the French Pyrenees on the border with Spain, there was a tangible fear of retaliation in Lisbon. This could have taken the form of an invasion by land, but more likely a bombing campaign against Lisbon and Portugal's second city, Oporto, in the north. There was an additional fear that the German U-boats would start to attack Portuguese shipping in the Atlantic, a move that would have almost certainly brought Portugal into the war.

The British tried to navigate their way through a series of complex problems related to the Azores, at the center of which was the role of acting as a broker for the United States.[5] Prior to the formal start of negotiations, Churchill had attempted, and failed, to get President Roosevelt to inform the Portuguese that the Americans were associated with the assurances that the British were offering the Portuguese.[6] Churchill also informed the president of the fact that the Portuguese wanted to limit the forces on the Azores to the British, so that they could legitimately claim that this had been offered under the terms of the Anglo-Portuguese alliance.[7] Naturally, this did not go down well in Washington, where there were growing calls for a much more robust approach towards Lisbon.

The practical results of this firmer American approach towards the Portuguese was seen when Pan Am was first encouraged to get landing rights on the Azores for its commercial aircraft.[8] The real reason for this request, however, was the interest of the Army Air Force to use these facilities as a ferrying point for the transfer of heavy military aircraft from the United States to European and African theaters when the government in Lisbon (it was hoped) gave authority.[9] On June 20, 1943, representatives of Pan Am had asked for the right to land aircraft on the Azores, which were on the way from America to Britain. The Portuguese National Air Council raised no objection and negotiations were opened with Lisbon on the use of the islands, in the first instance, as refueling stops for transatlantic commercial aircraft.[10]

The State Department asked for British backing for this scheme.[11] The Foreign Office gave it support, but suggested strongly that the timing of the request should be put off until after the conclusion of the British-Portuguese negotiations, which it argued were reaching a crucial stage.[12] The mild internal wrangling between the British and Americans complicated an already difficult set of negotiations. Privately, there was a suspicion in some American circles that Britain was trying to control the negotiations with Lisbon in order to try to gain postwar civil aviation advantages over the Americans for the Atlantic routes.[13]

Back in Lisbon, Salazar was setting the pace of the negotiations, much to the frustration of the British. While he had informed them at the outset that Britain would get what it wanted at the end of the negotiations, he showed little sign that this was going to happen any time soon. Salazar linked the agreement to the arrival of the British antiaircraft defenses and others, which Portugal had been promised by Ronald Campbell.[14] The British attempted to separate the two core issues.

In a meeting with Campbell and Roberts from the Foreign Office on August 7, Salazar made it clear that he would not allow any deal on the facilities without a similar deal on the defense of Portugal. In truth, the meeting with Campbell did not go well. While Salazar was concentrating on the details of the potential defense force for Portugal, Campbell was under enormous pressure to deliver an agreement, which appeared, at this stage, to be a distant prospect.[15]

At this point, both Eden and Churchill came together and decided that a deadline had to be imposed. An impatient Churchill penciled in August 15, but Eden argued that this date was premature, as the British military force could not arrive before September 1 at the earliest.[16] Eventually, after an intervention of the British Chiefs of Staff, the date of September 15 was agreed. Churchill made it clear that Salazar must be informed of the existence of this date through Campbell as well as being made aware of the impact on the Anglo-Portuguese alliance if Portugal did not accept the deadline. Churchill did offer something of a carrot to Salazar, arguing that if a deal could be reached that America would be willing to help out on the resulting economic benefits to Portugal.[17]

Salazar, however, was focusing on the security aspects of a deal and complained that the Portuguese military defenses would not be fully operational before October 15. He was eventually convinced to accept October 8, and the final agreement was signed by Salazar and Campbell on August 18, but was backdated to August 17. Upon the signing of the agreement, Eden sent a congratulatory message to Salazar stating that the use of the facilities was of great importance to the Allies and would help shorten the length of the war.[18] The British force arrived on the Azores on time and started to use the facilities, which British personnel had helped to build.[19]

———

Although the agreement was signed and implemented between the British and the Portuguese, the problem of the American demands remained to be resolved. The State Department reported that it welcomed the deal, but in private, they made it clear that America would have preferred a deal between Portugal and the Allies rather than Britain alone.[20] More specifically, the Americans reminded the British that any agreement that limited the use of the facilities to British aircraft alone was unacceptable to the United States.[21] The American military was still demanding an American occupation of the Azores, and at the beginning of September a

10,000-strong American force was getting ready for such an invasion. Once again, there were splits between the Foreign Office and Churchill. Eden felt that the Americans were demanding too much from the Portuguese.

Churchill felt, however, that the American demands were within reason and he was inclined to support them.[22] The prime minister did ask Roosevelt, however, that the Americans should try to allay Salazar's fears that they wanted to remain in the Azores on a permanent basis.[23] Later Churchill added that he was happy for the Americans to make their own request to Lisbon.[24] He promised to support the Americans to the full and would use the "friends" phrase, which was quoted in the Treaty of 1373 between Britain and Portugal, to try to pressure Salazar into helping an ally of Britain. He also suggested that a joint American-British approach by their respective ambassadors in Lisbon was the best approach, with the American ambassador taking the lead.

On November 4, 1943, President Roosevelt followed Churchill's advice and sent a personal letter to Salazar. The contents of the letter tried to allay Salazar's fear that if the Americans were granted facilities on the Azores they would remain there in the postwar era.[25] Roosevelt recited the time when, as undersecretary of the Navy, he had visited the Azores in 1918 to inspect the repair, refueling, and antisubmarine facilities, which the Americans had used. By 1919, the president added, all of those forces were withdrawn and bases dismantled. Keeping up the pressure, Roosevelt also sent a message to Churchill reminding him that the negotiations between the Portuguese and Americans would start in Lisbon.[26] Roosevelt wanted to impress upon Churchill to get Ronald Campbell to support the American chargé d'affaires in Lisbon, George Kennan.

At 5 PM on November 23, 1943, Salazar received a joint delegation of British and American officials in his office in Lisbon, at which the Americans tried to provide Salazar with a series of assurances.[27] There was also a degree of threat involved as the Americans argued that Portugal needed to consider how the postwar situation in Europe would look. The Americans had been trying to lobby Salazar for some time, but he was still refusing the U.S. direct access to the facilities on the Azores.

Prior the meeting, the Americans had not come to any agreement with the British on how best to conduct the negotiations.[28] Indeed, Kennan was given instruction to give the British a wide berth before the talks. All of this diplomatic maneuvering, as well as reflecting deep strains within the Allies, also revealed the division in Britain between Churchill and Eden over the issue of the American demands of Portugal.

For his part, Eden had sent a memo to Churchill, which had been prepared by the Foreign Office, reminding the prime minister that Portugal had taken serious risks in allowing British personnel onto the Azores. He went on to suggest that Portugal's behavior had been much better than that of most of the other neutrals—a clear reference to Ireland and Turkey. In a note to the American ambassador in London, Eden argued that Britain should help secure the same concessions over the Azores that it had extracted from the Portuguese for the Americans.[29] If Roosevelt wanted anything above and beyond this level, then the Americans should attempt to secure these additional concessions directly from the Portuguese.[30] In a stinging broadside, Eden suggested that the Americans must learn the very simple lesson that they could not get everything from Lisbon by bullying or bribery.

Salazar made it clear to the Americans that he could not afford to allow them access to the same facilities that he offered to the British.[31] He argued simply, and correctly, that if he did this, then he would have breached the terms of Portugal's neutrality. He did agree, however, that he was willing to offer the Americans similar facilities but under the terms of the deal with Britain.[32] This meant in reality that all the American units involved would have to be placed temporarily on loan to the British.

The dispute involving the United States rumbled on through a mixture of a lack of understanding as to exactly what the Americans wanted and the extent to which the Portuguese were willing to be flexible in allowing American personnel onto the islands under British supervision.[33] Eventually it was agreed that the American personnel on the Azores would wear two insignias. The first was the British insignia and the second was the American one. The latter insignia had to be smaller than the former.[34]

CHAPTER 24

The Cost of
Doing Business

THE REACTION OF THE GERMANS TO THE EFFECTIVE Allied occupation of the Azores was very mute indeed. This reflected the state of the war, but was also down to the careful diplomacy of the German ambassador, Baron von Hoyningen-Huene. The ambassador advised Berlin not to become angry with the Portuguese.[1] He also agreed with Salazar's argument that Portugal had no choice but to accept a fait accompli. Salazar's fear of German military action did not materialize.

The Portuguese ambassador in Berlin was summoned for a meeting with the German foreign minister. During a tense exchange, the ambassador was informed that, as the British were going to be able to use the Azores, Germany reserved the right to act as it saw fit without any consideration of Portuguese territorial waters.[2] The foreign minister then shifted tactics away from threat to the hope that German-Portuguese economic relations would be maintained and not damaged by developments in the Azores.

The Germans, while not happy with Lisbon, appeared to believe that Salazar's favor to the Allies would in turn make it easier to extract larger amounts of wolfram from Portugal for export to Germany. For his part, Salazar attempted to downplay the significance of the agreement over the Azores. He argued to the Axis powers that it dealt only with one port and one airfield and the restrictions on American use of the facilities were tight.[3]

The Joint Intelligence Sub-Committee (JIC), which produces advice for the British Cabinet on defense and security issues, produced an extremely insightful report on September 11, 1943, which appeared to confirm that the prospects of Germany taking military action against Portugal was remote.[4] In a prelude to the JIC report, on June 30, President Roosevelt had written to Winston Churchill on the same subject.[5] The president suggested that, as the Germans had not invaded the Iberian Peninsula when it had favorable circumstances, it was unlikely to try a ground invasion now that circumstances were against it. He added that what he feared most was that Germany would launch concentrated air and submarine attacks against Portugal in retaliation, and as a warning to other neutral nations not to follow a similar path to Portugal.

Growing ever more impatient with Salazar, Churchill replied three days later, disagreeing with a key part of Roosevelt's analysis.[6] He felt that German air attacks on Lisbon or Oporto would not have been in their interest. Any such attacks would have closed a valuable listening post for the Germans and would have allowed Britain to base air squadrons in Portugal. The latter would have strengthened the protection of Allied shipping convoys from German air attack and also strengthened British patrols in the Bay of Biscay.[7] Churchill's conclusion was that the Germans would not simply use air attacks out of spite.

The Joint Intelligence Committee's report supported the prime minister's analysis, finding that the risk of an attack from Spain was negligible, as was, given the commitments of Germany's land forces in the various theaters of war, a ground assault from France through Spain and into Portugal.[8] The JIC suggested that Germany could not even muster a meaningful naval offensive operation against Lisbon, and that the German Air Force, fighting in three theaters and increasingly having to defend German cities, could release only 100 to 150 aircraft for punitive operations against Portugal.

The secret report revealed that for all Salazar's understandable desire to try to secure the best conditions from Britain in terms of its commitment to the defense of Portugal, there was little real prospect of a major attack against its sovereignty or against its colonial possessions. In other words, Salazar had extracted a very good deal from the British. His handling of the Americans had, however, left a very bad taste in the mouth in Washington. From this point onwards, until the end of the war, Washington would, as a result, press Lisbon on all issues in a much more robust manner than the British.

On September 14, 1943, the Portuguese Ministry of Foreign Affairs announced that the Duke of Palmela would succeed Armindo Monteiro as the Portuguese ambassador to London. The *Times* of London described the appointment of the duke as ensuring the continuity of Anglo-Portuguese relations following the recall of Monteiro by Salazar.[9] The Foreign Office had gone to great lengths to try to further postpone the announcement, on the basis that it could be construed as reflecting a change of Portuguese policy at a time of agreement on the use of bases for the Azores. Salazar, however, was in no mood to accept such a delay.[10]

When Campbell gently inquired as to why Monteiro was being replaced, Salazar simply indicated to the ambassador that he felt that Monteiro had lost his balance. In truth, Salazar's appointment of the Duke of Palmela was a diplomatic masterstroke. While the British, and in particular the Foreign Office, harbored feelings of great affection for Monteiro, the Cambridge-educated Portuguese aristocrat Duke of Palmela was an altogether acceptable alternative to London.

The intrigues of Monteiro's recall, and his continued attempts to lobby support in London after learning his fate, led to a new round of speculation as to the existence of a Machiavellian plot in

London to replace Salazar. The Portuguese leader had complained to Campbell about Monteiro's attempts to gather support in London and suggested that this was one of the main reasons that he did not want to delay the announcement of the appointment of the Duke of Palmela.[11]

There remains no published documentary evidence, however, to suggest that Monteiro enjoyed anything more than strong support from the British government. Any idea of a British-backed plot to attempt to mount a challenge to Salazar, by pushing Monteiro as a viable alternative leader, would appear to overlook several important factors. Despite being extremely sympathetic to the personal plight of Monteiro, there remains little indication that the Foreign Office agreed with his viewpoint that Portugal should throw its lot in with the Allies.

The formal policy of the government in London remained that Portuguese neutrality was the best option. Having served in London for so long, Monteiro lacked any real powerbase back in Lisbon. His departure from London was the talk of Lisbon among the chattering classes during the summer of 1943, and he did become something of a cult figure for the anti-Salazar factions, but that was as far as it went.[12]

After returning to Lisbon, Monteiro soon left the city to spend time in the countryside away from the political intrigues of the capital. In discussing his case, Sampaio, the director-general of the Portuguese Foreign Ministry, merely indicated that in his opinion politicians never made good diplomats and that there nearly always came a time when the politician came to the fore. Monteiro slowly faded from the public eye and was soon replaced by other figures as the hero of the opposition forces in Lisbon. Monteiro's greatest legacy was to have helped keep Anglo-Portuguese relations on an even keel during the first part of the war, when they were put under enormous strain.

The appointment of the Duke of Palmela was warmly welcomed by London. (Churchill gave him an extended audience on their first meeting and a history lesson on his own aristocratic roots.) Among leading Portuguese figures, the response was less enthusiastic. Palmela's appointment was viewed by the Portuguese as a good one for Britain, but not so good for Lisbon.[13]

One leading official at the Portuguese Ministry of Foreign Affairs described the Duke of Palmela as a man of not much capacity. He added that it would be important to make significant matters very plain for him to comprehend and to clearly emphasize the benefits for Portugal in its dealings. Palmela, the official claimed, would faithfully transmit whatever he was told and understood that. He was not, however, a man who possessed the gift of expression in writing.[14]

As the Allied military campaign entered its crucial stage, the invasion of mainland Europe, the Duke of Palmela had an important role to play as a messenger between the British and Salazar over a number of issues. A question had arisen about the inclusion of Portuguese soldiers to help the Allies to retake Timor; it was still not resolved. There were increasing tensions between the Allies and Lisbon over the origins of the gold that the Bank of Portugal was receiving in payment for the wolfram sales to Germany. The pace and rhythm of the war was increasing and Salazar understood that everything was about to change.

CHAPTER 25

Nazi Gold

WHILE THE ALLIES CONCENTRATED ON PLANNING Overlord, the Allied invasion of mainland Europe, Salazar looked ever more closely at the impact of the end of the war on Lisbon. The agreements over the Azores, and the lack of any meaningful German military response, had removed the immediate threat to Portugal's neutrality. As the war moved towards its inevitable conclusion, however, Lisbon found itself once more in the spotlight. And this time it was for all the wrong reasons.

Away from the military fighting, three related issues dominated the Allied efforts against the Axis powers: the tracing of gold payments to the neutral countries by Germany; attempts to stop the Germans from smuggling looted assets out of Europe; and the adoption and implementation of a clear policy towards the issue of Axis war criminals. Salazar understood that the agreement over the Azores had more openly positioned Portugal in the Allied camp, but he was still reluctant to fully commit Portugal to every aspect of the Allied political agenda.

Salazar still clung to the hope of a German conditional surrender, which would preserve some order of a continental European power structure[1] and prevent what he saw as the carving up of Europe between the communists of the Soviet Union in the East, and the capitalists of the United States in the West. In a speech on February 8, 1944, Salazar argued that the establishment of large, new, international economic and political blocks was a threat to the independence and integrity of Portugal and its colonies.[2] The speech was interesting as it contained little to appease the Germans, but also showed little enthusiasm for an Allied victory.

Sitting alone in his office plotting Portugal's postwar politics, Salazar confided to British and American diplomats that he envisaged little prospect of the Soviet Union conducting itself as a decent member of the European family of nations.[3] For Salazar, the specter of part of Europe dominated by the communists was difficult to accept. He also feared that the local communists in Portugal would use any gains by the Soviet Union as a call to arms to challenge him.

To apparently complicate matters further for Salazar, there was a wave of strikes and social unrest that spread around the Lisbon area during May 1944. The strikes, which took place on May 8 and 9, were part of a concerted effort by the opposition to damage the regime.[4] They were also closely related to an equally worrying development for Salazar, the introduction of bread rationing on May 20, 1944. With other foodstuffs in increasingly short supply, bread had become the main food staple for many of the industrial workers based in the greater Lisbon area.

The government had good intelligence about the strikes, and the police had been put on alert before they broke out. American intelligence sources reported that over 1,000 people were arrested. The strikes spread to the east bank of the River Tagus into towns such as Barreiro, where the communists enjoyed widespread support. The wave of protest was brought under control after May 9.[5]

While the tightly state-controlled press naturally blamed the strikes on the communists, British intelligence initially suggested that the strikes were actually instigated by the Portuguese government, as a means of allowing the workers to vent their anger while not doing too much damage to the economy. Evidence to support the British theory included the limited nature of the strikes and the fact that government agents had been operating in many of the factories and plants that were the pivotal centers of the disturbance.[6] The Americans took the view that the strikes were genuine and were almost certainly the work of the Communist Party.[7] Two important points emerged from the strikes, however. The first was that the government appeared to have the situation relatively well under control, and that the unrest was part of a growing sense of dissatisfaction felt by many people towards the government. The days when the cafés of Rossio were full of exotic-looking cakes had disappeared. The PVDE was more and more frequently advising Salazar of the increasing linkage between the privations imposed by the war and the mounting internal opposition to the regime.[8]

As the threat of the Germans receded it was clear that the opposition, as well as the government, was making plans for the postwar situation in Lisbon. While Salazar enjoyed the support of the vast majority of senior officers in the armed services, he was relatively secure in power. It was equally clear, however, that he would have to offer some changes in both the composition and policies of his government if he were to have a long-term role.

Just as he had prepared for war, so was Salazar aware of the challenges ahead and started to prepare his regime for the postwar realities, and for the increasingly close attention that the Allies were paying to Lisbon and its wartime dealings with the Germans. As Allied victories on the battlefield increased, the Allied need to appease Salazar decreased. It was clear that the principal point of contention was going to be the degree to which Portugal could be said to have benefited economically from the war, and in particular whether the payments from Germany for its supply of wolfram should be considered as "ill-gotten gain."

———— •❖• ————

At the start of July 1943, the BBC (British Broadcasting Corporation) had broadcast a warning to Lisbon about the German gold.[9] The report warned that all gold bearing German insignia would be considered by the Allies as having been stolen and therefore contaminated.[10] It was a stern statement that was intended to make it clear to Lisbon that the origin of the gold that the Portuguese were now receiving was well known by the Allies. The statement led to near panic among Lisbon gold dealers, who demanded that the Bank of Portugal exchange gold bars bearing German marks for gold bars of unchallengeable origin.

When the Bank of Portugal did not agree to do this, the dealers began to arrange to have the gold melted down into new bars in order to sell it on. Some of the owners of the gold bars went to Portugal's second city, Porto, where there were good smelting facilities with no questions asked.[11] The dealers were afraid that if they did not disguise the origins of the gold they would lose their fortunes.

In July 1944, the BBC broadcast another item about the arrival in Lisbon of a shipment of German gold, which had been transported to Portugal from Switzerland.[12] The broadcast was in part another clear warning that the British government would not accept the situation regarding gold arriving from official or nonofficial German sources into Lisbon. The story of the shipments mentioned in the item was based on evidence from a Swiss source, and did not offer much in the way of detail or analysis. It was a low-key item that would nonetheless come to dominate the issue of the role of the neutral powers in World War II, and in Portugal's case the postwar period as well.

The BBC news item had been triggered by a letter received by the Foreign Office, calling for the introduction of an export ban on gold from Portugal. Officials from the Foreign Office, who had known for some time of the gold transactions involving Portugal, discussed the issue and concluded that the gold that had been imported into Lisbon for a number of years was in Portuguese banks and had not been exported. More specifically, the shipment of gold from Switzerland highlighted by the BBC had not been delivered to a Portuguese bank but had gone directly to the German legation in Lisbon.[13]

In private, both the American and British intelligence services had noted the arrival of this gold in Lisbon. From June 26 to July 4, four shipments of gold weighing 80 kilos each, totaling 320 kilos, arrived.[14] One of the shipments had arrived in the German diplomatic pouch, the others in unsealed bags carried by two guards. The gold was transferred immediately to the German embassy in Lisbon. The embassy had commissioned the casting of two large safes from a local company in the Benfica district of the city.[15] One safe was destined for the embassy itself, and the second was for the basement of a car sales dealership.

At the end of August, intelligence reported that the car dealership, headed by a Portuguese man, Diniz d'Almeida, had some 3,000 kilos of gold in its keeping.[16] D'Almeida's showroom was in the Avenida da Liberdade, on the same road as the city's best hotels where many of the refugees had stayed. The Americans believed that the car dealership, which sold Buicks, was a front—for the storage of German gold.[17] Allied Intelligence agents thought that the gold was eventually distributed among a number of German companies in Lisbon.[18] At around the same time, there were reports of a huge increase in the use of local banks' safe custody deposit boxes, specifically at Montepio Geral bank.[19]

When the Americans asked the Bank of Portugal to investigate this specific case of gold imports, the bank simply stated that they had no official knowledge of the import of gold in this way by the Germans.[20] Further investigation uncovered the fact that the local customs officials at the airport claimed to have no knowledge, or record, of the import of the gold either. The information supplied by local intelligence sources on this case highlighted the movement, but the Allies admitted that in many instances it was difficult to obtain definitive proof.[21] The Portuguese and German importers of gold went to great lengths to cover their tracks. The most favored method employed was to exchange the gold for other gold of a different origin.

The BBC broadcast was followed up by a series of articles in British newspapers on the same topic. The Portuguese ambassador to London, the Duke of Palmela, as a result, wrote to Salazar warning him.[22] The media had uncovered a story, the facts of which it did not fully understand at the time, any more than they understood the scale and importance of the shipments of gold to Lisbon.

The origins of the trail involving Portugal and the German gold could be traced back to 1940. The amount of gold involved was quite staggering. In 1939, Portugal's gold reserves had amounted to only 63.4 tons, but by the end of October 1945 they totalled 356.5 tons, nearly a 600 percent increase from the prewar figure. More specifically, during the war years Portugal received some 123.8 tons in gold, either directly or indirectly, from the Reichsbank alone. [23]

The increase in gold reserves was to a large extent created by the increase in Portugal's exports to Germany. In 1940 only some 1.79 percent of Portugal's exports were destined for Germany, but by 1942 this figure had increased to 24.38 percent. Right from the start of the war the question of how Germany paid Portugal for its goods was a bone of contention between the two countries. Salazar did not want to supply goods to Germany on credit, and European currency was becoming ever more contaminated by forged notes produced by printing presses in countries that Germany had occupied.

For Salazar and the Bank of Portugal, the most logical and safest form of payment for Portuguese goods was gold. The price of gold was much less volatile in the war compared with currency, and credit was much more complex to negotiate. In 1940, gold was an attractive prospect, but as the war progressed the Allies increasingly questioned the origins of the gold. As requests from the neutral powers to be paid in gold by Germany increased, it was clear that the Germans were drawing on gold reserves that had been seized from occupied countries.

Right from the start of the war, Germany had acquired gold reserves as it occupied countries. This gold was taken from national
banks, from private businesses, and from individuals.[24] The total
value of gold that the Germans looted from 1939 to 1945 was conservatively estimated by the British Ministry of Economic Warfare
to be between $545 and $550 million. This figure was primarily
based on the theft of gold from occupied national banks and did
not include the theft of gold from individuals. The Allied warnings
to Lisbon that resulted from this discovery of the gold, led to a
process of trying to cover up the origin of the gold, usually by melt-
ing it down. It also led to one of the world's biggest gold-laundering
operations involving German, Swiss, and Portuguese banks.

CHAPTER 26

Golden Triangle

I N EARLY 1942, THE BANK OF PORTUGAL APPROACHED Salazar in his office in Lisbon and informed him that, in their estimation, much of the currency that was being used by Germany to pay for Portuguese goods was forged. Indeed, the quality of the forged notes, which had initially been of a high quality were in decline as the German printing plates became older. What followed in six meetings, which took place between April 30, 1942, and May 27, 1942, were a set of negotiations, which centered upon a request by the Bank of Portugal to the Reichsbank, for Portugal to be paid almost exclusively in gold rather than hard currency.[1]

It took the Portuguese officials until the third meeting on May 18, 1942, to formally introduce the issue of the demand to be paid in gold for the sale of the wolfram to Germany.[2] They simply argued to their German counterparts that it was impractical to be paid in currency. At the fourth meeting held two days later on May 20, the Portuguese talked of transport difficulties in moving large amounts of currency from Germany to Portugal and formally requested payment in gold.[3] The gold was to be deposited in a complex scheme into the Swiss National Bank in Berne and transferred to the Bank of Portugal in Lisbon.

Six days later, during a long meeting on May 26, a detailed model for determining exactly how the gold would be transferred and a methodology for calculating the exchange value was drawn up.[4] In the final meeting, held on May 27, 1942, the respective heads of the Bank of Portugal and Reichsbank ironed out the details on the payment for Portuguese wolfram by Germany.[5] At the end of the six meetings the Bank of Portugal expressed its pleasure at the outcome.

Salazar understood that secrecy was of the utmost importance in his financial dealings with the Germans and wanted to make sure that there was no direct transfer of the gold from Germany to Portugal. The Germans also played along with this need for deception.[6] By late 1942 and early 1943, the British understood much of what was going on regarding the gold trade.[7] Using information that had been received from intercepted cables, as well as tracing the movements of Swiss and Portuguese bank returns and intelligence tipoffs from local agents, the Ministry of Economic Warfare, and the Bank of England began to see how the secret trades took place.

The method employed to avoid any direct contact was in hindsight remarkably simple. Central to the process was the Basel-based Bank for International Settlements (BIS). Three parties were involved in the process, BIS, the Swiss National Bank (SNB), and the main commercial banks.[8] A typical trade worked as follows: The Bank of Portugal handed over Portuguese escudos in exchange for gold, which the SNB, acting as a trustee for the Portuguese, had ready for shipment to Lisbon.[9]

At the other end of the chain, the Reichsbank used gold to acquire a large quantity of escudos through transactions with Switzerland's commercial banks. After selling the gold, the commercial banks made Swiss francs available to the Bank of Portugal, which in turn used them to buy gold from the SNB.[10] Not all the transactions required the physical transportation of the gold to Lisbon.[11] Transportation of gold during wartime was both risky and expensive. It was only due to sheer volume of the gold that Portugal was acquiring in both Basel and Berne that transportation of some of the gold became necessary.[12]

The Swiss banks were extremely willing partners in these transactions with Portugal and the other neutral powers that were trading with the Germans.[13] Indeed, Allied appeals to the Swiss during World War II to stop, or at least limit, its role in trading with the Germans fell on deaf ears. When Salazar eventually slowed Portugal's activities with the Germans, the Swiss showed no similar signs of slowing down and continued to trade without any qualms right up until the end of the war.

The closest the United States came to getting the Swiss to block all German assets came in February 1945, when the German war machine was all but defeated.[14] The American Treasury Department got an agreement from the Swiss to undertake a census of all existing German assets in Switzerland, to stop the purchase of additional gold and prevent the transfer of looted assets. One week later, however, the Swiss broke the agreement when the deputy head of the Reichsbank arrived in the country and managed to convince them to take more German gold.[15]

There were two developments in 1942 that complicated the Portuguese-Swiss-German gold triangle. The increased reliance by Germany on Portugal to supply it with its wolfram requirements meant that as the volume of wolfram trade increased, so did the need for corresponding gold transactions. On top of this, Allied intelligence was growing increasingly better at watching German economic activities in Lisbon.[16] Part of the reason for this success was the ability of Allied intelligence agencies to offer financial inducements to the local population in exchange for information concerning the dealings in gold. Allied successes in this area could also be attributed to the increased importance given to targeting this area, and the matching human and financial resources provided to match this new priority.[17]

From 1942, Allied intelligence agencies in both Portugal and Switzerland were supplying detailed evidence of Portugal's gold trade.[18] Prior to 1942, Allied intelligence noted several examples of trading in gold, but the picture was far from complete and the evidence gathered often relied upon only a single source of information. It is also clear that in Lisbon the British and Americans were openly sharing the fruits of their labor in gathering the evidence of the gold trade.[19] This was not always the case in other intelligence-related areas.

The British embassy in Lisbon cataloged a fairly comprehensive chronology of the gold trade.[20] What was evident from an early stage was the involvement of the large commercial banks in Lisbon in the operation, and the fact that Salazar encouraged the banks. Indeed, given the closeness of Salazar to leading bankers such as Ricardo Espírito Santo, the head of Banco Espírito Santo (BES), it would have been inconceivable for the Portuguese commercial banks to have acted in the way they did without the formal consent of Salazar. Espírito Santo admitted this point in his dinner meeting with James Wood, the U.S. financial attaché in Lisbon on the night of September 18, 1943.[21] Salazar was setting the parameters for all aspects of the economic relationship between Lisbon and Berlin.

Over dinner, Espírito Santo recalled asking Salazar whether or not his bank should suspend its business with the Germans. Salazar replied that he understood that the outcome of the war was clear in that the Allies were going to win, but that he thought it would not be gentlemanly to suspend all business with the Germans.[22] BES, like all the Lisbon banks, took its instruction from Salazar and nobody else. Even when a number of banks were hit by a series of scandals in 1944, Salazar maintained his tight control over their modus operandi by launching a series of investigations into the source of the irregularities.[23]

The British claimed on February 27, 1942 that Portuguese banks including BES, Fonsecas, and Santos e Viana were making great efforts to exchange the gold that they had recently received from Switzerland for British and American gold coin.[24] The report cited specific examples of the exchange of gold bars for gold coin, which took place between March 20, 1942, and the end of April 1942.

In early 1943, the British noted—wrongly, as it turned out—that the nondelivery of gold to Lisbon, which had been purchased by the Bank of Portugal, was due to Swiss fears that the Allies would hold it responsible in the future as the gold had originated from occupied countries. In July 1943, British intelligence discovered additional evidence that the Bank of Portugal had sold gold bars bearing the Reichsbank mark and the swastika to Lisbon exchange dealers.[25]

The Americans called for action against the Portuguese banks. Specifically, the American embassy wanted BES warned for alleged violation of an agreement it had signed on August 15, 1944.[26] The Americans did concede that the bank was making great efforts to reduce the amount of dealings it had with the Germans. The bank had pledged to close the accounts of the Germans that it held on its books. But when BES started to close the accounts of the Reichsbank, the Germans simply crossed the street and moved their deposits into accounts at Bank Lisbon and Acores. There were calls from the Americans, as a result, for this bank to be warned about its activities as well.[27]

The American State Department had for some time been calling for action against Ricardo Espírito Santo personally.[28] The British ambassador, Ronald Campbell, however, prevented any moves to place the man who had hosted the Duke and Duchess of Windsor on any Allied black list. Eventually, the American embassy in Lisbon came to agree with Campbell's view. Campbell argued that any moves against Espírito Santo would have serious political repercussions due to the bank's importance and Salazar's belief that under his policy of neutrality Portuguese banks should offer banking services to all sides.[29]

By the end of May 1944, Ricardo Espírito Santo, together with the other directors of BES, volunteered to cooperate with the Allies and asked which banking transactions should be discontinued.[30]

The Americans felt more than a little self-satisfied with this offer. They believed that the bank had been forced to take this course of action by Allied pressure.[31] The Allies replied to BES with a list of fifteen activities that needed to be stopped, which included all the bank's transactions with the Germans.[32] In this instance, BES was running ahead of the pack in terms of the reactions of other banks.

The Americans felt that once BES fell into line all the other banks would follow.[33] It was well known that the decision-making process in BES was much more rapid than in other banks. Ricardo Espírito Santo could make decisions on most issues,[34] in contrast to other banks that had to gain the approval of their respective boards of directors.[35] In June 1944, it was clear that Espírito Santo, like Salazar, was starting to prepare for the end of the war, and the Allied victory.

Over the summer of 1944, American unease with BES continued to manifest itself in a sense of frustration with the British attitude towards Ricardo Espírito Santo. The American embassy speculated that he had for some time been of great diplomatic use to the British ambassador, Ronald Campbell: Since Espírito Santo was close to Salazar he was able to relay things to Salazar that the British could not or would not say to him directly.[36] In terms of background it was true to say that Ricardo Espírito Santo remained closer in culture and background to the British than the Americans. He had spent time in London prior to the war and the British claimed that among his many desires was a hope for an ambassadorial appointment to London.[37]

On September 9, 1944, Allied intelligence agencies uncovered more deals involving the Bank of Portugal. This time it was an arrangement between the Bank of Portugal and the Portuguese government whereby gold held by the latter in New York was transferred into the bank's name against the transfer of an exact quantity of gold purchased by the bank from the Reichsbank (bearing bank and swastika markings) that was held in Lisbon.[38] The British embassy in Lisbon claimed that the objective of the bank was to try to get rid of the gold purchased through its arrangement with the Reichsbank and the Swiss National Bank.

Five days later on September 14, 1944, the British embassy in Lisbon received seemingly reliable detailed information to the effect that the Bank of Portugal had sold, and was continuing to sell, large quantities of gold, which was lying in its safe deposits. Senior figures at the bank were trying to persuade other banks and bankers, foreign exchange dealers, and even jewelers to buy the gold from it in order to melt it down.[39]

Although much of the intelligence material gathered by the Allies proved to be accurate, the evidence gathered was not always deemed to be comprehensive enough to take action against the various individuals and institutions concerned. There was an additional problem relating to the human intelligence-gathering side of the operation in that there appeared to be something of an industry among the local population in trying to make money by offering the Allies "juicy tidbits" of information, which in reality amounted to little more than coffee-shop gossip.

Once the tide of the war turned in favor of the Allies after 1943, there was also a sense that some individuals who used to be close in their dealings with the Germans were keen to please the Allies. There were instances of local industrialists and bankers trying to get their names removed from the Allied blacklist by informing on others. The most reliable source of information for the Allies remained the intercepted cables, which helped them piece together a much more accurate picture of gold transactions than Salazar ever envisaged.[40]

CHAPTER 27

Safehaven and
War Criminals

THE MOST ACUTE PROBLEM FOR SALAZAR IN TERMS
of the gold was the legitimacy of the origins of the gold that
the Germans were using to pay the Portuguese. It was clear that
the Germans were not only stealing gold from the central banks of
the countries that they had occupied during the war.[1]

By early as 1943, it was apparent that they were also stealing
gold from individual Jews. This gold originated from Holocaust victims' gold teeth, watches, rings, and various other pieces of jewel-
ery. The Prussian Mint and the Degussa Company in Frankfurt
subsequently melted down the gold. After this, the gold was cast
into gold bars and given the official stamp of the Reichsbank to
make it appear that it had originated from official sources. These
bars were subsequently sent on to the Swiss National Bank, who
traded them as they would any other gold bars.[2]

Towards the end of the war the Germans increased their efforts
to get gold out of Germany and France. Lisbon was a natural destination: The gold could be sold on the Lisbon exchange or smuggled
out of the country to South America. In September 1944, Allied intelligence reported a large increase in the number of irregular night
flights from Berlin to Barcelona and then on to Lisbon.[3]

Earlier in the same year, the Germans had put on several additional flights on the Berlin-Lisbon run using a large aircraft. A locally based Swedish diplomat stated that these flights had been used for the transportation of gold and other looted goods out of Berlin.[4] The diplomat claimed that there were hardly ever any passengers on these ghost flights, which were not advertised to the general public. Other sources confirmed that Lufthansa flights to Lisbon almost invariably carried some gold in unmarked bags in the holds of the large Condor aircraft.[5] The British embassy, as a result, wrote to Salazar in protest about the Lufthansa service demanding it be suspended.[6] In 1945, the Americans made the same protest, but again to no result.

Lisbon's Portela Airport was the scene of much smuggling towards the end of the war. It had opened during the war and handled air traffic from both the Allies and Axis powers. The airport was located only some seven kilometers from the city center and transfers to the city's glamorous hotels took only twenty minutes. Despite its proximity to the city, Portela still felt isolated. In the film *Casablanca,* Ilsa Lund (Ingrid Bergman) and Victor Laszlo (Paul Henreid) were to fly to Portela; in fact Portela Airport actually looked rather similar to the movie set version of Casablanca Airport.

Often at night the airport suffered from sea mists that come off the river or the Sintra hills. This naturally added to the shades-of-gray atmosphere of the place. Agents from both sides watched and recorded the details of all the flights. Portuguese customs officials were easy to bribe in order to get a copy of the plane's cargo lists.

Salazar's detachment from the emotions of the war and his cold rational negotiating methods were in some respects a major blessing to Lisbon in keeping Portugal out of the war. This detachment, however, at times gave the impression of a lack of compassion to the suffering associated with war. The plight of the Jews revealed the complexities of both Salazar's approach to the war and of his own personality.

Salazar made it a point of being well informed. In his joint roles of prime minister and minister of foreign affairs he made it his priority to be fully up to date on events by reading the various cables from his embassies. In this respect, it should be remembered that Portugal maintained full diplomatic relations with Germany for the duration of the war and had a well-staffed embassy in Berlin. Even prior to the outbreak of World War II, Salazar had been made aware of the increasing Nazi persecution of the Jews, and during the war itself he was closely informed about the developing tragedy of the Holocaust.

As early as November 1935, the Portuguese embassy in a cable to Salazar noted the growing hatred of the Jews and the desire of the Nazis to rid Germany of their influence.[7] In a detailed report on the New Order in Germany produced by the Portuguese legation in Berlin on November 15, 1941, the major difference between Portugal and Germany was seen in how each country treated the Jews.[8]

The report talked about the inhuman program being directed towards the Jews and of refined and premeditated cruelty towards them. The report also talked about the start of the program to cleanse German-occupied Europe of its Jews. Salazar, in his role as minister of foreign affairs, answered the report with a ten-page response. This written response did not mention the Jewish question and their suffering, instead focusing on the difference in church-state relations in each country.[9]

Both the British and American senior diplomatic representatives in Lisbon warned Salazar that the gold, which Portugal was receiving either directly or indirectly, was contaminated, and by 1944 was being stolen from victims of the Holocaust. Still Salazar insisted that the persecution of the Jews was an internal issue of the Third Reich. He argued that Portugal had signed agreements with Germany that required payment terms and that these were legitimate grounds for continuing to receive payment in whatever form from the Germans.

The Allies were not content with tracking the gold transactions from Germany through Switzerland to Lisbon. In October 1944, the Allies launched the Safehaven program. The British and American governments presented a series of points to the European neutral countries to take the required steps to implement the Bretton Woods Resolution VI.[10] In specific terms, the Portuguese were requested to freeze looted assets, discover and control Axis property in Portugal, and hold German assets for their eventual postwar authorities in Germany. Needless to say, Salazar was not overenthusiastic about Safehaven. Prior to the German surrender in May 1945 the Allies received no formal reply from Portugal.

In some ways the Allies made it easier for Salazar. The exact method for implementing the aims of Safehaven in Portugal was never completely agreed upon between the British and the Americans.[11] A number of conferences were held between American and British diplomats to try to thrash out how best to bring about an effective Safehaven program. The background to these attempts complicated the issue. The British were busy renegotiating the British-Portuguese Financial Payment Agreement, an economic agreement with the Portuguese, and the Americans were still dealing with the negotiations over access to the Azores. Only on May 7, 1945, a week after Hitler died, was the final version of the Allied Safehaven demands handed over to the Portuguese Foreign Ministry.[12]

Salazar's response to the Safehaven program was to promise much, but in reality not deliver as much as the Allies had hoped. It was only when the end of the fighting was fast approaching that Salazar gave the order to be proactive and whenever possible cooperate with Allied Safehaven groups working in Portugal. On March 22, 1945, Portugal issued a law that immobilized movable property that had been looted. On May 14, 1945, a law was passed that complied with almost all of the Allied demands made in the note that had been submitted on May 7 by the Allies. The decree required that German assets in Portugal be frozen, a census be set up to locate and catalog these assets, and the currency exchange be frozen.[13]

In spite of this apparent surge of goodwill from Lisbon as the war was about to end, the reality of Operation Safehaven in Lisbon was much more complicated. The Portuguese authorities gave only very limited cooperation to the Safehaven groups in Portugal.[14] It was clear that whatever the Portuguese government laid out in law there was still a great deal of activity going on in the city that was in direct conflict with the objectives of Safehaven.[15]

As the collapse of the German army and its eventual defeat appeared inevitable, there were changes in the German legation in Lisbon, which helped allow Salazar to distance himself from the Germans. The German ambassador, Baron von Hoyningen-Huene was recalled to Berlin for consultations with the Foreign Ministry in Berlin and did not return to his post. German ambassadors to the other European neutrals were also replaced around the same time. The proposed replacement for Hoyningen-Huene was rejected by Lisbon and the German's second choice never took up his office before the end of the war. As Ronald Campbell admitted, Hoyningen-Huene had been a worthy opponent. He had managed to ingratiate himself to important parts of Lisbon society, and enjoyed a good working relationship with Salazar.

As the pace of the war increased it appeared that Salazar, with his reluctance to embrace rapid change, was getting left behind. He refused to endorse the Allied statement on war criminals, which called for legal proceedings against those people deemed to have committed war crimes.[16] Once more, the British and American diplomatic missions in Lisbon went into overdrive in trying to convince him to come on board.

The Portuguese government argued that there was no clear definition of a war criminal. In a detailed response to the Allied demand, Salazar systematically attempted to dismantle each of the Allied points regarding war criminals. There was a fear, he pointed out, that there would be confusion between criminals whose acts had been repugnant, with individuals whose only crime was to have participated in governments that were viewed as legitimate at the time.[17] For Salazar the key issue was that he did not wish to take part as a neutral power in the "war of reprisals," which followed the ending of the fighting.[18]

Despite the increasing difficulties caused by food shortages, Salazar showed no sign of deviating from his investment in public works programs. While Allied soldiers were still clambering up the beaches in Normandy as part of Overlord, Salazar opened the new national football stadium (Estádio Nacional) in Oeiras near Lisbon on June 10, 1944. The stadium was located in a beautiful leafy suburb near the Marginal coast road that ran from Lisbon along its coastline out to Cascais. Around it was a park and forestland, which separated the stadium from the edge of the city. The stadium was meant to serve as a symbol of the regime's commitment to sport, especially football, and to the youth of Portugal. At the time, it was an ambitious project, with high-banked concrete end stands and an eight-lane running track, but, unusually, with an open east side, which allowed passersby to see inside the stadium without paying.

The stadium hosted its first football international game on March 11, 1945, a friendly international against Spain. The result was, helpfully, a draw: 2–2. The National Stadium remains in existence today, if a little tired looking and in need of renovation. Every May it still hosts the Portuguese Football Federation's Cup Final.[19] In its heyday, it was spectacular: Full to capacity for Portugal's international matches, with fans enjoying prematch picnics in the surrounding park and woods, it became one of the lasting symbols of the Salazar era.

As the war entered its final phase, the population of Lisbon was increasingly looking to the uncertainty of the postwar era. The sense of relief that the country had survived the threat of an Axis invasion was tapered with concern over how Salazar would manage the transformation to a peacetime administration. Aware of the need to reassure the population, Salazar remodeled his government in late 1944, and gave up the now much less meaningful portfolio of minister for defense. Still, Salazar's remoteness from his population and his desire to stick to his policy of neutrality appeared rather out of sync with the changing times. Naturally, the opposition movements sensed that this was their moment and mobilized accordingly, to ready themselves for the political struggle that would follow the conclusion of the war. In other words, the end of the war was likely to bring a lot of trouble for Salazar and his regime.

To make matters worse, at the moment the European war ended, Salazar's greatest virtue, his political judgment, appeared to, at least temporarily, desert him. Indeed, his actions at the end of the war managed to alienate even many of those who admired him. It took an intervention from Winston Churchill to end the resulting "open season" on Salazar from British sources who had been enraged by two actions in particular.

CHAPTER 28

There May Be
Trouble Ahead

PORTUGAL WAS ONE OF ONLY THREE EUROPEAN
countries to send condolences to Germany upon learning of
the death of Adolf Hitler on April 30, 1945.[1] The others were Ireland and Spain. Salazar also ordered that all flags on official buildings be flown at half-mast to mark the death of Hitler.[2] Needless to
say, when the existence of the message of condolence became public there were strongly worded protests from Lisbon's foreign diplomats. More interestingly, many well-connected Portuguese wrote
to Salazar complaining that the message showed the country in a
bad light.[3] The protests in Lisbon were not confined to the upper
classes. There were mass public demonstrations of anger against
Salazar's message of condolences to Germany that appeared to
show sympathy for the plight of Hitler.

In London, Salazar's message of condolence seriously irritated
officials in the British Foreign Office. Many government officials
understood the motives behind General Franco's message to Germany, and from a British perspective, Ireland, after its wartime an-
tics, was beyond the pale anyway. Ireland, as Salazar noted in his
diary, had gone further and declared a day of mourning to mark
the death of Hitler.[4] There was, however, a deep sense of betrayal

that Britain's oldest ally had sent such a communication to Berlin on the occasion of the death of a man who had destroyed much of Europe. Indeed, Salazar's message, and order to fly flags at half-mast, was a central feature in several accounts of his alleged personal sympathy towards the Axis powers.

A few days later Salazar did send a very different message to Churchill—on May 8, 1945—conveying the good wishes of the Portuguese government on the occasion of the Allied victory in Europe.[5] This prompted a series of discussions between the Foreign Office, the British embassy in Lisbon and the Prime Minister's Office. The Foreign Office had become increasingly disillusioned with Salazar during the final stages of the war. The message of condolence was the final insult in the eyes of some Foreign Office officials. It came on top of Salazar's reluctance to embrace the Allied policy towards disputed German gold, his only partial cooperation with Safehaven, and his lecturing the Allies of the problems of defining war criminals. The point that his case on the final issue was not without its merit mattered little to the Allied officials, who felt the time was right to put Lisbon back in its place.

Various strategies for a reply to Salazar's message to Churchill were discussed, including the highly unorthodox diplomatic tactic of not replying at all. Favored versions included references to the need for Portugal to be seen to be more openly supportive of the Allies' postwar agenda. Eventually, Eden consulted Churchill, who replied in a prime minister's minute with typical swagger, mixed with a dash of British humor:

> I think it would be wise to let them play around and not be too much down on them. Remember they ran a great risk in giving us the Azores when we could not give them a corresponding pledge to defend them from a land attack by Germany. After all if you are a 400-year-old ally, you must be allowed to kick about sometimes as you choose. I should treat them like well-loved children who make absurd grimaces.[6]

Eventually the message from Churchill to Salazar was delivered on May 17. Churchill thanked Salazar for his government's good wishes on the Allied victory. He then talked of the Azores and the Alliance of 1373 that had been used to grant the British access to the bases on the islands. Churchill described Portugal as "our ally," who had given the Allies assistance. Most importantly, he made no reference to any future demands being made on Lisbon, even though the Foreign Office had lobbied the Prime Minister's Office for a line or two to this effect.

———•••———

At the end of April 1945, in a sign of the increasingly difficult times that lay ahead for Salazar, a strange incident happened on the Spanish-French border, which was misreported by the *Times* of London. In a short two-paragraph article, on June 16, 1945, the paper reported that the leading Portuguese banker, Ricardo Espírito Santo had just been released by the French authorities and had returned to Lisbon.[7] The paper went on to state that Espírito Santo had gone to Paris some two months before and bought, for a large amount of money, a chateau, farms, and other properties, which he had paid for using French bank notes.[8]

According to the article, the French authorities asked Espírito Santo to explain where he had obtained the notes and how he had transported them to France. At the end of the questioning, the authorities had informed Espírito Santo that he would be detained in custody and would have to pay a (vast) fine of £250,000. Finally the article suggested that there had been a hitch in the transfer of the funds from the Portuguese government in Lisbon to Paris and that the French legation in Lisbon could not confirm if the fine had actually been paid.[9]

It turned out that the story was not accurate, and was based on sources with an axe to grind against both Espírito Santo and the bank he chaired.[10] The key issue lay in the article's claim that Espírito Santo had been fined £250,000, instead of the actual outcome, which was that he received an apology from the French for his short detention.[11] The news of the alleged fine led to a run on Espírito Santo's bank.[12] The bank lost several major Spanish clients, who read the story in the *Times* in Madrid. The circulation of Portuguese newspapers in Spain was practically nil and so there was no background or reaction pieces to analyze the original *Times* story. Given the rush to withdraw deposits from the bank and the political uncertainties of the time, Espírito Santo feared for the future of the bank.[13]

Espírito Santo, as a result, decided to sue the *Times* newspaper for £250,000. The resulting legal process surrounding this action brought to light all the festering frustration and attempted score settling of the French authorities and parts of the British Foreign Office towards the Portuguese banks and their role in the war. The aggressive tactics of the *Times*'s lawyers, and their desire to look beyond the alleged series of events in France to the role of Espírito Santo during the war, complicated and extended the case.

Upon his return to Lisbon on May 26, Espírito Santo had spoken directly to Ronald Campbell and told him what had happened in France with regard to his brief detention and subsequent apology from the authorities.[14] Campbell subsequently talked to Sampaio, the director-general of the Ministry of Foreign Affairs, who confirmed the banker's version of events. Everybody thought that was the end of the story until six weeks later when the *Times*'s account was published of "a banker in trouble."

Espírito Santo went straight to see Campbell again. The ambassador described Espírito Santo's state of mind in the meeting as bordering on the demented, and that he claimed that the article might well ruin him and the bank. He went on to argue that everybody believed the story as it had been published by the *Times*. Finally, he demanded to know what Campbell was planning to do about correcting the falsehoods. Later, Espírito Santo claimed that it was Campbell who had suggested he might sue the *Times*.[15] Campbell denied giving this advice, but did admit that he told Espírito Santo that if the article had been directed against him he probably would have taken that course of action.[16]

What followed was a protracted, and often bitter, process, which involved attempts to blacken the name of Espírito Santo, and at least one failed effort to have his name retrospectively put on the blacklist.[17] The affair also exposed the dangers and internal Allied politics of the blacklist, which, in reality, was three separate lists: American, British, and French. A joint committee involving American, British, and French officials met regularly in London with the view to producing a single Allied blacklist. The committee, however, failed to adopt a unified position on Espírito Santo.

The French appeared to be the most hostile to Espírito Santo, although there is evidence that this hostility was of a personal nature.[18] There were moves in Paris to have his name added to the French blacklist and the advice of the British Foreign Office was sought as to what the British attitude to such a move would be.[19] The Americans were harder on Espírito Santo than the British, but as the libel action was against a British newspaper they did not interfere directly.

The attitude of the British Foreign Office towards the case was a mixture of a sense of frustration at the poor quality of the article in the *Times* and a lack of sympathy for the plight of Espírito Santo. Foreign Office officials felt that the story, with its lack of credible evidence, would have been better suited to a more sensationalistic tabloid newspaper.[20] The *Times*, the Foreign Office concluded, should not have published the story without a better verification of the facts behind it. That said, when the *Times* decided to contest the case, the Foreign Office offered to do what it could to help.

When it became clear that the *Times* was having trouble putting up a good defense against the libel action, and the lawyers for the newspaper wanted to use Espírito Santo's wartime record against him, the Foreign Office cooperated with the lawyers.[21] The *Times*'s lawyers wanted British officials to testify in court and to produce certain documents that illustrated the alleged extent to which Espírito

Santo had financial dealings with the Germans during the war. It was agreed in principle that the Foreign Office would assist.

The Ministry of Economic Warfare was less keen to support the *Times* by giving evidence in court.[22] It argued that the British embassy's relationship with Espírito Santo was complex. Many people would find it difficult to understand how a banker who managed the accounts of the Germans had such a close relationship with the embassy. Officials in the MEW were also concerned that, despite his denials, Ronald Campbell had advised Espírito Santo to sue the *Times*. Eventually, and somewhat reluctantly, the MEW did agree to present some documents to the court and offered an official to give evidence.[23] The MEW's clearly stated preference, however, was for the *Times* to apologize to Espírito Santo on condition that the case was dropped.

Eventually, the case was resolved out of court and on Saturday, October 5, 1946, the *Times* published a full apology.[24] The apology to Espírito Santo stated that the charges against the banker were shown to have been without any foundation.[25] The case was closed, but the deep tensions that existed between the Allies over what to do about the Portuguese banks remained. Salazar had let it be known that he regarded the action against the most famous and charismatic of the Lisbon banking community as a move against himself and the Portuguese government.[26]

The transition from wartime to peacetime brought not only political problems but problems of a more personal nature to this most private of leaders. Salazar was starting to attract a lot of international exposure in the media, most of which was not wholly welcomed by him. A lot of the articles, which reflected on his personal life, turned out to be wide of the mark, or only partially factually correct. A case in point appeared on October 3, 1945, in the London tabloid newspaper, the *Daily Mail*, which reported in its society pages that Salazar had got married, improbably, to a widowed aristocrat and member of the former King of Portugal's court in London.[27]

CHAPTER 29

Should I Stay or
Should I Go?

THE *DAILY MAIL* STORY REFLECTED THE RUMORS that were circulating in Lisbon at the time of a serious relationship between Salazar and Carolina Asseca, daughter of the Viscount of Asseca. The origins of the story appeared to come from the Spanish embassy.[1] Among the chattering classes of Lisbon society, there was a deep sense of surprise at the so-called wedding. It had been presumed for some years that Salazar was a "lifelong bachelor," whose background in trainee priesthood and academia, as well as his lifestyle and long working hours, seemed to exclude the possibility of sharing his life with a woman.

The *Daily Mail* story of a wedding having already taken place was incorrect, but the romance was genuine enough. They had been writing regularly to each other and having long conversations on the phone.[2] She was present at certain official ceremonies and receptions, which added to the rumor mill. The following year, in its controversial article on Salazar and Portugal, *Time* magazine provided further details on the origins of Salazar's relationship with Carolina Asseca.[3] The magazine put Salazar on its cover with the title underneath, "Portugal's Salazar, Dean of Dictators."

The article inside the magazine was very harsh in tone on Salazar and his policies. Regarding his relationship with Carolina Asseca, it reported that it was Salazar's love of flowers that brought him close to her. When Salazar put on a reception for the mother of the last king of Portugal, Dom Manuel II, it was suggested that Carolina Asseca act as the official hostess. Salazar's advisers saw her as an aristocratic widow and being suitable to act in such a capacity. Like any good aristocratic Portuguese hostess, she took over the flower arranging duties for the party. Salazar was said to have been so impressed that he wrote her a brief thank you note. She replied with a long letter, to which Salazar replied asking for permission to call on her. They met for tea and the relationship blossomed from this point onwards. The gossipmongers in Lisbon speculated that, as a result of his relationship with Carolina Asseca, Salazar took more of an interest in his clothes and food, as well as the ceremonial side to his duties. In other words, Salazar was making more of an effort to be a little less austere.[4]

The article in *Time* magazine, with its strong criticism of the economic and social policies of the Portuguese government under the title "How Bad is Best," led to the magazine being temporarily banned in Portugal.[5] The central feature of the piece was that the Salazar government was just another European dictatorship that had failed.[6] To make matters worse for Salazar, the story was widely quoted and reprinted in the European press. Though a case could be made that the article unfairly criticized Salazar for things such as food shortages that were the consequence of Allied wartime policies, opposition figures in Portugal felt that it had not gone far enough.

Despite protests from the publisher of the magazine, Piero Saporiti, a forty-three-year-old Italian journalist who wrote the article, was thrown out of the country. In a situation that was reminiscent of the expulsion from Portugal of Edward Lucas, the *Times* correspondent in 1940, Saporiti was given a stay of expulsion. Eventually, after failing to persuade the authorities to revoke their decision, on October 3, 1946, he left Lisbon on a train bound for

France. To add insult to injury, he was stopped by the Portuguese police, who got on the train at the border with Spain. They announced that, as he did not have an exit visa to leave Portugal he could not proceed and should immediately get off the train. The journalist then displayed his expulsion document and asked what more of an exit visa could you need? He was allowed to remain on the train and headed for Paris.[7]

While the gossip surrounding Salazar's relationship with Carolina Asseca was still providing Lisbon high society with something to comment upon, there was a hugely important political aspect to the question of whether or not Salazar planned to marry her. Previously, Salazar had implied that he did not consider having a wife and children to be compatible with a life devoted to the public service of the state.[8] In other words, if Salazar married Asseca then it would be understood to be an indication that he would retire from office, head back to his home near Santa Comba Dão, and spend his time tending to his flowers. Such a move would have transformed the political landscape of Portugal and the Iberian Peninsula. A suggestion of marriage was, therefore, another way to subtly undermine his continued leadership.

Since the Allied appreciation for Salazar's conduct of the war had proved to be very short-lived, the end of the war appeared to be the perfect moment for Salazar to take the applause and gratitude of the Portuguese people and retire with honor to his home.[9] He was in already in his late fifties, and the effort of working up to eighteen hours a day during seemingly extended periods of crisis was starting to damage his health. The presence of a woman in his life whose company he enjoyed and who shared many of his rural interests acted as a further temptation.

Salazar was not a rich man, but his lack of interest in obtaining expensive material possessions, and his desire to leave Lisbon and spend a retirement in his modest home near Santa Comba Dão, meant that he would have been financially comfortable. Most men would have chosen this seemingly definitive moment in history to leave the stage.

Salazar, however, was no ordinary leader. He was determined to carry on and to try to develop the Estado Novo for the challenges of peacetime. There was too much unfinished business. His deep-rooted belief remained that he was the only man capable of managing the state, so he felt compelled to remain in office and devote himself once more to public service. There would be only a limited time allocated for flowers, whatever *Time* magazine suggested.

———

So Salazar stayed. Ronald Campbell, however, left Lisbon almost immediately at the end of the war. Salazar attended his farewell dinner on June 29, 1945, at which warm words were expressed on both sides about their mutual efforts to keep Portugal out of the war.[10] The next day, while Campbell's official car made the journey from the British embassy to Salazar's office in São Bento for a formal farewell meeting, the ambassador had a feeling of a job well done.[11]

As his car drove through Lisbon, Campbell saw the old apartment buildings of the Lapa area. The buildings were still in poor repair, but none had been victim to the bombs of the Luftwaffe. From the top of Lapa, the ambassador could see some of the changes that had taken place in the city during the war. To the west, in the far distance, was Belém where in 1940, as France fell to the Germans, Lisbon had hosted its huge international fair. The exhibition and fairgrounds had since been converted into permanent museums and parks for local Lisboetas to enjoy weekend strolls in the bright light that reflected off the River Tagus.

Campbell could also see the docks, whose noisy cranes were still busily unloading and loading ships—the very same cranes that in the event of an invasion of Lisbon, the SOE had planned to destroy. Missing from the docks was the human cargo. By 1945 the refugees had departed, and the scene had returned to some degree of normality. There were no more emotional farewells as ships slowly slipped out of port and headed down the river to the Atlantic Ocean, with their passengers facing uncertain journeys to unknown futures in the United States or in Palestine. Across the river, in the far distance, Campbell could see the dormitory towns of Lisbon such as Barreiro, hotbeds of the continuing communist opposition, and reminders of the pressing internal political problems to come for Salazar.

The Palace of São Bento was a magnificent white building, which was beautifully lit at night. The home of the National Assembly, it had survived the Lisbon earthquake of 1755. During World War II, the building was renovated inside, and outside there had been the addition of an impressive staircase along the entire front of the building. Salazar's office was located just behind the main building in a mansion house.

Compared to the splendor of the home of the National Assembly, Salazar's house was modest, fitting with his personality. The walled gardens with an old pond near the exit of the house offered both privacy and room to think, and Salazar enjoyed walking around them deep in thought. Sometimes, during the course of the afternoon, Salazar went for a stroll out of the house and headed up towards the Bairro Alto area of the city, or up the hill on the other side of the road to Lapa and the park of Jardim da Estrela, more often than not without bodyguards.[12]

Campbell had lost count of the number of times he had been to the house and to the office. On this occasion, his meeting with Salazar was brief; everything had already been said both in previous meetings to discuss arrangements for the ambassador's successor, and in public, at dinner the previous evening. The previous November, when news of the replacement of the German ambassador, Baron von Hoyningen-Huene, reached Lisbon, Campbell wrote to the British Foreign Office, and included a thoughtful tribute to Salazar that came to represent his personal viewpoint of Salazar and Portugal.[13] Campbell suggested that, had Portugal had a less courageous statesman than Salazar at the helm during 1940 and 1941, the country could have drifted into the German orbit, influencing the course and duration of the war.

On Portugal itself, he added, as small and insignificant as it appeared on the map of Europe, its geographical position gave it disproportionate importance in any war in which the British Empire had been engaged. He finished by reminding his masters in London that Britain would in all likelihood need her ancient ally again in future conflicts.[14]

Campbell's war had been an eventful one. At the start of the war, he was ambassador in Paris, and when the Germans invaded he decamped to Bordeaux along with the French government. Ironically, Campbell was in Bordeaux at the same time that the Portuguese consul, Aristides de Sousa Mendes, was issuing Portuguese transit visas to Jews against the wishes of Salazar. Indeed, their offices were only a few blocks apart. Sousa Mendes's wartime career was effectively over just as Campbell's was starting.

According to the records of the PVDE, Campbell had been in charge of 281 full-time embassy employees at the height of the war, which amounted to some 120 more than the German ambassador had under his command.[15] In 1943, the PVDE put the total number of foreign diplomats serving in Lisbon at 1,158 with Italy (103) and the United States (101) following Britain and Germany in having the highest number. Spain with 46 diplomats serving in Lisbon completed the list of the top five.

Campbell understood very early that he would one day have to get to Salazar to ask for access to the Azores. His whole diplomatic strategy in Lisbon had been based on securing Salazar's agreement to this access, and to limiting (not stopping) the supply of Portuguese wolfram to Germany. For Campbell, these had been the two issues where Portugal could make a huge difference to the conduct and duration of the war. The intelligence, and counterintelligence, plots were something of a sideshow to an ambassador who understood what his diplomatic masters in London needed from Salazar.

CHAPTER 30

Old Wine into
New Bottles

SALAZAR HAD CAREFULLY NOTED THE OUTCOME OF the British general election, which was held on July 5, 1945. The landslide victory of the Labour Party over the Conservative Party led by Winston Churchill sent shockwaves through Lisbon.[1] For Salazar, it was confirmation of the salient point that electorates would not necessarily return to power those individuals who would were most associated with having won the war. In Lisbon, there were fears among many of Salazar's close supporters that while the Portuguese public was happy with his handling of the war, and for preventing the physical horrors of war from reaching the country, the end of the war would lead to increased aspirations for a new beginning. In other words, the wartime accomplishments would belong to the past.

Salazar knew he would have to give the appearance of some type of liberal political and electoral reform. Change or die might have been too dramatic an analysis to events in Lisbon, but there was clearly a need to be seen having tried to do something. It was more like a case of old wine into new bottles. Salazar's diary reveals that over the summer months of 1945 he continued to work in Lisbon through a series of agreements and war-related issues.[2] He did not get to spend any lengthy holiday back home in Santa Comba Dão. Usually each summer Salazar had an extended stay at his home, which he viewed as vital for recharging his batteries for the year ahead. In the summer of 1945, the maximum time he was able to spend was four days towards the end of August.

On August 30, on Salazar's order, the Portuguese ambassador in London, the Duke of Palmela, transmitted to Winston Churchill an invitation to visit Portugal.[3] Churchill replied that he was very much looking forward to visiting "your lovely country." Despite the diplomatic tensions between Salazar over both the sale of wolfram to Germany and over the slow pace of the negotiations over the Azores, Churchill was widely viewed in Lisbon, as elsewhere, as the man who had done much to secure the Allied victory. A visit from the wartime hero would do much to emphasize that Portugal was back in the Allied fold.

The other issue that worried Salazar about the political demise of Churchill was whether there would be a degree of continuity in British foreign policy making under the new Labour government led by Clement Attlee. In private, Salazar feared that the government with its socialist social and welfare agenda might shift British foreign policy making in this direction as well. The presence of such a radical reforming government in London would, in all likelihood, stoke the fires for social and economic change in Lisbon.

In terms of foreign policy making, Salazar was extremely reassured by the speech given by the British foreign secretary, Ernest Bevin, on August 20.[4] The speech, heavily and favorably reported in the Portuguese press, went some way to providing Salazar with the reassurance he needed that the new British government would continue with existing British foreign polices.

Over the summer, Salazar had started to enter into the process of making some readjustments to the political workings in Lisbon in order to reflect the changes that were taking place in the world at the time.[5] A central feature of this process of reform was to allow a form of moderate opposition to come into being. British diplomats in Lisbon argued to the Foreign Office that he was trying to partially educate the Portuguese people in the art of parliamentary democracy, a system Salazar thought worked admirably in Britain, but one he felt was unsuitable to the Portuguese due to their temperament and political immaturity. Salazar talked about these changes in a speech he gave at a meeting of the directing committee of the National Union on September 8.

The central purpose was an attempt to recast Portugal fully back into the orbit of Britain and the Allies.[6] Salazar said that the harsh comments made against Spain, which were made by the Allies, were of less importance to him than what was not said about Portugal's conduct in the war. He tried to address the sense still held in some Allied circles of what was known as its "Portuguese Germanophiles" by reminding his audience that for weeks at a time in both 1940 and 1942, the Portuguese government was living with its bags all packed (to set up a government in exile in the Azores). This was why, as he put it, "It was necessary to throw a sop every now-and-again to Germany's friends in Lisbon." Finally, he promised greater freedom for the press at home and some kind of political amnesty.

In Lisbon, on October 6, 1945, Salazar dissolved the Portuguese National Assembly and set elections for November 18.[7] In his diary, Salazar noted that this was the only time during the Estado Novo that the National Assembly had been dissolved.[8] The following day he gave a long speech to members of the assembly in which he outlined his philosophy and vision.[9] The speech contained much detail, but it was clear that Salazar meant to go further down the path of democracy than General Franco and Spain, though not as far as transforming Portugal into a British-style democracy.[10] The reaction of the British government to the speech matched international response: that it betrayed no great faith in the future of democracy, and it remained to be seen whether the promises would be fulfilled.[11]

Salazar's position was helped enormously by the poor quality of the internal opposition he faced.[12] While there was some "effervescence" among those groups that were hostile to Salazar's regime, they lacked cohesion and viable national leaders. Overall, the opposition was too disunited and weak in leadership to exploit any of the opportunities that Salazar presented to them.[13] In reality, there was little need to take them seriously at this stage. As long as the armed forces remained behind Salazar there was little chance of removing him from power.[14]

The weakness of the opposition was confirmed during events that surrounded a political crisis caused by the elections.[15] The opposition were derided by the British Foreign Office as being a motley bunch, who all came with different motives.[16] None of them, the British added, had produced any constructive ideas, short of singing the praises of democracy and winning some applause for doing so.[17] The Americans added that the only motive that the opposition had was their own political ambition.[18]

The other major weakness of the opposition was its lack of funds. The wealthy in Portugal were almost united in their support of Salazar. Externally, the Soviet Union, anti-Salazar Portuguese in Brazil and in the United States were possible sources of financial aid for the opposition, but together they could not deliver the substantial amounts that were needed to mount a credible challenge.[19]

The British Foreign Office advised that the British government should not come down too hard on Salazar, who was at least moving in the right direction.[20] Understandably, the opposition was hugely critical of Britain for its support of Salazar at this time.[21] It was likewise hostile to the United States as it became clear that the Americans had little interest in helping the opposition change the regime in Lisbon.

The Allied attitude was best summed up by the phrase "better the devil you know." Neither Britain nor the United States had any real appetite to stir up internal trouble for Salazar. Both countries understood that one day their ambassadors would be going to

Salazar's office and asking for continued access to the Azores bases. The onset of the cold war meant that the Azores, Portugal, and Salazar remained extremely relevant to the military needs of Britain and the United States.

By the time the elections took place as arranged on November 18, 1945, the only candidates who agreed to stand were from Salazar's National Union. There was, as a result, never any doubt about the composition of the new Assembly.[22] The opposition had withdrawn from the process on November 10 after a bitter campaign that had been characterized by claim and counterclaim of wrongdoing by both sides. What was apparent was that during the campaign, Salazar decided to resort to his old authoritarian ways. There was widespread use of the secret police.

On October 27, the government had suspended all public meetings of the opposition groups, claiming that they were in effect preparing to overthrow Salazar by way of a coup.[23] Soon afterwards, Salazar shifted away from the experiment with partially democratic elections.[24] From Salazar's perspective, however, his efforts had not gone to waste. He had exposed the failings of the opposition, which boycotted the election, and showed to the outside world that he was still very much in charge.

Two days before the election, Lisbon was hit by a hurricane, which caused extensive damage to the outlying suburbs of the city. The inclement weather continued on the day of the election with torrential rain flooding parts of the city from early morning onwards. The outside tables of the cafés in the Rossio were all cleared and stacked neatly by the side of the pavement. Inside the cafés the mainly male population talked about the latest football match between Benfica and Sporting.

The foreign accents of the refugees had long since vanished, leaving almost no trace that they had once passed through the city on the way to their new lives. Although there were still food shortages, at least the coffee was not in short supply and the café goers were still able to enjoy their *bicas*. Outside in the pouring rain, the shoe shiners had been quick to pack their equipment away and offer another service to Lisboetas: cheap umbrellas.

There was no sense of drama on election day comparable to Britain or America, just a quiet and passive understanding that the wily doctor from Santa Comba Dão was working away in his office in São Bento, busily directing the country towards what he envisaged was its place in the world. The sodden city of Lisbon was entering the new postwar era with Salazar's authority intact. He would guide Portugal, for better or worse, for nearly twenty-three more years.

EPILOGUE

A few very basic economic statistics confirm the success story of Portugal's economy during World War II. Prior to the war, in the years from 1937 to 1939, Portugal had a trade deficit of around $40 million (exports $50 million and imports nearly $90 million).[1] By the end of 1942, the deficit had been transformed into a trade surplus of $68 million (exports $240 million and imports nearly $172 million). For the five-year period of the war from the end of 1939 to the end of 1944, Portugal had an overall trade surplus of nearly $45 million.[2]

In terms of the Portuguese banks, during the war years, the level of assets held in private banks doubled, and the assets in the Bank of Portugal more than tripled.[3] By 1943, revenue collected by the government in Lisbon mainly from export taxes had increased by some 44 percent from their level at the start of the war.[4] Put simply, the country had done very well out of the economic wars between the Allies and Axis powers.

There was, however, much unfinished business in Lisbon after the war, all of which took time and protracted negotiations to bring to some form of resolution. Three major issues were all hugely interrelated: negotiations over the return of the looted German gold that Portugal had received in payment for the wolfram and other goods; the question of the seized German assets in Portugal; and long-term access rights to the Azores military bases for the United States. Naturally, from his office in Lisbon, Salazar controlled Portugal's attitude and position towards these postwar negotiations.

The Portuguese attitude to the negotiations could best be characterized as trying to stall for as long as possible, and not to admit to having received any gold of questionable origins from Germany.[5] Prior to the start of the talks, the Portuguese government and the Bank of Portugal completely failed to respond to American requests for information about the gold. For its part, the Bank of Portugal stuck to its story that no monetary gold had been shipped from Germany to Portugal (meaning directly from Germany). As the Americans prepared their material for the negotiations they produced a detailed report, which drew upon testimony from Swiss bankers and Allied intelligence material. The report concluded, somewhat conservatively, that Portugal had acquired nearly 124 tons of gold, which was worth approximately $139 million, during the course of World War II.[6]

Using evidence from an undisclosed Swiss banker, the American State Department calculated that 20 tons of this windfall had come directly from gold looted by the Germans from Belgium. In addition, 104 tons had been acquired from the Swiss National Bank. Using Allied intelligence sources, around 72 percent (75 tons) of the gold from Switzerland had been looted by the Germans from occupied countries. The State Department report concluded, as a result, that the Allies should demand that Portugal return a figure of exactly 94.787 tons of gold ($106.6 million).[7]

As the author of the report admitted, the amount of gold the Bank of Portugal was thought to have received was probably underestimated by a lot. Allied intelligence reports put the figure of truck deliveries to the bank of up to 400 tons of gold from Switzerland. The problem with these intelligence reports was that many of them did not provide conclusive proof of the shipment of gold.

The negotiations between the Allies and Portugal started in Lisbon on September 3, 1946. There was no quick breakthrough in the talks, which lasted for years. Given that much of the Allied information on the gold was based on classified sources, they felt that they could ask Portugal to return only a figure of 44.864 tons of gold

($50.5 million).[8] This figure represented the amount of gold that the Allies *knew* Portugal had received after 1942, when it had become common knowledge that the German gold was looted. Portugal, however, offered to return only 3 tons of gold and stuck to this figure. The Bank of Portugal argued that the Allies could not conclusively prove that the gold it had received had been stolen.

The Allies attempted to tie the negotiations with the issue of seized German commercial assets in Portugal, which were said to be worth around $10.3 million.[9] Allied negotiators, however, made the mistake of agreeing to a Portuguese proposal that the liquidation of gold assets should be postponed until after a resolution had been found to the gold issue. The value of seized German commercial assets steadily fell as they were prevented from trading and this was one of the major reasons why the Allies reduced their demands for repayments of the gold.

Eventually, after years of haggling, an agreement was reached on June 24, 1953, whereby Portugal returned just 4 tons of gold (3.998 tons, to be exact).[10] The agreement represented a huge win for the Portuguese, who were able to keep the rest, and never had to reveal how much "the rest" amounted to. Since the report produced by the State Department in 1946 conservatively concluded that Portugal had received some 124 tons of gold during the war, this meant that in effect Portugal's net profit from the negotiations was at least 120 tons, and as much as 400 tons if the Allied intelligence estimate was accurate.

Such a one-sided conclusion to a complex, and extended, set of negotiations was a rare phenomenon. In truth, the American negotiators in the talks were hampered by the desire of the U.S. government to renew and extend access for American armed services to the bases in the Azores.[11] The American military identified the Azores as a vital bridge to helping with the rebuilding of Europe, and in the era of the cold war, helping maintain a strong American military presence in Europe and other theaters of the cold war conflict.

So the United States put the development of its strategic cold war needs over the pursuit of justice for the occupied countries that had gold stolen by the Germans from Central Banks and from individuals. The American set of priorities also abandoned the search for justice for victims of the Holocaust whose gold was stolen by the Germans.

As always, Salazar had made the Americans pay top dollar for access to the Azores. He understood the order of American priorities extremely well and used the negotiations over the Azores as a barrier to the gold. The Americans understood that if Salazar was displeased about the state of the gold negotiations, he would prove less flexible in the talks over the Azores. Questions over the morality of Portugal's gold remained largely ignored in Lisbon, as the state-controlled media was not allowed to make substantial reference to it. Salazar's attitude concerning the Holocaust had never changed: It was an internal issue of the Third Reich. It was nothing to do with Portugal, whose gold had been earned in return for the provision of wolfram and other goods to Germany.

In the meantime, the Bank of Portugal tried to get rid of some of the gold by dispersing it across Portugal and around the globe. Ironically, some of it was thought to have gone back to Switzerland.[12] There is evidence that other parts of the gold were secretly shipped to the Far East to Macau (then a Portuguese colony). Some of the gold turned up in very strange places. There are stories that the Bank of Portugal still has old gold bars with the stamp of the Reichsbank in its vaults. As most of these stories originated from ex-employees of the bank, it is difficult to fully confirm whether or not this is the case.

A BBC report broadcast on May 3, 2000, described how the Roman Catholic shrine in Fatima admitted that it had kept German gold until the mid 1980s.[13] The religious leaders at the shrine had asked a Portuguese bank in 1970 to melt down some of the gold from the shrine. According to the church, when it received the equivalent in gold bars back from the bank, it discovered that many of the bars had the Nazi insignia stamped on them. The church subsequently sold these bars between 1982–1986 in order to help finance building work at Fatima. The church wanted to upgrade the facilities at the shrine.

Even by the most conservative Allied estimates, Portugal at the end of World War II had enough gold reserves to help transform its economy and living conditions for its people. Yet Salazar appeared reluctant to actually use any of it. Instead, it sat in the vaults of the Bank of Portugal and other banks around the world. For decades after the war, Portugal continued to be a poor economy, with the major source of its income coming from trade with its colonies. In Lisbon, Salazar maintained his program of public works, which saw gradual improvements in the city's infrastructure. There were internal debates and disputes within the regime over the pace of the process of change and the direction of the economy. The wily old doctor was still governed by not spending what he believed the country could not afford. The gold stayed in the vaults.

The issue of the gold and trade in wolfram with Germany during World War II remains a deeply divisive issue in postauthoritarian, democratic Portugal. It came to international prominence through the work of Stuart Eizenstat and his team, in investigating the issue in order to seek justice for the victims of the Holocaust.[14] The international publicity, which surrounded the investigation, did not present Portugal in a very favorable light: Headlines included news coverage such as, "The Greatest Theft in History," from the BBC, and from the *New York Times*, "The Not So Neutrals of World War II."[15]

The undertones to this debate over the gold and Portugal's role in World War II were Portugal's historically difficult relations with the Jews, and charges that anti-Semitism remained rife in the country. These charges naturally led to a response from Lisbon, but one which very much fitted into the context of the country's antiauthoritarian politics, which dominated the political narrative at the time. Despite a national commission of inquiry into the gold issue, and credible research by historians on the banks, and in particular on the Bank of Portugal, the story of the legality and morality of the gold remains a largely unfinished one. What is clear is that it remains far too easy for Portugal's democratic politicians to merely dismiss the story as a hangover from the country's authoritarian past, and act as if it no longer concerns the country.

Salazar believed deeply that Portugal deserved to be paid for the goods and services it provided, and be allowed to keep the profit from this trade after the war. It would be a sign of the maturing nature of Portuguese democracy if the issues surrounding its trade in World War II were given a less politicized and a more open and fair critical assessment. Only then will the story of Lisbon during World War II have a real ending.

ACKNOWLEDGMENTS

As always, I am very grateful to David Lewis for continuing to support my position at University College London. I was extremely fortunate to be able to spend a great deal of time in Lisbon in order to conduct the research for this book. I wish to thank the British Academy for the award of a grant that allowed me to undertake this on the ground research in Lisbon as well as in London, Washington D.C., New York, Madrid, and Rio de Janeiro.

The book would not exist in its present form without the kind help that a number of individuals and archives gave me during the process of the research and writing of the book, which took place over a three-year period.

A special mention must go to Miguel Champalimaud for his friendship, deep knowledge of Portuguese history, and great enthusiasm for the project. The book has greatly benefited from his help. Also to Duncan and Elizabeth Barker, who were fantastic hosts to me in Rio de Janeiro and did so much to make my trip to Brazil such a success for this book, and for future projects.

In Lisbon, I would like to thank all the staff at Torre do Tombo (the Portuguese national archive) for their assistance in handling my frequent requests for documents and for constantly forgiving my inability to remember what each color of document request form signified. The long process of discovering the wonders and possibilities of Torre do Tombo has turned out to be one of the great pleasures in writing this book. The archive is a fine testament to the process of opening up information in Portugal. The documents from the archive of António de Oliveira Salazar, as well as the PIDE secret police archives, were a source of hugely valuable information.

I would also like to thank the staff at Cascais Municipality Archives who were kind enough to provide me with some rarely seen photographs of the area during World War II. The archive contains important information and hotel records for the period.

There are a number of people to whom I owe a huge debt of gratitude for their help during my research in Lisbon. To Francisco Sousa da Câmara for originally suggesting to me that the Americans and the British remain extremely interested in the history of Portuguese neutrality during World War II. Also to Luís de Almeida for encouraging me to write a book on Portuguese history. To José Mateus for his boundless enthusiasm and comprehensive knowledge of the history of the Portuguese banking system. Jaime Nogueira Pinto, who took the time to explain Salazar's philosophy to me, as well the importance of his colonial policies in assessing his legacy. Paula Serra helped me understand how Portugal works (and doesn't work). To one of Lisbon's best photographers, Ana Baião, for the photographs. Nick Racich helped with his knowledge of the recent history of the banks in Lisbon.

A very special note of thanks must be given to Carlos Alberto Damas, the head of the Historical Archive at Banco Espírito Santo. The fact that the archive is one of the best run in Portugal is down to many years of his hard work and organizational skills. He provided me with a lot of documentary material for the book and his knowledge of the history of the bank is encyclopaedic. Thanks also to the current vice president of the bank, José Manuel Espírito Santo, for talking to me at length about the issues relating to the bank in World War II and for opening up the archive to me.

In London, the staff at the Public Records Office (National Archives) in Kew were, as ever, very helpful and enthusiastic in helping direct me to the huge volume of documentary material that Portugal and its role in World War II had created. I was particularly grateful for the guidance on the various locations for the security files of MI5 and MI6, which were new areas of research to me. Likewise, the staff at the Wiener Library in London were very helpful in directing me to the material on Wilfrid Israel and the Jewish refugees in Lisbon.

In Portugal, I would like to thank Frederico, and his father, Francisco Champalimaud for helping me find my "room with a view," from where I wrote up much of this book. To Udo and Marion Kruse for all their kindness and support. Likewise, to Mafalda Champalimaud for her assistance with Portuguese family trees. Thank you also to my lawyer, Francisco Costa Reis, for showing me the way to the next stage. To Claire Chung for her energy and support for the project. I am extremely grateful to Ricardo Arrenega at Quinta da Marinha Health & Racket Club, whose expert training made sure that I stayed fit and healthy throughout the writing of the book.

I would like to thank my friends at Oitavos Dunes for their support, and for understanding why I disappeared for long periods of time during the writing stage of the book: Axel Bernstorff, Davis Bader, Ian Whittle (who bought a copy of the book before I had finished writing it), John and Roxanna Lawson, J. P. Salzmann, João Marim, Luís Cameira, Mike Callahan, Norman and Arona Brenn, Pierre and Marie-France Gaudreault, and William Branth. Thanks must also go to Jack and Craig.

In Brazil, a number of people very kindly helped me navigate my way through the archives. I am especially grateful to Jaime Antunes da Silva, director general of the National Archives based in Rio de Janeiro, for giving me so much of his time and explaining exactly in which archives I needed to look for material. To Sátiro Nunes for helping me specifically with the photographs and documentation in the National Archives. Tenente Coronel José Luiz Cruz Andrade, director Military Archives, helped me enormously with this book and a future project.

In the United States, the staff at the United States Holocaust Memorial Museum (USHMM) were very good in helping me locate material on the Jewish refugees in Lisbon during World War II. Judith Cohen, director of the photographic collection at USHMM, helped identity some wonderful images of the Jewish refugees in Lisbon. Also thank you to Michael Berkowitz for originally finding these photographic files. At the U.S. National Archives in Maryland I am extremely grateful to the staff who assisted me in locating the files I needed in order to write this book. The lack of a good centralized computer system in the archive made the help provided by the team there absolutely invaluable.

At PublicAffairs, it has been a great pleasure working with my editor, Clive Priddle, whose input has enormously helped this project develop into its final form. I am grateful, too, to Melissa Raymond, my production editor. Also to Niki Papadopoulos who, although no longer with PublicAffairs, was of great help at the start of the project. It has been a pleasure dealing with such a professional publisher. My thanks most also go to my agent, David Patterson, at the Foundry Literary and Media Agency in New York. I am very much looking forward to working on new projects with him and the team at Foundry. Matt Freeman and Helena Shaw have done a marvelous job developing and maintaining my website.

Finally, and most important of all, I owe a huge debt of gratitude to my family for their continued love and support: to my mother and to my parents-in-law, Pat and Gillian Castle Stewart, my wife, Emma, and my children, Benjamin and Hélèna. The book is dedicated to my wife and children with an apology for my long absences at my writing desk.

PHOTO CREDITS

Page 1: Calouste Gulbenkian Foundation, CFT003003770

Page 2: Calouste Gulbenkian Foundation, CFT16401159

Page 3: (top) Calouste Gulbenkian Foundation, CFT16401154; (bottom) Courtesy of Arquivo Municipal de Lisboa, BEK003619

Page 4: (top) Courtesy of ANTT/National Archive Torre do Tombo; (bottom) Calouste Gulbenkian Foundation, CFT003101549

Page 5: (top) Arquivo Municipal de Cascais, PAS408; (bottom) Calouste Gulbenkian Foundation, CFT16400794

Page 6: Calouste Gulbenkian Foundation, CFT003071106

Page 7: (top) Fundacão de Aristide de Sousa Mendes; (bottom) United States Holocaust Memorial Museum, 16197

Page 8: United States Holocaust Memorial Museum, 59615

Page 9: United States Holocaust Memorial Museum, 34483

Page 10: (top) Courtesy of Arquivo Municipal de Lisboa, A22194, Kurt Pinto; (bottom) Calouste Gulbenkian Foundation, CFT16401128

Page 11: (top) Centro de Estudos da História do BES; (bottom) Centro de Estudos da História do BES

Page 12: Centro de Estudos da História do BES

Page 13: (top) Calouste Gulbenkian Foundation, CFT003016090; (bottom) National Archives and Records Administration (NARA, United States)

Page 14: (top) German Federal Archives (Bundersarchiv), Picture 183–2011–0509–501; (bottom) With the kind permission of Viscount John Eccles

Page 15: (top) Arquivo Municipal de Cascais; (bottom) Arquivo Municipal de Cascais, PAS295

Page 16: The National Archives, KV2/1273 (United Kingdom)

Page 17: (top) Arquivo Municipal de Cascais, CAP275; (middle) Arquivo Municipal de Cascais; (bottom) ©Bettmann/Corbis

Page 18: (top) With the kind permission of the family of Jack Beevor; (bottom) Courtesy of CriticalPast

Page 19: (top) Courtesy of CriticalPast; (bottom) Calouste Gulbenkian Foundation, CFT164054946

Page 20: Hotel Aviz

Page 21: (top) Courtesy of CriticalPast; (bottom) Courtesy of Arquivo Municipal de Lisboa, B093861

Page 22: (top) Courtesy of CriticalPast; (bottom) Calouste Gulbenkian Foundation, CFT003005184

Page 23: (top) Calouste Gulbenkian Foundation, CFT003110610; (bottom) Calouste Gulbenkian Foundation, CFT16401124

Page 24: Calouste Gulbenkian Foundation, CFT003003756

A NOTE ABOUT SOURCES

The vast majority of documents used in this book originate from archives in Lisbon (and Cascais), London, Rio de Janeiro, and Washington, D.C. (College Park, Maryland). In Lisbon, I made use of the National Archives at Torre do Tombo, which houses, among its many collections, the papers related to António de Oliveira Salazar. The Portuguese leader maintained a near daily diary during his time in office. The diary was more of a record of his daily appointments, interspersed with a few observations and comments. The diary was written in his own hand, and remains extremely hard to decipher in places. That said, it provided an excellent record for the timings and dates of meetings, which form a central part of this book.

Other useful papers from the archive include Salazar's official correspondence in the various governmental roles he held during World War II. At times, this correspondence remains incomplete as the archive contains the correspondence from the sender, but not the replies from Salazar. A certain amount of reading between the lines is required when this occurs. To some extent, the Diplomatic Archives, which are located in another part of Lisbon, helped fill in some of the gaps. The PIDE (Secret Police) archives are also located at Torre do Tombo. These files relating to the reports of the PVDE during the war proved very useful in both looking at the external and internal threats to the Salazar regime.

In London the range of documents used from the National Archive illustrates the centrality of Lisbon to many different facets of the war. The Foreign Office papers provided a lot of detail of relevant meetings and events. The papers of Anthony Eden proved more useful in helping to identify key areas in which Lisbon became important to the Allies, as did the cabinet papers, which are now available online. Documents relating to the various intelligence agencies operating in Lisbon proved useful in piecing together the complex operations they undertook in the city. British intercepts of German and Portuguese cables were invaluable to developing an understanding of the extent of the trade between the two countries.

In the United States, a whole range of documents were examined including both the general and classified records of the U.S. embassy in Lisbon. Records

247

relating to the Nazi Gold and Safehaven were also used in conjunction with the British and Portuguese documents. Interestingly, it was in this area that the documentary sources from the Allies started to diverge in the various perceptions of Salazar. State Department records provided important background, particularly over wolfram and the negotiations over the Azores.

Overall, nearly 50,000 pages of documents have been photographed, downloaded, or photocopied, and then read for this book from the various archives. Secondary source material from books and articles from both English and Portuguese sources provided invaluable background and detail for the book, as did autobiographies and memoirs of the participants. Material from various newspapers also added some flavor to the plot. As a result of all this material, each of the major subjects in this book could have constituted a full-length treatment of its own. Difficult and careful choices have had to be made, as a result, as to what to include in the book and what to leave out in order to make this book a digestible size.

Introduction

1. "Lisbon: Europe's Bottleneck," *Life Magazine*, April 28, 1941, p. 80.
2. Ibid.

Chapter 1—Sitting Out the War

1. Malcolm Muggeridge, *Chronicles of Wasted Times: An Autobiography* (Vancouver: Regent College Publishing, 2006), p. 413.
2. Public Records Office, National Archive, Kew, London, Foreign Office/ 371/24064/ From Walford Selby to Foreign Office, September 2, 1939.
3. Ibid.
4. PRO/FO/371/24064/ Selby, September 2, 1939.
5. PRO/FO/371/24064/ From Selby to Foreign Office, September 1, 1939.
6. PRO/FO/371/24064/ Selby, September 2, 1939.
7. PRO/FO/371/24064/From Foreign Office to Selby, September 4, 1939.
8. PRO/FO/371/24064/ Selby, September 2, 1939.
9. Arthur Koestler, *Arrival and Departure* (London: Penguin, 1943), p. 14.
10. David Eccles, *By Safe Hand: The Letters of Sybil and David Eccles*, 1939– 1942 (London: Bodley Head, 1983), p. 105.
11. Koestler, *Arrival and Departure*, p. 15.
12. Eccles, *By Safe Hand*, p. 105.
13. Ibid., p. 100.
14. Ibid., p. 105.
15. Malcolm Muggeridge, *Like It Was: a Selection from the Diaries of Malcolm Muggeridge* (London: Collins, 1981), p. 183.
16. Eccles, *By Safe Hand*, p. 105.
17. "Lisbon: Europe's Bottleneck," *Life Magazine*, April 28, 1941, p. 77.

18. Muggeridge, *Chronicles of Wasted Time*, p. 412.
19. National Archives and Records Administration (NARA), College Park, Maryland, United States of America/RG131/346/General Records of the Embassy in Lisbon, From Crocker to Wood, Lisbon, December 31, 1943.
20. Ibid., p. 3.
21. NARA/RG131/346/Classified Records of the Embassy in Lisbon, From James Wood to Edward Crocker, December 31, 1943, p. 3.
22. Ibid.
23. Ibid., p. 4.
24. Carlos Alberto Damas, *Hotel Tivoli Lisbon: Tradition and Modernity in the Lisbon Hotel Industry, 1933–2008* (Lisbon: Banco Espírito Santo, 2008), pp. 192–196.
25. NARA/RG84/15/ Classified General Records of U.S. Embassy in Lisbon, 1924–1961, War History Report of the U.S. Embassy Lisbon, August 1, 1946, p. 2.
26. PRO/FO/371/34714/ Records of Leading Personalities in Portugal, June 10, 1943, pp. 21–22.

Chapter 2—The Most Beautiful Dictator

1. David Eccles, *By Safe Hand: the Letters of Sybil and David Eccles, 1939–1942* (London: Bodley Head, 1983), p. 107.
2. António Ferro, *Salazar: Portugal and Her Leader* (London: Faber and Faber, 1939), pp. 200–201.
3. Ibid.
4. See, for example, *O Século*, May 21, 1938, from Helena Matos, *Salazar: A Propaganda, 1934–1938* (Lisboa: Circulo de Leitores, 2010), pp. 270–271. This work and her later volume are full of examples of the development and use of Salazar's image.
5. Paul H. Lewis, "Salazar's Ministerial Elite, 1932–1968," *The Journal of Politics* 40, no. 3 (August 1978), p. 632.
6. NARA/RG84/94/ General Records of U.S. Embassy in Lisbon/Background on Portugal's Position in May 1940/ Political Situation, May 15, 1944, pp. 4–5.
7. Hugh Kay, *Salazar and Modern Portugal: A Biography* (New York: Hawthorn, 1970), p. 79.
8. Ibid., p. 196.
9. Ibid., p. 197.
10. Kay, *Salazar and Modern Portugal*, p. 79.
11. PRO/FO/371/34714/ Records of Leading Personalities in Portugal, June 10, 1943, pp. 21–22.
12. Filipe Ribeiro de Meneses, *Salazar: A Political Biography* (New York: Enigma Books, 2009), p. 223.
13. On Salazar's childhood, see Kay, *Salazar and Modern Portugal*, pp. 9–13.

14. Ibid., p. 26.
15. Meneses, *Salazar*, p. 18.
16. Christine Garnier, *Férias com Salazar* (Lisbon: A. M. Pereira e Grasset e Fasquelle, 1952), p. 176.
17. Ibid.
18. Ibid., p. 177.
19. Meneses, *Salazar*, p. 13.
20. PRO/FO/371/34714/ Records of Leading Personalities in Portugal, June 10, 1943, pp. 21–22.
21. NARA/RG84/94/ General Records of U.S. Embassy in Lisbon/Background on Portugal's Position in May 1940/ Political Situation, May 15, 1944, p. 5.
22. Ibid., pp. 4–5.
23. PRO/FO/371/34714/ Records of Leading Personalities in Portugal, June 10, 1943, pp. 21–22.
24. Ibid.
25. Ibid.
26. Paul Preston, *Franco: A Biography* (London: Basic Books, 1994), p. 454.
27. Ibid.

Chapter 3—Preparing for the Worst

1. PRO/FO/371/24064/ The Role of Portugal in the Event of War, Committee of Imperial Defence, Chiefs of Staff Subcommittee, September 1, 1939, p. 2.
2. PRO/FO/371/23161/ Address by Dr. Salazar to the National Assembly, October 9, 1939, p. 8.
3. António de Figueiredo, *Portugal: Fifty Years of Dictatorship* (London: Penguin, 1975), p. 91.
4. "Portugal and the War," *Times* (London), October 10, 1939.
5. PRO/FO/371/23161/ Address by Dr. Salazar, p. 3.
6. William Manchester, *William Spencer Churchill: Alone, 1932–1940* (Boston: Little Brown, 1988), pp. 247–248.
7. Niall Ferguson, *The Pity of War* (London: Penguin, 1998), p. 295.
8. Ibid., p. 299.
9. Margaret Macmillan, *Peacemakers: Six Months That Changed the World* (London: John Murray, 2003), p. 115.
10. Ibid.
11. Walford Selby, *Diplomatic Twilight, 1930–1940* (London: John Murray, 1953).
12. Ibid., p. 123.
13. David Eccles, *By Safe Hand: The Letters of Sybil and David Eccles, 1939–1942* (London: Bodley Head, 1983), p. 97.
14. Ibid., p. 173.
15. Selby, *Diplomatic Twilight*, p. 110.
16. See Patrick Wilcken, *Empire Adrift: The Portuguese Court in Rio de Janeiro, 1808–1821* (London: Bloomsbury, 2004).

17. Ibid., pp. 248–250.
18. On role of scorched earth policy, see Charles Esdaile, *Napoleon's Wars: An International History, 1803–1815* (London: Penguin, 2007), pp. 355–356.
19. See Niall Ferguson, *The House of Rothschild: Money's Prophets, 1798–1848* (New York: Penguin, 1998), pp. 84–88.
20. Samuel Hoare, *Ambassador on a Special Mission* (London: Collins, 1946), p. 125.
21. Paul Preston, *Franco: A Biography* (London: Basic Books, 1994), p. 427.
22. Portugal/Torre do Tombo/Arquivo Oliveira Salazar/CO/IN-8B/5/ Press Cuttings and PVDE Reports, August 1939.
23. Preston, *Franco*, p. 428.

Chapter 4—Mixed Messages

1. Filipe Ribeiro de Meneses, *Salazar: A Political Biography* (New York: Enigma Books, 2009), p. 232.
2. PRO/FO/371/23162/ Selby to Foreign Office, German Propaganda in Portugal, November 16, 1939.
3. Ibid., p. 2.
4. Malcolm Muggeridge, *Chronicles of Wasted Times: An Autobiography* (Vancouver: Regent College Publishing, 2006), p. 410.
5. Ibid., p. 413.
6. Christian Leitz, *Nazi Germany and Neutral Europe during the Second World War* (Manchester: Manchester University Press, 2000), p. 150.
7. PRO/FO/24488/Postal Censorship, Report on Portugal No. 7, April 17, 1940, p. 2.
8. PRO/War Office/208/2051/ Spain and Portugal (Annex), May 9, 1940.
9. PRO/FO/371/24488/Postal Censorship, Report on Portugal No. 7, April 17, 1940, p. 2.
10. PRO/FO/371/24488/ From Selby to Foreign Office, May 16, 1940.
11. PRO/FO/371/24488/ Portugal: Request for Change of Policy in H. M. Embassy, June 12, 1940.
12. PRO/FO/371/39596/ From Campbell to FO, November 23, 1944.
13. Ibid.
14. Ibid.
15. Leitz, *Nazi Germany and Neutral*, p. 150.
16. Muggeridge, *Chronicles of Wasted Times*, p. 411.
17. Ibid.
18. PRO/WO/208/2051/ From Selby to War Cabinet, May 3, 1940.
19. PRO/WO/208/2051/ Spain and Portugal (Annex), May 9, 1940.
20. Ibid.
21. PRO/Cabinet Office/67/7/5/ Minutes of War Cabinet Meeting, May 6, 1940.
22. Ibid.

Chapter 5—Forget About Your Troubles

1. David Corkill and José Carlos Pina Almeida, "Commemoration and Propaganda in Salazar's *Portugal: The Mundo Português Exposition of 1940*," *Journal of Contemporary History* 44, no. 3 (2009), p. 381.
2. Marina Tavares Dias, *Lisboa nos Anos 40: Longe de Guerra* (Lisboa: Quimera, 2005), p. 47.
3. Ibid., p. 28.
4. PRO/FO/371/34714/Portuguese Personalities Report, June 10, 1943, p. 11.
5. Ibid.
6. Dias, *Lisboa nos Anos 40*, pp. 34–35.
7. António de Figueiredo, *Portugal: Fifty Years of Dictatorship* (London: Penguin, 1975).
8. PT/TT/AOS/CO/IN-8B/1/ PVDE Report, Lisbon, January 27, 1940, p. 4.
9. Figueiredo, *Portugal*, 91.
10. PT/TT/AOS/O Diário de Salazar/ November 16, 1943.
11. Corkill and Almeida, "Commemoration and Propaganda," p. 388.
12. Ibid.
13. Ibid., p. 392.
14. PRO/FO/371/24488/ Selby to Foreign Office, August 12, 1940.
15. Ibid.
16. PRO/FO/371/34714/Portuguese Personalities Report, June 10, 1943, p. 11.
17. Ibid.
18. David Eccles, *By Safe Hand: The Letters of Sybil and David Eccles, 1939–1942* (London: Bodley Head, 1983), pp. 116–117.
19. Ibid., p. 99.

Chapter 6—Wartime Refugees

1. Arthur Koestler, *Arrival and Departure* (London: Penguin, 1971), p. 15.
2. "Lisbon: Europe's Bottleneck," *Life Magazine*, April 28, 1941, p. 84.
3. Koestler, *Arrival and Departure*, p. 19.
4. Arthur Koestler, *Scum of the Earth* (London: Eland, 2006), p. 242.
5. Douglas Wheeler, "And Who Is My Neighbour? A World War II Hero of Conscience for Portugal," *Luso-Brazilian Review* 26, no. 1 (Summer 1989), p. 120.
6. Winston Churchill, *The Second World War: Vol. 2, Their Finest Hour* (London: Folio Society, 2000), p. 174.
7. Avraham Milgram, "Portugal, the Consuls, and the Jewish Refugees, 1938–1941," *Yad Vashem Studies XXVII* (Jerusalem, 1999), pp. 123–156.
8. Jose Alain Fralon, *A Good Man in Evil Times: The Story of Aristides de Sousa Mendes—the Man Who Saved the Lives of Countless Refugees in World War II* (New York: Carroll and Graf, 2001), pp. 55–56.
9. Ibid.
10. Wheeler, "And Who Is My Neighbour," p. 120.

11. For a summary of the development of the 30,000 number, see Milgram, "Portugal, the Consuls, and the Jewish Refugees, 1938–1941." Milgram quotes as the original source of this figure an article by Harry Ezratty in which Ezratty claimed that Sousa Mendes had saved the lives of 30,000 refugees out of which 10,000 were Jewish, "The Portuguese Consul and the 10,000 Jews," *Jewish Life* (September–October 1964), pp. 17–19.

12. PT/TT/AOS/CO/IN-8C/5/PVDE Report on Movements of Foreigners on Portugal's Borders for 1940.

13. Milgram, "Portugal, the Consuls, and the Jewish Refugees," p. 144.

14. Figure quoted from ibid.

Chapter 7—Retired, Outcast

1. Filipe Ribeiro de Meneses, *Salazar: A Political Biography* (New York: Enigma Books, 2009), p. 240.

2. From Pereira to Salazar, June 20, 1940, *Correspondência de Pedro Teotónio Pereira para Salazar: Vol. 2, 1940–1941* (Lisbon: Presidência Do Conselho de Ministros Comissão Do Livro Negro Sobre O Regime Fascista, 1989), pp. 48–49.

3. Arthur Koestler, *Scum of the Earth* (London: Eland, 2006), pp. 184–194.

4. Rui Afonso, *Aristides de Sousa Mendes: Um Homen Bom* (Lisbon: Texto, 2009), p. 179.

5. For copy of document, see Miriam Assor, *Aristides de Sousa Mendes: Um Justo Contra a Corrente* (Lisbon: Guerra e Paz, 2009), p. 99.

6. From Selby to Ministry of Foreign Affairs Lisbon, June 20, 1940, in Avraham Milgrim, *Portugal, Salazar e os Judeus* (Lisbon: Gradiva, 2010), p. 102.

7. Avraham Milgram, "Portugal, the Consuls, and the Jewish Refugees, 1938–1941," *Yad Vashem* 27 (Jerusalem 1999), p. 147.

8. Jose Alain Fralon, *A Good Man in Evil Times: The Story of Aristides de Sousa Mendes—the Man Who Saved the Lives of Countless Refugees in World War II* (New York: Carroll and Graf, 2001), pp. 110–111.

9. Ibid., p. 111.

10. Meneses, *Salazar*, p. 239.

11. Douglas Wheeler, "And Who Is My Neighbour? A World War II Hero of Conscience for Portugal," *Luso-Brazilian Review* 26, no. 1 (Summer 1989), p. 127.

12. For documents, see Assor, *Aristides de Sousa Mendes*, p. 117.

13. PT/TT/AOS/CP/178/ Letter from Aristides de Sousa Mendes to Salazar, April 2, 1941.

14. Fralon, *A Good Man in Evil Times*, p. 144.

15. Wheeler, "And Who Is My Neighbour," p. 130.

16. For an elaboration of this theory, see the early work of Rui Afonso.

17. Irene Flunser Pimentel, *Judeus em Portugal durante II Guerra Mundial: Em Fuga de Hitler e do Holocausto* (Lisbon: A Esfera dos Livors, 2006), p. 82.

18. PT/TT/AOS/CO/NE-4/ From Portuguese Embassy in Berlin to MFA Lisbon.

19. PT/TT/AOS/CO/NE-4//Report on "The New Order," by Portuguese Delegation in Berlin, November 15, 1941.

Chapter 8—The Jewish Question

1. On Franco's attitude, and the complex attitude of the Spanish right, towards the Jews, see Isabelle Rohr, *The Spanish Right and the Jews, 1898–1945: Anti-Semitism and Opportunism* (Brighton and Portland: Sussex Academic Press, 2008).

2. PRO/FO/371/24495/ From Embassy in Lisbon to Foreign Office, August 23, 1940.

3. PRO/FO/371/24495/ From Foreign Office to World Jewish Congress, September 24, 1940.

4. Douglas Wheeler, "In the Service of Order: the Portuguese Secret Police and the British, German and Spanish Intelligence, 1932–1945," *Journal of Contemporary History* 18, no. 1 (January 1983), p. 12.

5. NARA/RG84/1941:123–885.91/Classified General Records of the U.S. Embassy in Lisbon, 1924–1961/The Role of the International Police Organisation in Lisbon and its Attitude towards the Belligerents and the United States, December 5, 1941.

6. Wheeler, "In the Service of Order," p. 4.

7. PRO/FO/371/24495/Minute from Embassy in Lisbon to Foreign Office, October 24, 1940.

8. PRO/FO/371/24495/Correspondence from Foreign Office to Embassy in Lisbon, November 2, 1940.

9. PRO/FO/371/24495/Draft Minute from Foreign Office to Embassy in Lisbon, December 17, 1940.

10. PRO/AIR/40/1626/Secret Memo/ Foreign Office, April 1, 1941.

11. PRO/AIR/40/1626/Secret Memo/S.O.2/Mr Britain, January 17, 1941.

12. PRO/AIR/40/1626/Secret Memo/International Police at Lisbon/ April 5, 1941.

13. PRO/AIR/40/1626/Secret Memo/ Foreign Office, April 26, 1941.

14. PRO/AIR/40/1626/From Embassy in Lisbon to Foreign Office, May 13, 1941.

15. PRO/AIR/40/1626/Campbell to Foreign Office, July 17, 1941.

16. PRO/AIR/40/1626/Foreign Office to Lisbon, September 1, 1941.

17. PRO/AIR/40/1626/From Campbell to Salazar, October 29, 1941.

18. PRO/AIR/40/1626/Campbell to Foreign Office, November 27, 1941.

19. NARA/RG226/106/29/ From German Minister in Berlin to Foreign Office Berlin, August 9, 1941.

20. Ibid.

21. NARA/RG84/1941:123–885.91/Classified General Records of the U.S. Embassy in Lisbon, 1924–1961/The Role of the International Police Organisa-

tion in Lisbon and its Attitude towards the Belligerents and the United States, December 5, 1941.

22. PRO/AIR/40/1626/Campbell to Foreign Office, July 17, 1941.
23. Ibid.
24. Wheeler, "In the Service of Order," p. 7.
25. Ibid.
26. PRO/FO/371/31182/Records of Leading Personalities in Portugal 1942, September 25, 1942, p.14.
27. PT/TT/AOS/IN-8/30/PVDE Report on *Times* Journalist Walter Edward Lucas.
28. Ibid.
29. Filipe Ribeiro de Meneses, *Salazar: A Political Biography* (New York: Enigma Books, 2009), p. 252.
30. PT/TT/AOS/IN-8/30/PVDE Report on *Times* Journalist Walter Edward Lucas.
31. *Koenigsberger Allgemeine Zeitung*, January 7, 1941.
32. PT/TT/AOS/IN-8/30/PVDE Report on *Times* Journalist Walter Edward Lucas.
33. Ibid.
34. David Eccles, *By Safe Hand: The Letters of Sybil and David Eccles, 1939–1942* (London: Bodley Head, 1983), pp. 208–209.
35. PRO/FO/371/31182/Records of Leading Personalities in Portugal 1942, September 25, 1942, p. 14.

Chapter 9—On the Run

1. Philip Ziegler, *King Edward VIII: The Official Biography* (London: Collins, 1990), pp. 420–422.
2. Antony Beevor and Artemis Cooper, *Paris: After the Liberation, 1944–1945* (London: Penguin, 2007), p. 9.
3. Ibid.
4. Ziegler, *King Edward VIII*, pp. 420–422.
5. Ibid., p. 420.
6. Walter Schellenberg, *The Memoirs of Hitler's Spymaster* (London: Andre Deutsch, 2006), p. 133.
7. PT/TT/AOS/CO/NE-1A/18 King Carol II of Rumania arrives in Portugal July 1940.
8. Ibid.
9. "Life Visits a Haven for Exiled Royalty," *Life Magazine*, February 19, 1951, p. 130.
10. For a detailed account of the difficulties, see Samuel Hoare, *Ambassador on a Special Mission* (London: Collins, 1946).
11. Michael Bloch, *The Duke of Windsor's War* (London: Weidenfeld and Nicolson, 1982), p. 76.
12. From Pereira to Salazar, June 20, 1940, *Correspondência de Pedro Teotónio Pereira para Salazar: Vol.2, 1940–1941* (Lisbon: Presidência Do Conselho

de Ministros Comissão Do Livro Negro Sobre O Regime Fascista, 1989), pp. 48–49.

13. David Eccles, *By Safe Hand: The Letters of Sybil and David Eccles, 1939–1942* (London: Bodley Head, 1983), p. 144.

14. Bloch, *The Duke of Windsor's War*, p. 76.

15. Hoare, *Ambassador on a Special Mission*, p. 22.

16. Ibid.

17. Ibid., p. 34.

18. Ibid., p. 36.

19. Bloch, *The Duke of Windsor's War*, p. 79.

20. Ibid.

21. Richard Wigg, *Churchill and Spain: the Survival of the Franco Regime, 1940–1945* (Brighton and Portland: Sussex Academic Press, 2008), p. 14.

22. Ziegler, *King Edward VIII*, p. 422.

23. Paul Preston, *Franco: A Biography* (London: Basic Books, 1994), p. 366.

24. Ibid.

25. Ziegler, *King Edward VIII*, p. 426.

26. Lord Moran, *Churchill at War, 1940–1945* (London: Robinson, 2002), p. 116.

27. Carlos Alberto Damas, "Conspiração e Fantasia em Lisboa: Ricardo Espírito Santo e o Duque De Windsor," *Historia*, no. 62 (December 2003), p. 7.

28. When the Duke of Kent was asked if he wished to meet his brother before his own departure from Lisbon he is reported by a Portuguese diplomat assigned to his party to have answered, "Good God, no." Carlos Alberto Damas, "The Duke of Windsor and Ricardo Espírito Santo 1940," Centro de Investigação e Documentação da Historia, BES, Lisbon, undated, p. 1.

29. "Lisbon: Europe's Bottleneck," *Life Magazine*, April 28, 1941, p. 80.

30. *Hotel Palácio: Boletins de Alojamento de Estrangeiros*, (Cascais: Câmara Municipal de Cascais), 2004, p. 89.

31. Ibid., p. 133.

32. *Grande Hotel e Hotel Atlântico: Boletins de Alojamento de Estrangeiros*, (Cascais: Câmara Municipal de Cascais), 2005.

33. Ibid.

34. Carlos Alberto Damas, *Hotel Tivoli Lisbon: Tradition and Modernity in the Lisbon Hotel Industry, 1933–2008* (Lisbon: Banco Espírito Santo, 2008), p. 64.

35. Ibid, p. 65.

Chapter 10—Operation Willi

1. Michael Bloch, *Operation Willi: The Plot to Kidnap the Duke of Windsor, July 1940* (London: Weidenfeld and Nicolson, 1986), p. 70.

2. Ibid., p. 71.

3. Charles Higham, *Mrs Simpson: Secret Lives of the Duchess of Windsor* (London: Pan Books, 2004), p. 326.

4. David Eccles, *By Safe Hand: The Letters of Sybil and David Eccles, 1939–1942* (London: Bodley Head, 1983), pp. 110–111.
5. Higham, *Mrs Simpson*, p. 326.
6. PT/TT/AOS/O Diário de Salazar/ August 1, 1940, and August 6, 1940.
7. PT/TT/AOS/CO/NE-1A/17/Report of the PVDE on the Visit of the Duke of Windsor to Portugal.
8. "Traps for Duke of Windsor," *Times* (London), August 1, 1957.
9. Philip Ziegler, *King Edward VIII: The Official Biography* (London: Collins, 1990), p. 424.
10. Walter Schellenberg, *The Memoirs of Hitler's Spymaster* (London: Andre Deutsch, 2006), pp. 135–136.
11. Ibid., p. 130.
12. Ibid.
13. Martin Allen, *Hidden Agenda: How the Duke of Windsor Betrayed the Allies* (London: Macmillan, 2000), pp. 269–270.
14. Schellenberg, *The Memoirs of Hitler's Spymaster*.
15. Ibid., pp. 138–139.
16. Ziegler, *King Edward VIII*, p. 426.
17. Allen, *Hidden Agenda*, p. 265.
18. PT/TT/AOS/O Diário de Salazar.

Chapter 11—The Portuguese Banker

1. See Michael Bloch, *Operation Willi: The Plot to Kidnap the Duke of Windsor, July 1940* (London: Weidenfeld and Nicolson, 1986).
2. Martin Allen also suggests that Espírito Santo was a man with German sympathies, see Martin Allen, *Hidden Agenda: How the Duke of Windsor Betrayed the Allies* (London: Macmillan, 2000), 257.
3. PRO/FO/371/26804/From Campbell to Foreign Office, June 9, 1941.
4. PT/TT/AOS/CO/NE-1A/17/Report of the PVDE on the Visit of the Duke of Windsor to Portugal, July 5, 1940.
5. Ibid., July 5 and 6, 1940.
6. Ibid., July 5, 1940.
7. Ibid., July 6, 1940.
8. Ibid.
9. Ibid., July 10 and 24, 1940.
10. Ibid., July 8, 1940.
11. Bloch, *Operation Willi*, p. 112.
12. Ibid., p. 113.
13. PT/TT/AOS/CO/NE-1A/17/Report of the PVDE on the Visit of the Duke of Windsor to Portugal, July 10, 1940.
14. Ibid., July 12, 1940.
15. Ibid., July 11, 1940.
16. Ibid., July 12, 1940.
17. Ibid., July 13, 1940.

18. Bloch, *Operation Willi*, pp. 114–115.
19. Ibid.
20. PT/TT/AOS/CO/NE-1A/17/Report of the PVDE on the Visit of the Duke of Windsor to Portugal, July 23, 1940.
21. David Eccles, *By Safe Hand: The Letters of Sybil and David Eccles, 1939–1942* (London: Bodley Head, 1983), p. 132.
22. Ibid., p. 133.
23. Ibid., p. 139.
24. PT/TT/AOS/CO/NE-1A/17/Report of the PVDE on the Visit of the Duke of Windsor to Portugal, July 20, 1940.
25. Ibid., July 13, 1940.
26. Ibid., July 20, 1940.
27. Ibid., July 26, 1940.
28. Bloch, *Operation Willi*, p. 191.
29. Ibid.
30. Walford Selby, *Diplomatic Twilight, 1930–1940* (London: John Murray, 1953), p. 122.
31. Richard J. Evans, *The Third Reich at War: How the Nazis Led Germany from Conquest to Disaster* (London: Penguin, 2009), p. 137.
32. Ibid., pp. 137–138.

Chapter 12—Spanish Connections

1. PT/TT/AOS/O Diário de Salazar, September 3, 1940.
2. PRO/FO/371/36794/Report of Chiefs of Staff on Possible Military Help to Portugal, April 29, 1941.
3. For a detailed account, see Patrick Wilcken, *Empire Adrift: The Portuguese Court in Rio de Janeiro, 1808–1821* (London: Bloomsbury, 2004).
4. PRO/HS/6/978/Operation Panicle, May 19, 1941.
5. David Eccles, *By Safe Hand: The Letters of Sybil and David Eccles, 1939–1942* (London, Bodley Head, 1983).
6. PRO/FO/371/24491/Situation in Portugal and the Iberian Peninsula, June 24, 1940, p. 349.
7. On Spanish detailed plans for invasion, see Manuel Ros Agudo, *A Grande Tentação: Os Planos de Franco para Invadir Portugal* (Lisbon: Casa das Letras, 2009).
8. Filipe Ribeiro de Meneses, *Salazar: A Political Biography* (New York: Enigma Books, 2009), p. 254.
9. Eccles, *By Safe Hand*, pp. 103–104.
10. PT/TT/AOS/CP-64/Letter from Churchill to Salazar, September 24, 1940.
11. NARA/RG84/40/ General Correspondence of U.S. Embassy in Lisbon, 1941. From Fish to State Department, January 15, 1941, p. 1.
12. Ibid., p. 3.
13. Ibid., p. 2.
14. Ibid.

15. NARA/RG56/23/Classified Correspondence of Embassy in Lisbon, From Wood to U.S. Treasury, September 27, 1943, p. 4.
16. Ibid.
17. NARA/RG56/2/ General Records of the Embassy in Lisbon, Some Notes on the Situation in Portugal, July 31 1945, p. 8.
18. F. Norton Brandão, "Epidemiology of Venereal Disease in Portugal during the Second World War," *British Journal of Venereal Diseases* 36, no. 2 (1960), p. 136.
19. NARA/RG84/41/General Records of the Embassy in Lisbon/ From Fish to State Department, May 1, 1941, p. 1.
20. Ibid., p. 2.
21. Ibid., p. 1.
22. Ibid., p. 3.
23. Ibid., p. 1.
24. Ibid., p. 4.
25. Ibid., p. 5.

Chapter 13—Secret Jewish Rescue Lists

1. Peggy Guggenheim, *Out of This Century: Confessions of an Art Addict, the Autobiography of Peggy Guggenheim* (London: Andre Deutsch, 2005), p. 245.
2. Rosemary Bailey, *Love and War in the Pyrenees: A Story of Courage, Fear and Hope, 1939–1944* (London: Weidenfeld and Nicolson, 2008), p. 114.
3. Guggenheim, *Out of This Century*, p. 236.
4. Ibid.
5. Varian Fry, *Surrender on Demand* (Boulder, CO: Johnson Books, 1997), p. 186.
6. Ibid., p. 185.
7. Ibid.
8. Ibid., p. 184.
9. Ibid., p. 185.
10. Isabelle Rohr, *The Spanish Right and the Jews: Antisemitism and Opportunism* (Brighton and Portland: Sussex Academic Press, 2008), p. 108.
11. Guggenheim, *Out of This Century*, p. 235.
12. Ibid., p. 233.
13. Rohr, *The Spanish*, p. 108.
14. Guggenheim, *Out of This Century*, pp. 236–237.
15. Ibid., p. 236.
16. Rohr, *The Spanish*, p. 108.
17. Irwin Unger and Debi Unger, *The Guggenheims: A Family History* (New York: Harper Perennial, 2005), p. 419.
18. Guggenheim, *Out of This Century*, p. 237.
19. Mary Dearborn, *Peggy Guggenheim: Mistress of Modernism* (London: Virago, 2006), p. 209.
20. Unger and Unger, *The Guggenheims*, p. 419.

21. Guggenheim, *Out of This Century*, p. 244.
22. Ibid., p. 242.
23. Ibid., p. 243.
24. Ibid.
25. Dearborn, *Peggy Guggenheim*, p. 210.
26. Unger and Unger, *The Guggenheims*, p. 419.
27. Vicki Caron, *Uneasy Asylum: France and the Jewish Refugee Crisis, 1933–1942* (Stanford: Stanford University Press, 1999), p. 262.
28. Fry, *Surrender on Demand*, p. 198.
29. Ibid., pp. 199–200.
30. Ibid., pp. 202–203.
31. Ibid., p. 235.
32. Bailey, *Love and War in the Pyrenees*, p. 117.
33. Fry, *Surrender on Demand*, p. 235.
34. Douglas Wheeler, "In the Service of Order: The Portuguese Secret Police and the British, German and Spanish Intelligence, 1932–1945," *Journal of Contemporary History* 18, no. 1 (January 1983), p. 11.
35. Ibid., pp. 11–12.
36. Ibid., p. 12.
37. PRO/KV/1273/Emergency Certificate: Arthur Koester, November 10, 1940.
38. David Cesarani, *Arthur Koestler: The Homeless Mind* (London: Random House, 1998), p. 168.
39. PRO/KV/1273/Form for Interrogation: Arthur Koestler, November 7, 1940, p. 2.
40. Ibid., p. 3.
41. Michael Scammell, *Arthur Koestler: The Indispensable Intellectual* (London: Faber and Faber, 2009), pp. 223–224.
42. Ibid., p. 224.
43. NARA/RG56/23/Classified Correspondence of Embassy in Lisbon, From Wood to U.S. Treasury, September 27, 1943, p. 4.
44. Scammell, *Arthur Koestler*, p. 191.
45. Ibid.
46. PRO/KV/1273/Form for Interrogation: Arthur Koestler, November 7 1940, p. 3.
47. Cesarani, *Arthur Koestler*, p. 170.
48. PRO/KV/1273/Form for Interrogation: Arthur Koestler, November 7 1940, p. 1.
49. Ibid.
50. Ibid., p. 3.
51. Scammell, *Arthur Koestler*, pp. 194–195.

Chapter 14—Double Dealing

1. Christine Garnier, *Férias com Salazar* (Lisbon: A. M. Pereira e Grasset e Fasquelle, 1952), p. 63.

2. Ibid., p. 63.
3. Hugh Kay, *Salazar and Modern Portugal* (New York: Hawthorn Books, 1970), p. 171.
4. For an example of this British frustration, see PRO/FO/115/4018/From Eden and Halifax to Lisbon, March 16, 1944.
5. PT/TT/AOS/CO/NE-74/9/Record of Meeting between Salazar and Eccles, March 17, 1942.
6. NARA/RG84/15/Classfied Records of Embassy in Lisbon, War History of the U.S. Embassy in Lisbon, August 1, 1946, p. 34.
7. See William Medlicott, *The Economic Blockade* (London: HMSO, 1952).
8. Kay, *Salazar and Modern Portugal*, p. 172.
9. Leonard Caruana and Hugh Rockoff, "A Wolfram in Sheep's Clothing: Economic Warfare in Spain, 1940–1944," *The Journal of Economic History* 63, no. 1 (March 2003), p. 104.
10. Kay, *Salazar and Modern Portugal*, p. 173.
11. David Eccles, *By Safe Hand: The Letters of Sybil and David Eccles, 1939–1942* (London: Bodley Head, 1983), p. 98.
12. PT/TT/AOS/Diário de Salazar/ Entries from 1941-end 1944. See for example entries into diary for February 29, 1944; March 2, 1944; March 3, 1944; March 6, 1944; March 7, 1944; March 9, 1944; and March 13, 1944.
13. Douglas Wheeler, "The Price of Neutrality: Portugal, the Wolfram Question and World War II–Part Two," *Luso-Brazilian Review* 23, no. 2 (Winter 1986), p. 107.
14. Christian Leitz, *Nazi Germany and Neutral Europe during the Second World War* (Manchester: Manchester University Press, 2000), p. 156.
15. António Telo, *Portugal Na Segunda Guerra, 1941–1945, Vol. 1* (Lisbon: Vega, 1991), pp. 188–189.
16. NARA/RG84/15/Classified Records of Embassy in Lisbon, War History of the U.S. Embassy in Lisbon, August 1, 1946, p. 40.
17. Wheeler, "The Price of Neutrality," p. 115.
18. NARA/RG84/15/Classified Records of Embassy in Lisbon, War History of the U.S. Embassy in Lisbon, August 1, 1946, p. 40.
19. Nicholas Tarling, "Britain, Portugal and East Timor in 1941," *Journal of South East Asian Studies* 27, no. 1 (March 1996), p. 135.
20. Llewellyn Woodward, *British Foreign Policy in the Second World War* (London: H. M. Stationery Office, 1962), p. 376.
21. Werner Levi, "Portuguese Timor and the War," *Far Eastern Survey* 15, no. 14 (July 17, 1946), p. 221.
22. Woodward, *British Foreign Policy*, p. 376.
23. Ibid.
24. Tarling, "Britain, Portugal and East Timor," p. 137.
25. Levi, "Portuguese Timor and the War," p. 222.
26. Woodward, *British Foreign Policy*, p. 377.
27. Levi, "Portuguese Timor and the War," p. 222.
28. Tarling, "Britain, Portugal and East Timor," p. 137.

29. Woodward, *British Foreign Policy*, p. 377.
30. Tarling, "Britain, Portugal and East Timor in 1941," p. 138.
31. Woodward, *British Foreign*, p. 378.
32. Wheeler, "The Price of Neutrality," p. 108.
33. Leitz, *Nazi Germany and Neutral*, p. 159.
34. Telo, *Portugal Na Segunda Guerra*, p. 189.
35. Leitz, *Nazi Germany and Neutral*, p. 159.
36. Ibid.
37. Telo, *Portugal Na Segunda Guerra*, p. 190.
38. Wheeler, "The Price of Neutrality," p. 110.
39. PT/TT/AOS/CO/NE-4C1/5/From Duke of Palmela to Salazar, December 18, 1943.

Chapter 15—Under Pressure

1. Leonard Caruana and Hugh Rockoff, "A Wolfram in Sheep's Clothing: Economic Warfare in Spain, 1940–1944," *The Journal of Economic History* 63, no. 1 (March 2003), p. 119.
2. Douglas Wheeler, "The Price of Neutrality: Portugal, the Wolfram Question and World War II–Part Two," *Luso-Brazilian Review* 23, no. 2 (Winter 1986), p. 101.
3. J. K. Sweeney, "The Portuguese Wolfram Embargo: A Case Study in Economic Warfare," *Military Affairs* 38, no. 1 (February 1974), p. 26.
4. Ibid.
5. NARA/RG56/23/Classified Records of the Embassy in Lisbon, From Wood to White, August 27, 1943, p. 2.
6. Ibid.
7. Wheeler, "The Price of Neutrality," p. 102.
8. NARA/RG56/2/ Some Notes on the Situation in Portugal, July 31, 1944, p. 1.
9. Ibid.
10. Ibid., p. 19.
11. NARA/State Department Special Interrogation Mission, Baron Oswald von Hoyningen-Huene, October 2, 1944, p. 3.
12. Ibid., p. 7.
13. Sweeney, "The Portuguese Wolfram Embargo," p. 24.
14. PRO/FO/371/26795/From Campbell to Eden, July 2, 1941.

Chapter 16—Shocked to Discover That Spying Is Going On

1. "Lisbon: Europe's Bottleneck," *Life Magazine*, April 28, 1941, p. 78.
2. Ibid.
3. Ibid.
4. *Hotel Palácio: Boletins de Alojamento de Estrangeiros* (Cascais: Câmara Municipal de Cascais, 2004), pp. 176–177.
5. PRO/ADM/223/490/From Hillgarth to DNI, November 20, 1941.

6. Andrew Lycett, *Ian Fleming* (London: Phoenix, 2008), p. 169.
7. PRO/ADM/223/490/From Fleming to Godfrey, Admiralty, August 11, 1941.
8. David Eccles, *By Safe Hand: The Letters of Sybil and David Eccles, 1939–1942* (London: Bodley Head, 1983), p. 303.
9. PRO/ADM/223/490/From Fleming to Godfrey, Admiralty, August 11, 1941.
10. Ibid.
11. Lycett, *Ian Fleming*, p. 127.
12. Ibid., 128.
13. PRO/ADM/223/490/From Fleming to Godfrey, Admiralty, August 11, 1941.
14. Neville Wylie, "An Amateur Learns His Job? Special Operations Executive in Portugal, 1940–1942," *Journal of Contemporary History* 36, no. 3 (July 2001), pp. 450–452.
15. PRO/HS/6/987/German Espionage Activities in Portugal, from Campbell to Salazar, April 1, 1942, pp. 2–3.
16. For an example, see PRO/HS/6/987/Memorandum, November 24, 1942, pp. 1–2.
17. M. R. D. Foot, *SOE: Special Operations Executive, 1940–1946* (London: Pimlico, 1999), p. 1.
18. Ibid., p. 34.
19. Ibid., p. 35.
20. Ibid., p. 36.
21. PRO/HS/6/981/Memorandum on Wolfram, February 5, 1944, p. 1.
22. PRO/HS/6/981/Top Secret Memorandum From OB.004, April 25, 1944, p. 1.
23. Wylie, "An Amateur Learns His Job?," p. 444.
24. J. G. Beevor, *SOE: Recollections and Reflections, 1940–1945* (London: Bodley Head, 1981), p. 31.
25. Ibid.
26. Ibid., p. 36.
27. Ibid., p. 37.
28. Ibid., p. 39.
29. PRO/HS/6/978/Memorandum on Changes to Operation Panicle, July 5, 1941, p. 1.
30. PRO/HS/6/978/Operation Panicle, May 19, 1941, p. 3.
31. PRO/FO/371/36794/Report of Chiefs of Staff on Possible Military Help to Portugal, April 29, 1941.
32. PRO/HS/6/978/Memorandum on Changes to Operation Panicle, July 5, 1941, p. 1.
33. Ibid., p. 2.
34. Ibid.
35. PRO/HS/6/978/Operation Panicle, May 19, 1941, Appendix 1.
36. PRO/HS/6/978/Memorandum on Changes to Operation Panicle, July 5, 1941, p. 2.
37. Ibid.
38. PRO/HS/6/978/Operation Panicle, May 19, 1941, Appendix 1.

39. PRO/HS/6/978/Operation Panicle, May 19, 1941.
40. Wylie, "An Amateur Learns His Job?," p. 449.
41. PRO/HS/6/943/SOE Activities in Portugal, November 12, 1945, p. 1.
42. PRO/HS/6/987/From Campbell to Foreign Office, March 5, 1942.
43. Ibid.
44. Ibid.
45. Ibid.
46. PRO/HS/6/943/SOE Activities in Portugal, November 12, 1945, p. 1.
47. PRO/HS/6/987/From Campbell to Foreign Office, March 11, 1942.
48. Ibid., March 14, 1942.
49. PRO/HS/6/987/From Campbell to Foreign Office (Memo 1), March 17, 1942.
50. Ibid.
51. PRO/HS/6/987/From Campbell to Foreign Office, (Memo 2) March, 17, 1942.
52. Ibid.
53. PRO/HS/6/987/From Campbell to Foreign Office, March 21, 1942.
54. PRO/HS/6/987SOE Memorandum, March 21, 1942.
55. Ibid.
56. PRO/HS/6/987/Foreign Office to Campbell, March 25, 1942.
57. PRO/HS/6/987/SOE Memorandum, March 21, 1942.
58. PRO/HS/6/987/From Cadogan to Jebb, MEF, March 26, 1942.
59. PRO/HS/6/987/From Campbell to Foreign Office, March 22, 1942.
60. Ibid., March 17, 1942.
61. Ibid., March 22, 1942.
62. Ibid., March 26, 1942.
63. Ibid.
64. PRO/HS/6/987/SOE/From AD to CEO, March 28, 1942.
65. PRO/HS/6/943/SOE Activities in Portugal, November 12, 1945, p. 2.
66. PRO/HS/6/987/Foreign Office to Campbell, March 25, 1942.
67. PRO/HS/6/987/From Campbell to Foreign Office, March 27, 1942.
68. PRO/HS/6/943/SOE Activities in Portugal, November 12, 1945, p. 2.
69. PRO/HS/6/987/SOE/From AD to CEO, March 28, 1942.
70. PRO/HS/6/987From Lisbon to SOE, March 27, 1942.
71. PRO/HS/6/987/SOE/From AD to CEO, March 28, 1942.
72. PRO/HS/6/987/From Jebb to Cadogan, March 31, 1942, p. 2.
73. PRO/HS/6/987/Foreign Office to Campbell, March 31, 1942.

Chapter 17—The Dossier

1. J. G. Beevor, *SOE: Recollections and Reflections, 1940–1945* (London: Bodley Head, 1981), p. 41.
2. PRO/HS/6/987/From Campbell to Foreign Office, April 2, 1942.
3. Beevor, *SOE*, p. 41.
4. PRO/HS/6/987/From Campbell to Foreign Office, April 2, 1942.

5. Kim Philby, *My Silent War: The Autobiography of a Spy* (New York: The Modern Library, 2002), pp. 56–57.

6. In his account of events Philby mistakenly describes Sampaio as the Minister of Foreign Affairs, a portfolio actually held by Salazar.

7. Philby, *My Silent War*, p. 58.

8. Ibid., p. 59.

9. Beevor, *SOE*, p. 41.

10. PRO/HS/6/987/From Campbell to Foreign Office, April 21, 1942.

11. Beevor, *SOE*, pp. 42–43.

12. Ibid.

13. Ibid.

14. PRO/HS/6/987/Report on German Espionage Activities in Portugal, April 1, 1942, p. 1.

15. Ibid., p. 2.

16. PRO/HS/6/987/Subsection/German Sabotage Organisation in Portugal, April 1, 1942, p. 2.

17. PRO/HS/6/987/Subsection/German Influence in the PVDE, April 1, 1942, p. 3.

18. PRO/KV/3/171/From White to London, August 5, 1941.

19. PRO/KV/3/175/Result of Police Investigation into Axis Espionage in Lisbon, July 1, 1943, p. 1.

20. PRO/ADM/223/490/Salazar to Campbell, May 29, 1943.

21. PRO/KV/3/175/Result of Police Investigation into Axis Espionage in Lisbon, July 1, 1943, p. 1.

22. Ibid., p. 2.

23. Philby, *My Silent War*, p. 59.

24. PRO/ADM/223/490/From Campbell to Foreign Office, June 21, 1943.

Chapter 18—Agents and Double Agents

1. Ben Macintyre, *Agent Zigzag: The True Wartime Story of Eddie Chapman: Lover, Betrayer, Hero, Spy* (London: Bloomsbury, 2007), p. 201.

2. PRO/KV/3/171/German Intelligence Organisation in the Iberian Peninsula, February 19, 1941, p. 9.

3. Keith Jeffery, *MI6: The History of the Secret Intelligence Service, 1909–1949* (London: Bloomsbury, 2010), p. 409.

4. PRO/KV/3/175/Extract from Report on Abwehr Organisation on Portugal, July 28, 1945, p. 1.

5. Ibid., p. 2.

6. PRO/KV/3/171/German Intelligence Organisation in the Iberian Peninsula, February 19, 1941, p. 9.

7. Nigel West, *MI6: British Secret Intelligence Service Operations, 1909–1945* (London: Panther, 1985), p. 311.

8. M. R. D. Foot, *SOE: Special Operations Executive, 1940–1946* (London: Pimlico, 1999), p. 35.

9. West, *MI6*, p. 311.
10. Ibid., p. 229.
11. Kim Philby, *My Silent War: The Autobiography of a Spy* (New York: The Modern Library, 2002), p. 78.
12. Jeffery, *MI6: The History*, p. 408.
13. On the issue of a stay-behind force there was clearly some overlap with the activities of SOE.
14. Jeffery, *MI6: The History*, p. 408.
15. Ibid., p. 409.
16. West, *MI6*, p. 306.
17. Philby, *My Silent War*, p. 57.
18. Ibid., p. 58.
19. West, *MI6*, p. 306.
20. Ibid., p. 307.
21. Thomas Holt, *The Deceivers: Allied Military Deception in the Second World War* (London: Phoenix, 2005), p. 59.
22. Ibid., p. 60.
23. Christopher Andrew, *The Defence of the Realm: The Authorised History of MI5* (London: Allen Lane, 2009), p. 253.
24. Ibid., p. 254.
25. Nicholas Rankin, *Churchill's Wizards: The British Genius for Deception, 1914–1945* (London: Faber and Faber, 2009), p. 482.
26. Ibid.
27. Andrew, *The Defence of the Realm*, p. 254.
28. Rankin, *Churchill's Wizards*, pp. 482–483.
29. Andrew, *The Defence of the Realm*, p. 254.
30. Rankin, *Churchill's Wizards*, p. 482.
31. Andrew, *The Defence of the Realm*, p. 254.
32. Jeffery, *MI6*, p. 570.
33. Andrew, *The Defence of the Realm*, p. 254.
34. Jeffery, *MI6*, p. 570.
35. Ben Macintyre, *Operation Mincemeat: The True Spy Story that Changed the Course of World War II* (London: Bloomsbury, 2010), p. 162.
36. PRO/KV3/175/Abwehr Report from Lisbon, March 1, 1944, p. 1.

Chapter 19—Death of a Hollywood Star

1. PRO/BW/1/20/From British Council to Mrs. Howard, June 3, 1943.
2. PRO/BW/1/20/Foreign Office Memorandum on Leslie Howard, June 15, 1971.
3. PRO/BW/1/20/From British Institute Madrid to British Council London, June 4, 1943.
4. Ibid., May 28, 1943, p. 1.
5. PRO/BW/1/20/Spain and Portugal: Mr. Leslie Howard, February 24, 1943.
6. PRO/BW/1/20/From British Institute Madrid to British Council London, May 28, 1943, p. 1.

7. PRO/BW/1/20/Spain and Portugal: Mr. Leslie Howard, February 24, 1943.
8. PRO/BW/1/20/From British Institute Madrid to British Council London, May 28, 1943, p. 2.
9. Ibid., p. 3.
10. Naomi Shepherd, *A Refuge from Darkness: Wilfrid Israel and the Rescue of the Jews* (New York: Pantheon, 1984), pp. 249–250.
11. Ibid., p. 250.
12. Ibid.
13. Winston Churchill, *The Second World War: VOL. 4, The Hinge of Fate* (London: Folio Society, 2000), p. 667.
14. Shepherd, *A Refuge from Darkness*, p. 249.
15. Douglas Wheeler, "World War II: Leslie Howard May Have Helped Britain Win," *St. Louis Post*, May 4, 2005.
16. Keith Jeffery, *MI6: The History of the Secret Intelligence Service, 1909–1949* (London: Bloomsbury, 2010), p. 747.
17. Ibid., p. 563.
18. Ibid., p. 747.
19. "The Man Who Told Berlin," *The Evening Standard*, December 13, 1943.
20. PRO/KV/2/1930/SIS File on Weltzein, 1941–1943.
21. PRO/KV/2/1930/ SIS Memorandum, February 14, 1942.
22. PRO/KV/2/1930/SIS File on Axis Agents Operating in Portugal, 1941–1942.
23. PRO/KV/2/1930/ SIS Memorandum, October 22, 1942.
24. Douglas Wheeler, "In the Service of Order: The Portuguese Secret Police and the British, German and Spanish Intelligence, 1932–1945," *Journal of Contemporary History* 18, no. 1 (January 1983), pp. 10–11.

Chapter 20—Farewell to Friends

1. PRO/BW/1/20/ From Director of British Council to Foreign Office, June 4, 1943.
2. The presence of detailed flower arrangements on the table is a Portuguese tradition for formal meals such as celebrations, holy days, and birthdays.
3. Isabelle Rohr, *The Spanish Right and the Jews, 1898–1945: Antisemitism and Opportunism* (Brighton and Portland: Sussex Academic Press, 2008), p. 123.
4. WL/1514/5/Correspondence from Wilfrid Israel to Diana Israel, March 1943.
5. Naomi Shepherd, *A Refuge from Darkness: Wilfrid Israel and the Rescue of the Jews* (New York: Pantheon, 1984), p. 239.
6. PRO/FO/371/36635/Foreign Office Minute, April 5, 1943.
7. PRO/FO/371/36633/From Campbell to Foreign Office, March 16, 1943.
8. PRO/FO/371/36633/From Foreign Office to Campbell, March 11, 1943.
9. Shepherd, *A Refuge from Darkness* (New York: Pantheon, 1984), p. 240.
10. Ibid., p. 241.
11. Ibid., p. 244.

12. PRO/FO/371/36639/Results of the Work of Mr. Wilfrid Israel, June 7, 1943.
13. PRO/FO/371/36639/From Jewish Agency to Foreign Office, June 7, 1943.
14. PRO/FO/371/36639/Hoare to Eden, June 7, 1943.
15. NARA/RG84/77/General Records of the Embassy in Lisbon, Report of the Aeronautic Board, September 7, 1943, p. 3.
16. NARA/RG84/77/General Records of the Embassy in Lisbon, From Fish to State Department, February 23, 1943.
17. NARA/RG84/77/General Records of the Embassy in Lisbon, Report of the Aeronautic Board, September 7, 1943, p. 16.
18. Ibid., p. 3.
19. NARA/RG84/77/General Records of the Embassy in Lisbon, From Embassy to Sampaio, Ministry of Foreign Affairs Lisbon, May 31, 1943.
20. "Trials: Ten Years Later," *Time*, March 23, 1953.
21. NARA/RG84/77/General Records of the Embassy in Lisbon, Internal Memo from Booker, February 26, 1943.
22. NARA/RG84/77/General Records of the Embassy in Lisbon, Report of the Aeronautic Board, September 7, 1943, p. 17.
23. "Trials: Ten Years Later."

Chapter 21—Ancient Alliance

1. PT/TT/AOS/Diário de Salazar, November 7, 1943.
2. António de Figueiredo, *Portugal: Fifty Years of Dictatorship* (London: Penguin, 1975), p. 99.
3. Ibid.
4. Hugh Kay, *Salazar and Modern Portugal: A Biography* (New York: Hawthorn, 1970), p. 160.
5. PT/TT/AOS/CO/NE/1C/6/From Churchill to Salazar, November 7, 1942.
6. Ibid.
7. Ibid.
8. PRO/FO/371/34656/From Campbell to Foreign Office, April 1, 1943.
9. PT/TT/AOS/CO/NE/1C/6/From Roosevelt to Salazar, November 8, 1942.
10. Kay, *Salazar and Modern Portugal*, p. 160.
11. PRO/FO/371/34657/Foreign Office Aide Memoire, June 29, 1943.
12. PRO/FO/371/34656/From Campbell to Foreign Office, April 1, 1943.
13. PRO/FO/371/34657/Foreign Office Aide Memoire, June 29, 1943.
14. PRO/FO/371/34656/From Campbell to Foreign Office, April 1, 1943.
15. PRO/FO/371/34656/From Campbell to Eden, June 11, 1943.
16. PRO/FO/371/34656/From Campbell to Foreign Office, April 1, 1943.
17. PRO/FO/371/34690/From Campbell to Foreign Office, March 24, 1943.
18. PRO/FO/371/34656/From Campbell to Foreign Office, April 1, 1943.
19. Llewellyn Woodward, *British Foreign Policy in the Second World War* (London: H. M. Stationery Office, 1962), p. 375.
20. Ibid., p. 378.
21. Ibid., p. 379.

22. PRO/FO/371/34657/Foreign Office Aide Memoire, June 29, 1943.
23. Woodward, *British Foreign Policy*, p. 379.
24. PRO/WO/106/2934/Operation Lifebelt: Alternative Plan, Report by Joint Chiefs of Staff, July 8, 1943.
25. PRO/FO/371/34656/From Campbell to Foreign Office, April 1, 1943.

Chapter 22—Reluctant Participant

1. António de Oliveira Salazar, *Pensamento e Doutrina Politica Textos Antológicos* (Lisbon: Verbo, 2007), p. 371.
2. PRO/FO/371/34657/Foreign Office Aide Memoire, June 29, 1943.
3. Salazar, *Pensamento e Doutrina*, p. 371.
4. Ibid., p. 372.
5. PT/TT/AOS/Diário de Salazar, June 23, 1943.
6. PRO/FO/371/34656/From Campbell to Foreign Office, June 24, 1943.
7. Salazar, *Pensamento e Doutrina*, p. 374.
8. PRO/FO/371/34656/From Campbell to Foreign Office, June 24, 1943.
9. Salazar, *Pensamento e Doutrina*, p. 372.
10. PRO/FO/371/34657/Foreign Office Aide Memoire, June 29, 1943.
11. Salazar, *Pensamento e Doutrina*, pp. 372–373.
12. PRO/FO/371/34656/From Campbell to Foreign Office, June 24, 1943.
13. Salazar, *Pensamento e Doutrina*, p. 373.
14. Llewellyn Woodward, *British Foreign Policy in the Second World War* (London: H. M. Stationery Office, 1962), p. 380.
15. PRO/FO/371/34658/Views of the Ministry of Economic Warfare, June 30, 1943.
16. Ibid.
17. Ibid.
18. PRO/FO/371/34657/Campbell to Foreign Office, June 26, 1943.
19. PRO/FO/371/34657/Foreign Office Minute, June 29, 1943.
20. PRO/FO/371/34657/Campbell to Foreign Office, June 26, 1943.
21. PRO/FO/371/34657/Campbell to Foreign Office, June 27, 1943.
22. Fernando Rosas, Júlia Leitão, and Pedro de Oliveira, *Armindo Monteiro e Oliveira Salazar: Correspondência Politica, 1926–1955* (Lisbon: Editorial Estampa, 1996), pp. 409–412.
23. PRO/FO/371/34657/From Foreign Office to Campbell, June 28, 1943.
24. Ibid.
25. Rosas, Leitão, and Oliveira, *Armindo Monteiro e Oliveira Salazar*, pp. 413–433.
26. Ibid., p. 414.
27. Ibid., p. 422.
28. Ibid., p. 422.
29. PT/TT/AOS/Diário de Salazar, July 1, 1943.
30. Rosas, Leitão, and Oliveira, *Armindo Monteiro e Oliveira Salazar*, p. 435.
31. Ibid., p. 438.

32. Franco Nogueira, *Salazar: Volume 3, As Grandes Crises, 1936–1945* (Porto: Civilização Editora, 2000), p. 452.

Chapter 23—A Painful Set of Negotiations

1. PT/TT/AOS/Diário de Salazar, July 3, 1943.
2. António de Oliveira Salazar, *Pensamento e Doutrina Politica Textos Antológicos* (Lisbon: Verbo, 2007), p. 378.
3. António Ferro, *Salazar: Portugal and Her Leader* (London: Faber and Faber, 1939), p. 328.
4. PRO/FO/371/34657/Draft Minute from the Prime Minister to Lord Selborne, June 28, 1943.
5. Ibid.
6. PRO/FO/371/34657/ Foreign Office Minute, United States Guarantee of Portuguese Colonial Integrity, August 11, 1943.
7. Llewellyn Woodward, *British Foreign Policy in the Second World War* (London: H. M. Stationery Office, 1962), p. 380.
8. Ibid.
9. From Admiral D. Leahy, Chief of Staff to the Commander of the Army and Navy to the Secretary of State, July 7, 1943, *Foreign Relations of the United States*, Vol. 2, 1943, p. 538.
10. Ibid.
11. From the Secretary of State to Winant, Ambassador in Britain, July 26, 1943, *FRUS 2*, p. 539.
12. From Winant to the Secretary of State, August 5 1943, *FRUS 2*, p. 540.
13. Aide Memoire from the State Department to the British Embassy in Washington, September 27, 1943, *FRUS 2*, p. 545.
14. Salazar, *Pensamento e Doutrina*, p. 378.
15. Ibid.
16. Woodward, *British Foreign Policy*, p. 381.
17. PRO/PREM/3/362/3/Minute from Winston Churchill, July 19, 1943.
18. Salazar, *Pensamento e Doutrina*, p. 382.
19. Woodward, *British Foreign Policy*, p. 381.
20. From the Secretary of State to Caffery, Ambassador in Britain, October 6, 1943, *FRUS 2*, p. 548.
21. From the Secretary of State to Winant, August 12, 1943, *FRUS 2*, p. 541.
22. From Churchill to President Roosevelt, October 8, 1943, *FRUS 2*, p. 550.
23. Ibid., p. 551.
24. Ibid., p. 554.
25. From President Roosevelt to Salazar, November 4, 1943, *FRUS 2*, p. 564.
26. From President Roosevelt to Embassy in London, November 8, 1943, *FRUS 2*, p. 565.
27. Salazar, *Pensamento e Doutrina*, pp. 385–387.
28. From Kennan to Secretary of State, November 22, 1943, *FRUS 2*, p. 566.

29. Aide Memoire from the British Embassy in Washington to the Department of State, August 18, 1943, *FRUS 2*, p. 543.
30. Woodward, *British Foreign Policy*, p. 382.
31. PRO/FO/371/34657/Memorandum from Secretary of State to Winant, June 29, 1943.
32. From Kennan to Secretary of State, November 23, 1943, *FRUS 2*, p. 567.
33. Woodward, *British Foreign Policy*, p. 382.
34. Ibid., p. 383.

Chapter 24—The Cost of Doing Business

1. NARA/State Department Special Interrogation Mission, Interview with Baron von Hoyningen-Huene, October 11, 1945, p. 3.
2. NARA/RG457/8/Magic Diplomatic Summary, November 2, 1943.
3. Ibid.
4. PRO/WO/106/2935/War Cabinet Joint Intelligence Sub-Committee, Attack on Portugal, September 11, 1943.
5. From Roosevelt to Churchill, June 30, 1943, *Foreign Relations of the United States*, Vol. 2, 1943, p. 536.
6. From Churchill to Roosevelt, July 3, 1943, *Foreign Relations of the United States*, Vol. 2, 1943, p. 537.
7. Ibid.
8. PRO/WO/106/2935/War Cabinet Joint Intelligence Sub-Committee, Attack on Portugal, September 11, 1943, p. 1.
9. PRO/FO/371/34706/ "Portugal Ambassador to Britain," *Times*, September 15, 1943.
10. PRO/FO/371/34706/From Campbell to Foreign Office, September 12, 1943.
11. PRO/FO/371/34706/From Campbell to Foreign Office, September 9, 1943.
12. PRO/FO/371/34706/Campbell to Foreign Office, October 16, 1943.
13. PRO/FO/371/34706/Campbell to Foreign Office, October 21, 1943.
14. Ibid.

Chapter 25—Nazi Gold

1. NARA/RG84/94/General Records of the Embassy in Lisbon/From Norweb to State Department, May 25, 1944.
2. NARA/RG84/94/General Records of the Embassy in Lisbon/From Crocker to State Department, February 15, 1944.
3. NARA/RG84/94/General Records of the Embassy in Lisbon/From Norweb to State Department, August 24, 1944.
4. NARA/RG84/102/General Records of the Embassy in Lisbon/From Crocker to Secretary of State, May 13, 1944.
5. Ibid.

6. Ibid.
7. NARA/RG226/893/From the Naval Attaché to Washington, Brief, May 15, 1944.
8. PT/TT/AOS/CO/IN-8D-17B/ 21ST Report of the PVDE, June 23, 1943, p. 10.
9. António Telo, *A Neutralidade Portuguesa e o Ouro Nazi* (Lisbon: Quetzal Editores, 2000), p. 215.
10. NARA/RG84/90/General Records of the Embassy in Lisbon, Gold Imports into Portugal: Two Aspects, October 12, 1944, p. 2.
11. NARA/RG56/23/Sale of Contaminated Gold by Bank of Portugal, July 27, 1943.
12. PRO/FO/371/39642/Foreign Office Minute, BBC Report Gold Shipment to Lisbon, July 4, 1944.
13. Ibid.
14. NARA/RG84/90/General Records of the Embassy in Lisbon, From Norweb to Secretary of State, July 18, 1944; also July 10, 1944.
15. NARA/RG84/90/General Records of the Embassy in Lisbon, Memorandum, Gold from Germany, July 10, 1944.
16. NARA/RG84/90/General Records of the Embassy in Lisbon, From Ives to Dexter, Memorandum, August 26, 1944.
17. Ibid.
18. NARA/RG84/90/General Records of the Embassy in Lisbon, Memorandum, Gold from Germany, July 10, 1944.
19. NARA/RG84/90/General Records of the Embassy in Lisbon, Supplementary to Memorandum, Gold from Germany dated July 10, 1944, and July 12, 1944.
20. NARA/RG84/90/General Records of the Embassy in Lisbon, From Norweb to Secretary of State, July 18, 1944, also July 10, 1944.
21. NARA/RG84/90/General Records of the Embassy in Lisbon, From Dickerson to State Department, October 12, 1944.
22. Filipe Ribeiro de Meneses, *Salazar: A Political Biography* (New York: Enigma Books, 2009), p. 331.
23. António Louça and Ansgar Schafer, "Portugal and the Nazi Gold: The Lisbon Connection in the Sale of Looted Gold by the Third Reich," *Yad Vashem*, Jerusalem, n.d., p. 2.
24. History Notes: Nazi Gold Information from the British Archives, no. 11, Foreign and Commonwealth Office, January 1997, p. 1.

Chapter 26—Golden Triangle

1. PT/TT/AOS/CO/NE-2/16/Record of Meetings on German Payments for Wolfram, April 30–May 27, 1942.
2. Ibid., May 18, 1942.
3. Ibid., May 20, 1942.
4. Ibid., May 26, 1942.

5. Ibid., May 27, 1942.
6. Tom Bower, *Nazi Gold: The Full Story of the Fifty Year Swiss-Nazi Conspiracy to Steal Billions from Europe's Jews and Holocaust Survivors* (London: HarperCollins, 1997), p. 53.
7. History Notes: Nazi Gold Information from the British Archives, no. 11, Foreign and Commonwealth Office, January 1997, p. 4.
8. Christian Leitz, *Nazi Germany and Neutral Europe during the Second World War* (Manchester: Manchester University Press, 2000), p. 161.
9. History Notes: Nazi Gold Information from the British Archives, No. 11, Foreign and Commonwealth Office, January 1997, p. 4.
10. Leitz, *Nazi Germany and Neutral Europe*, p. 161.
11. António Louça and Ansgar Schafer, "Portugal and the Nazi Gold: The Lisbon Connection in the Sale of Looted Gold by the Third Reich," *Yad Vashem*, Jerusalem, n.d., p. 3.
12. Ibid., p. 4.
13. Stuart Eizenstat, *Imperfect Justice: Looted Assets, Slave Labor, and the Unfinished Business of World War II* (New York: PublicAffairs, 2003), p. 50.
14. Ibid., p. 104.
15. Ibid.
16. NARA/RG84/90/General Records of the Embassy in Lisbon/Suggestions of Making and Inventory of Enemy Assets in Portugal, September 6, 1944.
17. Ibid.
18. Bower, *Nazi Gold*, p. 53.
19. NARA/RG84/90/General Records of the Embassy in Lisbon/Flight of Axis Capital, August 23, 1944.
20. NARA/RG84/90/General Records of the Embassy in Lisbon, Gold Imports into Portugal: Two Aspects, October 12, 1944.
21. NARA/RG56/23/From Wood to White, Assistant Secretary of Treasury, September 27, 1943.
22. Ibid.
23. NARA/RG226/744/ From Naval Attaché to Washington, Brief, February 15, 1944.
24. NARA/RG84/90/General Records of the Embassy in Lisbon, Gold Imports into Portugal: Two Aspects, October 12, 1944, p. 1.
25. Ibid.
26. NARA/RG131/346/From Post to Fleischer, Activities of Portuguese Banks, December 22, 1944.
27. Ibid.
28. NARA/RG131/346/ From Embassy in Lisbon to Secretary of State, March 3, 1943.
29. Ibid.
30. NARA/RG169/91/From London to Secretary of State, Washington, June 1, 1944.
31. NARA/RG169/91/From American Embassy London to Secretary of State, June 22, 1944.

32. NARA/RG169/91/From London to Secretary of State, Washington, June 1, 1944.
33. NARA/RG56/23/Memorandum, Control of Banks in Portugal, June 8, 1944.
34. NARA/RG56/23/Classified Correspondence of Embassy in Lisbon, From Wood to U.S. Treasury, September 27, 1943, p. 2.
35. Ibid., p. 4.
36. NARA/RG56/2/Some Notes on the Situation in Portugal, July 31, 1944, p. 6.
37. PRO/FO/371/49534/Leading Personalities in Portugal, September 20, 1947.
38. NARA/RG84/90/General Records of the Embassy in Lisbon, Gold Imports into Portugal: Two Aspects, October 12, 1944, p. 3.
39. Ibid.
40. History Notes: Nazi Gold Information from the British Archives, Foreign and Commonwealth Office, No. 11, January 1997, p. 4.

Chapter 27—Safehaven and War Criminals

1. Stuart Eizenstat, *Imperfect Justice: Looted Assets, Slave Labor, and the Unfinished Business of World War II* (New York: PublicAffairs, 2003), p. 50.
2. Ibid.
3. NARA/RG256/190/From Naval Attaché to Washington, Brief, September 1, 1944.
4. Ibid.
5. Ibid.
6. PT/TT/AOS/CO/NE-2/26/US Embassy to Ministry of Foreign Affairs Lisbon, February 12, 1945.
7. PT/TT/AOS/CO/NE-4/2/ Economic Situation in Germany, November 16, 1935.
8. PT/TT/AOS/CO/NE-4/4/From Embassy in Berlin to Ministry of Foreign Affairs in Lisbon, Report on the New Order in Germany, November 15, 1941.
9. Ibid.
10. NARA/RG131/346/Safehaven—Portugal, July 27, 1946, p. 1.
11. Ibid.
12. Ibid., p. 2.
13. Ibid.
14. Ibid., p. 6.
15. Ibid., pp. 6–7.
16. NARA/RG84/92/General Records of the Embassy in Lisbon/From Norweb to Secretary of State, September 30, 1944.
17. Ibid.
18. NARA/RG84/92/General Records of the Embassy in Lisbon/From Crocker to Secretary of State, October 1, 1944.
19. The biggest match the stadium hosted was the 1967 European Cup final when Glasgow Celtic defeated Inter Milan 2–1.

Chapter 28—There May Be Trouble Ahead

1. PT/TT/AOS/CO/NE-2/54/Reports on Death of Hitler, May 3–5, 1945.
2. PT/TT/AOS/O Diário de Salazar, May 3, 1945.
3. PT/TT/AOS/CO/NE-2/54/Reports on Death of Hitler, May 3–5, 1945.
4. PT/TT/AOS/O Diário de Salazar, May 3, 1945.
5. PRO/FO/954/21/From Salazar to Churchill, May 17, 1945.
6. PRO/FO/954/21/Prime Minister's Minute, May 10, 1945.
7. "Real Estate Deals in France: A Banker in Trouble," *Times*, June 15, 1945.
8. Ibid.
9. Ibid.
10. PRO/FO/371/49534/Foreign Office Minute, October 18, 1945.
11. PRO/FO/371/49534/From Foreign Office to Campbell, October 22, 1945.
12. PRO/FO/371/49534/From Reynolds in Lisbon to Stoneham and Sons, London, July 4, 1945.
13. Ibid.
14. PRO/FO/371/49534/From Campbell to Foreign Office, November 5, 1945.
15. PRO/FO/371/49534/From Foreign Office to Campbell, October 22, 1945
16. PRO/FO/371/49534/From Campbell to Foreign Office, November 5, 1945.
17. PRO/FO/371/49534/Memorandum, Ricardo Espírito Santo versus the *Times*, October 19, 1945.
18. NARA/RG226/110/Report on Ricardo Espírito Santo, July 7, 1945.
19. PRO/FO/371/49534/From Millar to Foreign Office, October 19, 1945.
20. PRO/FO/371/49534/Report, Ricardo Espírito Santo versus the *Times*, October 18, 1945.
21. Ibid., February 4, 1946.
22. PRO/FO/371/60291/From Villiers, MEW to Millar, Foreign Office, February 7, 1946.
23. PRO/FO/371/60291/From MEW to Culross and Trelawny Solicitors, March 21, 1946.
24. "Senhor Espírito Santo," *Times*, October 5, 1946.
25. Ibid.
26. NARA/RG226/110/Report on Ricardo Espírito Santo, July 7, 1945.
27. Filipe Ribeiro de Meneses, *Salazar: A Political Biography* (New York: Enigma Books, 2009), p. 334.

Chapter 29—Should I Stay or Should I Go?

1. Filipe Ribeiro de Meneses, *Salazar: A Political Biography* (New York: Enigma Books, 2009), p. 334.
2. Franco Nogueira, *Salazar: Volume 4, O Ataque, 1945–1958* (Porto: Civilização Editora, 2000), p. 11.
3. "Portugal: How Bad Is Best," *Time*, July 22, 1946, pp. 28–33.
4. Ibid.

5. Meneses, *Salazar*, p. 334.
6. "A Letter from the Publisher," *Time*, November 4, 1946.
7. Ibid.
8. Nogueira, *Salazar: Volume 4*, p. 11.
9. Ibid., p. 10.
10. PT/TT/AOS/PT/TT/AOS/O Diário de Salazar, June 29, 1945.
11. Ibid., June 30, 1945.
12. "Portugal: How Bad Is Best," pp. 28–33.
13. PRO/FO/371/39596/From Campbell to Foreign Office, November 23, 1944.
14. Ibid.
15. PT/TT/AOS/CO/IN-8C/17/PVDE Figures on Diplomatic and Consular Corps 1943.

Chapter 30—Old Wine into New Bottles

1. The Labour Party won an overall majority of 145 seats in the House of Commons.
2. PT/TT/AOS/PT/TT/AOS/O Diário de Salazar, July–August 1945.
3. PT/TT/AOS/PT/TT/AOS/O Diário de Salazar, August 30, 1945.
4. PRO/FO/371/49475/From O'Malley to Secretary of State, August 22, 1945.
5. PRO/FO/371/49475/From O'Malley to Bevin, September 14, 1945.
6. PRO/FO/371/49475/From O'Malley to Bevin, September 8, 1945.
7. Franco Nogueira, *Salazar: Volume 4, O Ataque, 1945–1958* (Porto: Civilização Editora, 2000), p. 12.
8. PT/TT/AOS/PT/TT/AOS/O Diário de Salazar, October 6, 1945.
9. Nogueira, *Salazar: Volume 4*, p. 12.
10. PRO/FO/371/49475/From Lisbon to Bevin, Speech by Salazar on October 7, 1945.
11. PRO/FO/371/49475/Foreign Office Minute, October 19, 1945.
12. PRO/FO/371/49475/From Lisbon to Foreign Office, August 2, 1945.
13. PRO/FO/371/49475/From Clarke in Lisbon to Bevin, October 13, 1945.
14. PRO/FO/371/49475/From Lisbon to Foreign Office, August 2, 1945.
15. PRO/FO/371/49475/From O'Malley to Foreign Office, October 22, 1945.
16. PRO/FO/371/49475/Foreign Office Minute, November 6, 1945.
17. PRO/FO/371/49475/From Embassy in Lisbon to Bevin, October 29, 1945.
18. NARA/RG84/14/General Records of the Embassy in Lisbon, From Lisbon to Secretary of State, Portuguese Opposition Movement, December 31, 1946.
19. Ibid.
20. PRO/FO/371/49475/Foreign Office Minute, November 7, 1945.
21. NARA/RG84/14/General Records of the Embassy in Lisbon, From Lisbon to Secretary of State, Portuguese Opposition Movement, December 31, 1946.
22. PRO/FO/371/49475/From Embassy in Lisbon to Foreign Office, October 24, 1945.

23. Filipe Ribeiro de Meneses, *Salazar: A Political Biography* (New York: Enigma Books, 2009), p. 379.
24. PRO/FO/371/49475/From O'Malley to Bevin, December 19, 1945.

Epilogue

1. NARA/RG165/2845/Records of Military Intelligence Division/Portuguese Foreign Trade during the War, March 13, 1944.
2. NARA/RG84/2/General Records of the Embassy in Lisbon, German External Assets in Portugal, 1947–1956, April 20 1945.
3. "Allied Relations and Negotiations with Portugal," *U.S. State Department Report*, undated, p. 1.
4. NARA/RG84/2/General Records of the Embassy in Lisbon, German External Assets in Portugal, 1947–1956, April 20, 1945.
5. "Allied Relations and Negotiations with Portugal," p. 16.
6. NARA/RG131/346/Foreign Funds Control, Memorandum on Gold Acquisitions by Portugal during World War II, July 2, 1946.
7. Ibid.
8. "Allied Relations and Negotiations with Portugal," p. 16.
9. António Louça and Ansgar Schafer, "Portugal and the Nazi Gold: The Lisbon Connection in the Sale of Looted Gold by the Third Reich', *Yad Vashem*, Jerusalem, p. 9.
10. "Allied Relations and Negotiations with Portugal," p. 25.
11. Ibid., p. 18.
12. Louça and Schafer, "Portugal and the Nazi Gold," p. 11.
13. "Catholic Shrine Had Nazi Gold Haul," *BBC News*, May 3, 2000.
14. On this, see Stuart Eizenstat, *Imperfect Justice: Looted Assets, Slave Labor, and the Unfinished Business of World War II* (New York: PublicAffairs, 2003).
15. "The Not So Neutrals of World War II," *New York Times*, January 26, 1997; "Neutral Countries Prolonged War," *CBC News*, November 13, 1998; "Neutral Nations Kept Nazi Forces Going," *Los Angeles Times*, June 3, 1998.

BIBLIOGRAPHY

UNPUBLISHED DOCUMENTS AND PHOTOGRAPHS

National Archives (Public Records Office) Kew, London

ADM—Records of the Admiralty, Naval Forces, Royal Marines, Coastguard, and related bodies, 1939–1945.

AIR—Records created or inherited by the Air Ministry, the Royal Air Force, and related bodies, 1939–1945.

BT—Records of the British Board of Trade and of successor and related bodies.

BW—Records of the British Council, 1943.

CAB—Records of the British Cabinet Office, 1939–1945.

CO—Records of the Colonial Office, Commonwealth and Foreign and Commonwealth Offices, Empire Marketing Board, and related bodies.

DEFE—Records of the Ministry of Defence.

DO—Records created or inherited by the Dominions Office, and of the Commonwealth Relations and Foreign and Commonwealth Offices, 1939–1945.

FO—Records created and inherited by the Foreign Office, 1938–1946.

GFM—Copies of captured records of the German, Italian, and Japanese Governments.

HO—Records created or inherited by the Home Office, Ministry of Home Security, and related bodies, 1939–1945.

HS—Records of Special Operations Executive, 1939–1945.

HW—Records created and inherited by British Government Communications Headquarters (GCHQ), 1939–1945.

KV—Records of the Security Service, 1939–1945.

PREM—Records of the British Prime Minister's Office, 1939–1945.

T—Records created and inherited by HM Treasury, 1939–1945.

WO—Records created or inherited by the War Office, Armed Forces, Judge Advocate General, and related bodies, 1939–1945.

Arquivo Nacional, Torre do Tombo, Lisboa, Portugal

AOS-Arquivo Salazar
Diários 1936–1946

Comissão do Livro Branco do Ministério dos Negócios Estrangeiros
Correspondência Diplomática. 1935–1946
Correspondência Oficial. 1928–1946
Correspondência Oficial Especial. 1934–1946
Correspondência Particular 1928–1946
Papéis Pessoais 1936–1946
PIDE (Secret Police)
Arquivo Geral
Direcção dos Serviços de Estrangeiro.
Gabinete do Director
Propaganda Apreendida, 1936–1946
SPD Subdelegação de Ponta Delgada 1942–1945.

Arquivo Municipal Lisboa, Lisboa, Portugal

Photographs of Lisbon, 1939–1945.

Arquivo Histórico Municipal de Cascais, Cascais, Portugal

AFTG—Arquivos Fotográficos
CAM—Colecção Antiga do Município
CAP—Colecção António Passaporte
CCGC—Colecção César Guilherme Cardoso
CFCB—Colecção Família Castelo Branco
CSAG—Colecção Sérgio Álvares da Guerra

The Wiener Library, London

Mf Doc 2—International Committee of the Red Cross: G59 Israélites, 1939–1961.
Mf Doc 56—World Jewish Congress: Central Files, 1919–1976.
548—Wilfred Israel Papers, 1940s.
585—Documents Re Nazis in Spain, 1933–1936.
660—Thomas Cook & Son Ltd: Storage Record Book, 1914–1969.
683—Jewish Refugees In Portugal: Various Papers, 1930's.
1072—Reports and Correspondence Re Gurs and Other French Concentration
   Camps, 1940s.
1100—Nsdap Auswaertigesamt: Papers on Jews in Spain and Portugal, 1930s.
1206—Hepner and Cahn: Family Papers, 1874–1950s.
1514—Wilfrid Israel: Correspondence, 1937–1943.
1579—Frank Family: Copy Red Cross Telegrams.

U.S. Holocaust Memorial Museum (USHMM), Washington, D.C.

General Correspondence between Jewish Refugees in Lisbon and Officials and
   Relatives.
Series RG-60: Video footage of Jewish refugees in Lisbon and Caldas da Rainha,
   the port of Lisbon, the Pan Am Clipper arriving and António Oliveira de
   Salazar holding political meetings.

Steven Spielberg Film and Video Archive at USHMM
U.S. Holocaust Memorial Museum Photograph Archive, Washington, D.C.
W/S/59581–86458: Photographs of Jewish Refugees in [and departing] Lisbon during World War II.

U.S. National Archives, College Park, Maryland

Foreign Relations of the United States—Relevant Parts of volumes on Portugal, 1939–1948. Also available online at http://digicoll.library.wisc.edu.

RG 84 Entry 3126—General Records of the U.S. Embassy Lisbon Portugal, 1936–1945.

RG 84 Entry 3127—Classified General Records of the U.S. Embassy in Lisbon Portugal, 1941–1949.

RG 84 Entry 3128—Top Secret General Records of the U.S. Embassy in Lisbon, 1945–1949.

RG 84 Entry 3129A—Top Secret Subject Files related to Operation Safehaven, 1947–1948, and German external Assets, 1950–1952.

RG 84 Entry 3130—General Records Relating to War Refugees, 1942.

RG 84 Entry 3131—Files Relating to War Refugees, 1944–1945.

RG 84 Entry 3138—Records Relating to German External Assets in Portugal, 1947–1956.

RG 84 Entry 3139—Files of the Financial Attachés, James E. Wood, 1942–1945.

RG 84—Classified Records of the U.S. Embassy in Madrid, 1940–1963.

RG 84—Classified Records of the U.S. Embassy in Paris, 1944–1963.

RG 226—Records of the Office of Strategic Services, Relevant files to Portugal and Operation Safehaven.

Centro de Historia BES, Banco Espírito Santo, Lisboa, Portugal

Documentation about World War II.
Photographic Archive of the family.
Transcripts of Exerts of the Diary of Salazar, 1933–1946.

PUBLISHED DOCUMENTS

Correspondência de Pedro Teotónio Pereira para Oliveira Salazar, Volume 1, 1931–1939. Mira e Sintra: Presidência do Conselho de Ministros, Comissão do Livro Negro Sobre o Regime Fascista, 1987.

Correspondência de Pedro Teotónio Pereira para Oliveira Salazar, Volume 2, 1940–1941. Mira e Sintra: Presidência do Conselho de Ministros, Comissão do Livro Negro Sobre o Regime Fascista, 1989.

Grande Hotel e Hotel Atlântico: Boletins de Alojamento de Estrangeiros. Cascais: Câmara Municipal de Cascais, 2005.

Hotel Palácio: Boletins de Alojamento de Estrangeiros. Cascais: Câmara Municipal de Cascais, 2004.

MAGAZINES, NEWS AGENCIES, NEWSPAPERS, AND TELEVISION NEWS

Associated Press
BBC News
British Pathe News
Daily Express
Daily Mail
Daily Telegraph
Diário da Manha
Diário de Lisboa
Diário de Noticias
Diário Popular
El Pais
Expresso
Financial Times
Grande Reportagem
Harper's
Jornal do Comercio
Life Magazine
New York Times
Novidades
O Sábado
O Século
O Voz
Primeiro de Janeiro
Republica
Reuters
RTP News
San Francisco Chronicle
The Atlantic
The Economist
The Guardian
The Tablet
The Times (London)
Time
Visão
United Press
Washington Post

FICTION AND VERSE BOOKS

Beauvoir, Simone de. *The Mandarins*. London: Flamingo, 1982.
Fleming, Ian. *Casino Royale*. London: Penguin, 2006.
Gabbay, Tom. *The Lisbon Crossing: A Novel*. New York: William Morrow, 2007.

Koestler, Arthur. *Arrival and Departure*. London: Penguin, 1971.

Mercier, Pascal. *Night Train to Lisbon*. London: Atlantic, 2008.

Pessoa, Fernando. *Poesia Inglesa 1*: Lisboa: Assírio e Alvim, 2000.

———. *Poesia Inglesa 2*: Lisboa: Assírio e Alvim, 2000.

Saramago, José. *Blindness*. Austin, New York, San Diego, and London: Harcourt, 2004.

———. *The Stone Raft: A Novel*. New York, San Diego, and London: Harcourt Brace, 1995.

———. *The Year of the Death of Ricardo Reis*. London: Harvell, 1992.

Wilson, Robert. *A Small Death in Lisbon*. New York: Berkley Books, 2002.

———. *The Company of Strangers*. London: HarperCollins, 2002.

NONFICTION BOOKS AND ARTICLES

Afonso, Rui. *Um Homem Bom: Aristides de Sousa Mendes*. Alfragide: Texto, 2009.

Agudo, Manuel Rós. *A Grande Tentacao: Os Planos de Franco para Invadir Portugal*. Alfragide: Casa das Letras, 2009.

Allen, Martin. *Hidden Agenda: How the Duke of Windsor Betrayed the Allies*. London: Macmillan, 2000.

———. *The Hitler/Hess Deception: British Intelligence's Best-Kept Secret of the Second World War*. London: HarperCollins, 2003.

Allen, Peter. *The Crown and the Swastika: Hitler, Hess and the Duke of Windsor*. London: Robert Hale, 1983.

Anderson, James M. *The History of Portugal*. Westport, CT, and London: 2000.

Andrew, Christopher. *The Defence of the Realm: The Authorized History of MI5*. London: Allen Lane, 2009.

Araújo, Rui. *O Diário Secreto que Salazar Não Leu*. Cruz Quebrada: Oficina do Livro, 2008.

Asprey, Robert. *The Rise and Fall of Napoleon Bonaparte: Volume One—the Rise*. London: Little, Brown, 2000.

———. *The Rise and Fall of Napoleon Bonaparte: Volume Two—the Fall*. London: Little, Brown, 2001.

Assor, Miriam. *Aristides de Sousa Mendes: Um Justo Contra a Corrente*. Lisboa: Guerra e Paz, 2009.

Baigent, Michael and Richard Leigh. *The Inquisition*. London: Penguin, 2000.

Bailey, Rosemary. *Love and War in the Pyrenees: A Story of Courage, Fear, and Hope, 1939–1944*. London: Weidenfeld and Nicolson, 2008.

Beauvoir, Simone de, ed. *Quiet Moments in a War: The Letters of Jean-Paul Sartre to Simone de Beauvoir, 1940–1963*. London: Penguin, 1995.

Beevor, Antony. *Stalingrad*. London: Penguin, 1999.

———. *The Battle for Spain: The Spanish Civil War, 1936–1939*. London: Weidenfeld and Nicolson, 2006.

———. *D-Day: The Battle for Normandy*. London: Viking, 2009.

Beevor, Anthony and Artemis Cooper. *Paris: After the Liberation, 1944–1949*. London: Penguin, 2007.

Beevor, J. G. *SOE: Recollections and Reflections, 1940–1945*. London: Bodley Head, 1981.

Benoliel, Joshua. *1873–1932: Repórter Fotográfico*. Lisboa: Câmara Municipal de Lisboa, 2005.

Bercuson, David J., and Holder H. Herwig. *One Christmas in Washington: Churchill and Roosevelt Forge the Grand Alliance*. London: Phoenix, 2006.

Bermeo, Nancy Gina. *The Revolution within the Revolution: Workers Control in Rural Portugal*. Princeton, NJ: Princeton University Press, 1986.

Bethencourt, Francisco, and Diogo Ramada Curto, eds. *Portuguese Oceanic Expansion, 1440–1800*. New York: Cambridge University Press, 2007.

Birmingham, David. *A Concise History of Portugal*. Cambridge: Cambridge University Press, 2007.

———. *Portugal and Africa*. Athens, OH: Ohio University Press, 1999.

Bloch, Michael. *Operation Willi: The Plot to Kidnap the Duke of Windsor, July 1940*. London: Weidenfeld and Nicolson, 1986.

———. *The Duchess of Windsor*. London: Weidenfeld and Nicolson, 1996.

———. *The Duke of Windsor's War*. London: Weidenfeld and Nicolson, 1982.

———. *The Secret File of the Duke of Windsor*. London: Corgi Books, 1989.

Bower, Tom. *The Full Story of the Fifty-Year Swiss-Nazi Conspiracy to Steal Billions from Europe's Jews and Holocaust Survivors*. New York: Harper-Collins, 1997.

Brandão, Fernando de Castro. *António de Oliveira Salazar: Uma Cronologia*. Lisbon: Prefacio, 2011.

Brandão, F. Norton. "Epidemiology of Venereal Disease in Portugal during the Second World War." *British Journal of Venereal Diseases* 36, no. 2 (1960): 136–138.

Breitman, Richard. "A Deal with the Nazi Dictatorship?: Himmler's Alleged Peace Emissaries in Autumn 1943." *Journal of Contemporary History* 30 (1995): 411–430.

Briggs, Asa. *History of England: England in the Age of Improvement*. London: Folio Society, 2000.

Buck, Paul. *Lisbon: A Cultural and Literary Companion*. Oxford: Signal Books, 2002.

Burleigh, Michael. *Sacred Causes: Religion and Politics from the European Dictators to Al Qaeda*. London: HarperPerennial, 2006.

———. *The Third Reich: A New History*. London: Pan, 2001.

Burman, Edward. *The Inquisition: The Hammer of Heresy*. Stroud: Sutton, 2004.

Burns, Jimmy. *Papa Spy: Love, Faith, and Betrayal in Wartime Spain*. London: Bloomsbury, 2009.

Caldwell, Robert. "The Anglo-Portuguese Alliance Today." *Foreign Affairs* 21, no. 1 (October 1942): 149, 157.

Cannadine, David. *In Churchill's Shadow: Confronting the Past in Modern Britain*. London: Penguin, 2003.

Cantwell, John. *The Second World War: A Guide to Documents in the Public Record Office.* London: The National Archives, 1998.

Caron, Vicki. *Uneasy Asylum: France and the Jewish Refugee Crisis, 1933–1942.* Stanford, CA: Stanford University Press, 1999.

Carpozi, George J. R. *Nazi Gold: The Real Story of How the World Plundered Jewish Treasures.* Far Hills: New Horizon Press, 1999.

Carr, Raymond. *Modern Spain, 1875–1980.* Oxford, Oxford University Press, 1986.

Carrilho, M., et al., eds. *Portugal Na Segunda Guerra Mundial.* Lisbon: Dom Quixote, 1989.

Carter, Miranda. *Anthony Blunt: His Lives.* London: Pan Books, 2002.

Caruana, Leonard, and Hugh Rockoff. "A Wolfram in Sheep's Clothing: Economic Warfare in Spain, 1940–1944," *The Journal of Economic History* 63, no. 1 (March 2003): 100–126.

Carvalho, Manuel de Abreu Ferreira. *Relatório dos Acontecimentos de Timor, 1942–45.* Lisboa: Instituto da Defesa Nacional, 2003.

Castro, Pedro Jorge. *Salazar e os Milionários.* Lisboa: Quetzal, 2009.

———. *Salazar e os Milionários.* Lisbon: Quetzal Editores, 2009.

Chandler, David G. *The Campaigns of Napoleon: Volume Two: the Zenith, September 1805–September 1812.* London: Folio Society, 2002.

Chaves, Miguel de Mattos. *Portugal e a Construção Europeia: Mitos e Realidades.* Lisboa: Sete Caminhos, 2005.

Churchill, Winston. *The Second World War (Abridged Version).* London: Pimlico, 2002.

———. *The Second World War: Volume Five, Closing the Ring.* London: Folio Society, 2000.

———. *The Second World War: Volume Four, the Hinge of Fate.* London: Folio Society, 2000.

———. *The Second World War: Volume One, the Gathering Storm.* London: Folio Society, 2000.

———. *The Second World War: Volume Six, Triumph and Tragedy.* London: Folio Society, 2000.

———. *The Second World War: Volume Three, the Grand Alliance.* London: Folio Society, 2000.

———. *The Second World War: Volume Two, the Finest Hour.* London: Folio Society, 2000.

Churchill, Winston S., ed. *Never Give In: The Best of Winston Churchill's Speeches.* London: Pimlico, 2003.

Clausewitz, Carl von. *On War.* London: Everyman's Library, 1993.

Corkill, David, and Jose Carlos Pina Almeida. "Commemoration and Propaganda in Salazar's Portugal: the Mundo Portuguese Exposition of 1940." *Journal of Contemporary History* 44, no. 3 (2009): 381–399.

Costa, Fernando. *Portugal e a Guerra Anglo-Boer.* Lisboa: Edições Cosmos, 1998.

Dacosta, Fernando. *Máscaras de Salazar.* Cruz Quebrada: Casa das Letras, 2007.

Damas, Carlos Alberto. "Ricardo Espírito Santo e o Duque de Windsor:" *Historia*, no. 62 (December 2003): 46–51.

———. "Espírito Santo e Os Windsor em 1940." *Grande Reportagem*, pp. 96–101.

———. *Hotel Tivoli Lisboa, 1933–2008*. Lisboa: Centro de Historia do Grupo Banco Espírito Santo, 2008.

———. *Manuel Ribeiro Espírito Santo Silva: Fotobiografia, 1908–1973*. Lisboa: Centro de Historia do Grupo Banco Espírito Santo, 2008.

Damas, Carlos Alberto, and Augusto De Ataíde. *O Banco Espírito Santo: Uma Dinastia Financeira Portuguesa, 1886–1973*. Lisboa: Banco Espírito Santo, 2004.

De Sousa, Maria Leonor Machado, ed. *A Guerra Peninsular em Portugal: Relatos Britânicos*. Casal de Cambra: Calei dos Copio, 2008.

Deakin, F. W. *The Brutal Friendship: Mussolini, Hitler, and the Fall of Italian Fascism*. London: Penguin, 1962.

Dearborn, Mary. *Peggy Guggenheim: Mistress of Modernism*. London: Virago Press, 2008.

Delgado, Humberto. *The Memoirs of General Delgado*. London: Cassell, 1964.

Diamond, Hanna. *Fleeing Hitler: France 1940*. Oxford: Oxford University Press, 2007.

Dias, Marina Tavares. *Lisboa nos Anos 40: Longe da Guerra*. Lisboa: Quimera Editores, 2005.

Disney, A. R. *A History of Portugal and the Portuguese Empire, Volume One*. Cambridge: Cambridge University Press, 2009.

———. *A History of Portugal and the Portuguese Empire, Volume Two*. Cambridge: Cambridge University Press, 2009.

Doerries, Reinhard. *Hitler's Last Chief of Foreign Intelligence: Allied Interrogations of Walter Schellenberg*. London and Portland: Frank Cass, 2003.

Duggan, Christopher. *A Concise History of Italy*. Cambridge: Cambridge University Press, 1997.

Eccles, David. *By Safe Hand: The Letters of Sybil and David Eccles, 1939–42*. London: the Bodley Head, 1983.

Eden, Anthony. *Full Circle: The Memoirs of Sir Anthony Eden*. London: Cassell, 1960.

Edmondson, John. *France: A Traveller's Literary Companion*. London: In Print, 1993.

Eisenhower, Dwight D. *Crusade in Europe*. London: Heinemann, 1948.

Eizenstat, Stuart E. *Imperfect Justice: Looted Assets, Slave Labour and the Unfinished Business of World War II*. New York: PublicAffairs, 2003.

Esdaile, Charles. *Napoleon's Wars: An International History, 1803–1815*. London: Allen Lane, 2007.

Evans, Richard E. *The Third Reich at War: How the Nazis Led Germany from Conquest to Disaster*. London: Penguin, 2009.

Faria, Miguel Figueira de. *Alfredo da Silva e Salazar*. Lisboa: Bertrand Editora, 2009.

Ferguson, Niall. *Empire: How Britain Made the Modern World*. London: Penguin, 2004.

———. *The Ascent of Money: A Financial History of the World*. London: Penguin, 2007.

———. *The House of Rothschild: Money's Prophets, 1798–1848*. New York: Penguin, 1998.

———. *The House of Rothschild: The World's Banker, 1849–1999*. New York: Penguin, 1998.

———. *The Pity of War*. London: Penguin, 1999.

———. *The War of the World*. London: Penguin, 2007.

Ferro, António. *Salazar: Portugal and Her Leader*. London: Faber and Faber, 1939.

Figueiredo, António de. *Portugal: Fifty Years of Dictatorship*. London: Penguin, 1975.

Foot, M. R. D. *SOE: The Special Operations Executive, 1940–1946*. London: Pimlico, 1999.

Fralon, Jose-Alain. *A Good Man in Evil Times: The Story of Aristides de Sousa Mendes, the Man Who Saved the Lives of Countless Refugees in World War II*. New York: Carroll and Graf, 2001.

Fry, Varian. *Surrender on Demand*. Boulder: Johnson Books, 1997.

Garcia, Maria Madalena. *Arquivo Salazar: Inventario e Índices*. Lisboa: Editorial Estampa, 1992.

Garnier, Christine. *Férias com Salazar*. Lisboa: Parceria A. M. Pereira e Grasset e Fasquelle, 1952.

———. *Salazar in Portugal: An Intimate Portrait*. New York: Farrar, Straus, and Young, 1954.

Gilbert, Martin. *A History of the Twentieth Century Volume One: 1900–1933*. London: HarperCollins, 1997.

———. *Churchill and America*. New York: Free Press, 2005.

———. *Churchill: A Life: Volume Two*. London: Folio Society, 2004.

———. *D-Day*. Hoboken, NJ: Wiley, 2004.

Ginsburg, Paul. *A History of Contemporary Italy: Society and Politics, 1943–1988*. London: Penguin, 1990.

Glancey, Jonathan. *Spitfire: The Biography*. London: Atlantic Books, 2007.

Glass, Charles. *Americans in Paris: Life and Death under German Occupation, 1940–1944*. London: Harpers Press, 2009.

Greene, Richard, ed. *Graham Greene: A Life in Letters*. London: Little, Brown, 2007.

Guggenheim, Peggy. *Out of This Century: Confessions of an Art Addict*. London: Andre Deutsch, 2005.

Gurriarán, José António. *Um Rei no Estoril: Dom Juan Carlos e a Família Real Espanhola no Exílio Português*. Lisboa: Dom Quixote, 2001.

Hayward, James. *Mitos e Lendas da Segunda Guerra Mundial*. Lisboa: A Esfera dos Livros, 2007.

Henriques, João, Miguel and Olga Bettencourt, and Teresa Ramirez, eds. *The History of Sailing in Cascais: From the First Regatta to the Internationalisation of Sailing*. Lisbon: Edicoes Inapa, 2007.

Henriques, Mendo Castro, and Gonçalo De Sampaio e Mello, eds. *Salazar, António, De Oliveira: Pensamento e Doutrina Politica*. Lisboa: Verbo, 2010.

Herz, Norman. *Operation Alacrity: The Azores and the War in the Atlantic*. Annapolis, MD: Naval Institute Press, 2004.

Higham, Charles. *Mrs Simpson: Secret Lives of the Duchess of Windsor*. London: Pan Books, 2004.

Hildebrand, Klaus. *The Foreign Policy of the Third Reich*. Berkeley and Los Angeles: University of California Press, 1973.

———. *The Third Reich*. London: George Allen and Unwin, 1985.

Hinsley, F. H. *British Intelligence in the Second World War* (Abridged Version). London: Her Majesty's Stationery Office, 1993.

Hoare, Samuel. *Ambassador on Special Mission*. London: Collins, 1946.

———. *Nine Troubled Years*. London: Collins, 1954.

Holland, James. *Fortress Malta: An Island under Siege, 1940–1943*. London: Phoenix, 2004.

Holt, Thaddeus. *The Deceivers: Allied Military Deception in the Second World War*. London: Phoenix, 2005.

Hyland, Paul. *Backwards Out of the Big World*. London: HarperCollins, 1996.

Hynes, Samuel, Anne Matthews, Nancy Caldwell Sorel, and Roger J. Spiller, eds. *Reporting World War II: Part One: American Journalism, 1938–1940*. New York: Library of America, 1995.

Ingrams, Richard. *Muggeridge: The Biography*. London: HarperCollins, 1995.

Jack, Malcolm. *Lisbon: City of the Sea, a History*. New York: I. B. Tauris, 2007.

Janeiro, Helena Pinto. *Salazar e Pétain: Relações Luso-Francesas durante a II Guerra Mundial, 1940–44*. Lisboa: Edições Cosmos, 1998.

Jardim, Rita. "Memoria Duque de Windsor: Operação Willi." *Grande Reportagem*, pp. 116–121.

Jeffery, Keith. *MI6: The History of the Secret Intelligence Service, 1909–1949*. London: Bloomsbury, 2010.

Johnson, Paul. *Napoleon*. London: Phoenix, 2002.

Justino, Ana Clara, ed. *O Século XX em Revista*. Lisboa: Câmara Municipal de Cascais, 2002.

Kaplan, Marion. *The Portuguese: The Land and Its People*. Manchester: Carcanet, 2006.

Kassow, Samuel D. *Who Will Write Our History? Rediscovering a Hidden Archive from the Warsaw Ghetto*. London: Allen Lane, 2009.

Kay, Hugh. *Salazar and Modern Portugal*. New York: Hawthorn Books, 1970.

Koestler, Arthur. *Scum of the Earth*. London: Eland Publishing, 2006.

Laqueur, Walter. *Generation Exodus: The Fate of the Young Jewish Refugees from Nazi Germany*. Hanover and London: Brandeis University Press, 2001.

Leal, Ernesto Castro. *António Ferro: Espaço Politico e Imaginário Social, 1918–32*. Lisboa: Edições Cosmos, 1994.

Lee, Laurie. *Red Sky at Sunrise: An Autobiographical Trilogy*. London: Penguin, 1993.

Leitz, Christian. "Nazi Germany and the Luso-Hispanic World." *Contemporary European History* 12, no. 2 (May 2003): 183–196.

———. *Nazi Germany and Neutral Europe during the Second World War*. Manchester: Manchester University Press, 2000.

Lewis, Paul H. "Salazar's Ministerial Elite, 1932–1968," *Journal of Politics* 40, no. 3 (August 1978): 622–647.

Lima, Mário João e José Soares Neves. *Cascais e a Memória dos Exílios*. Lisboa, Câmara Municipal de Cascais, 2005.

Livermore, H. V. *A New History of Portugal*. Cambridge: Cambridge University Press, 1966.

Lob, Ladislaus. *Dealing with Satan: Rezso Kasztner's Daring Rescue Mission*. London: Jonathan Cape, 2008.

Louça, António, and Ansgar Schafer. "Portugal and the Nazi Gold: The Lisbon Connection in the Sales of Looted Gold by the Third Reich." *Yad Vashem*, Jerusalem, no publication date.

Louça, António, and Isabelle Paccaud. *O Segredo da Rua d' o Século Ligações Perigosas de um Dirigente Judeu com a Alemanha Nazi, 1935–1939*. Lisboa, Fim de Século, 2007.

Louça, António. *Hitler e Salazar: Comercio em Tempos de Guerra, 1940–1944*. Lisboa: Terramar, 2000.

Louro, Sónia. *O Cônsul Desobediente*. Parede: Saída de Emergência, 2009.

Lycett, Andrew. *Ian Fleming*. London: Phoenix, 1996.

MacDonagh, S. J. "A Professor in Politics: Salazar and the Regeneration of Portugal." *Irish Monthly*, 1940, pp. 417–427.

Macintyre, Ben. *Agent Zigzag: The True Wartime Story of Eddie Chapman: Lover, Betrayer, Hero, Spy*. London: Bloomsbury, 2007.

———. *Operation Mincemeat: The True Spy Story that Changed the Course of World War II*. London: Bloomsbury, 2010.

Macmillan, Margaret. *Peacemakers: Six Months That Changed the World*. London: John Murray, 2002.

Makovsky, Michael. *Churchill's Promised Land: Zionism and Statecraft*. New Haven and London: Yale University Press, 2007.

Manchester, William. *The Last Lion: Winston Spenser Churchill, Alone 1932–1940*. Boston, New York, and London: Little, Brown, 1988.

Matos, Helena. *Salazar: A Construção do Mito, 1928–1933*. Lisboa: Circulo de Leitores, 2010.

———. *Salazar: A Propaganda, 1934–1938*. Lisboa: Circulo de Leitores, 2010.

Mattoso José e Fernando Rosas. *Historia de Portugal, Sétimo Volume: O Estado Novo, 1926–1974*. Lisboa: Editorial Estampa, 1998.

Maxwell, Kenneth. *The Making of Portuguese Democracy*. Cambridge: Cambridge University Press, 1995.

Mayson, Richard. *Port and the Douro*. London: Octopus, 2004.

Meneses, Filipe Ribeiro de. *Salazar: A Political Biography*. New York: Enigma Books, 2009.

———. *União Sagrada e Sidonismo: Portugal em Guerra, 1916–18*. Lisboa: Edições Cosmos, 2000.

Milgram, Avraham. "Portugal: the Consuls, and the Jewish Refugees, 1938–1941." *Yad Vashem Studies* 27 (Jerusalem, 1999): 123–156.

———. *Portugal, Salazar e os Judeus*. Lisboa: Gradiva, 2010.

Mocatta, Frederic David. *The Jews of Spain and Portugal and the Inquisition*. General Books, 2009.

Monteiro, Armindo. "Portugal in Africa," *Journal of the Royal African Society* 38, no. 151 (April 1939): 259–272.

Moran, Lord. *Churchill at War, 1940–45*. London: Robinson, 2002.

Muggeridge, Malcolm, ed. *Ciano's Diary, 1939–1943*. London: Heinemann, 1947.

———. *Chronicles of Wasted Time: An Autobiography*. Vancouver: Regent College Publishing, 2006.

———. *Like It Was: A Selection from the Diaries of Malcolm Muggeridge*. London: Collins, 1981.

Neillands, Robin. *Wellington and Napoleon: Clash of Armies, 1807–1815*. Barnsley: Pen and Sword, 2003.

Nicholas Lynn. *Europa Saqueada: O Destino dos Tesouros Artisticos Europeus no Terceiro Reich e na Segunda Munidal*. Sao Paulo: Compania Das Letras, 1996.

Nogueira, Franco. *Salazar: Volume 1, A Mocidade e os Princípios, 1889–1928*. Porto: Civilização Editora, 2000.

———. *Salazar: Volume 2, Os Tempos Áureos, 1928–1936*. Porto: Civilização Editora, 2000.

———. *Salazar: Volume 3, As Grandes Crises, 1936–1945*. Porto: Civilização Editora, 2000.

———. *Salazar: Volume 4, O Ataque, 1945–1958*. Porto: Civilização Editora, 2000.

———. *Salazar: Volume 5, A Resistência, 1958–1964*. Porto: Civilização Editora, 2000.

———. *Salazar: Volume 6, O Ultimo Combate, 1964–1970*. Porto: Civilização Editora, 2000.

Norwich, John Julius. *The Middle Sea: A History of the Mediterranean*. London: Vintage, 2007.

Nunes, João Paulo Avelãs. *O Estado Novo e o Volfrâmio, 1933–1947*. Coimbra: Imprensa da Universidade de Coimbra, 2010.

Oliveira, Pedro Aires. *Armindo Monteiro: Uma Biografia Politica*. Lisboa: Bertrand Editora, 2000.

Overy, Richard. *The Dictators: Hitler's Germany, Stalin's Russia*. London: Penguin, 2005.

Page, Martin. *The First Global Village: How Portugal Changed the World*. Cruz Quebrada: Casa das Letras, 2002.

Paice, Edward. *Wrath of God: The Great Lisbon Earthquake of 1755*. London: Quercus, 2008.

Paxton, Robert O. *The Anatomy of Fascism*. London: Penguin, 2005.

Payne, Stanley G. *A History of Spain and Portugal, Volume One*. Madison and London: University of Wisconsin Press, 1973.

———. *A History of Spain and Portugal, Volume Two*. Madison and London: University of Wisconsin Press, 1973.

———. *A History of Fascism, 1914–45*. London: Routledge, 2001.

Petropoulos, Jonathan. *Royals and the Reich: The Princes von Hessen in Nazi Germany*. New York: Oxford University Press, 2006.

Philby, Kim. *My Silent War: The Autobiography of a Spy*. New York: the Modern Library, 2002.

Picaper, Jean-Paul. *No Rasto Dos Tesouros Nazis*. Lisbon: Edicoes 70, 1998.

Pignatelli, Marina. *Interioridades e Exterioridades dos Judeus de Lisboa*. Lisboa: Instituto Superior de Ciências Sociais e Políticas, 2008.

Pimentel, Irene Flunser. *Cardeal Cerejeira: O Príncipe da Igreja*. Lisboa: A Esfera dos Livros, 2010.

———. *Judeus em Portugal durante a II Guerra Mundial: Em Fuga de Hitler e do Holocausto*. Lisboa: A Esfera dos Livros, 2006.

Pinto, Jaime Nogueira. *António de Oliveira Salazar: O Outro Retrato*. Lisboa: A Esfera dos Livros, 2008.

———. *O Fim do Estado Novo e os Origens do 25 de Abril*. Algés, Lisboa: Difel, 1995.

Preston, Paul. *Comrades: Portraits from the Spanish Civil War*. London: HarperPerennial, 2006.

———. *Franco*. London: Basic Books, 1994.

———. *Juan Carlos: Steering Spain from Dictatorship to Democracy*. London: Harper Perennial, 2005.

———. *The Spanish Civil War, 1936–39*. London: Weidenfeld and Nicolson, 1986.

———. *The Spanish Civil War: Reaction, Revolution and Revenge*. London: HarperPerennial, 2006.

Raby, Dawn Linda. "The Portuguese Presidential Election of 1949: A Successful Governmental Maneuver?" *Luso-Brazilian Review* 27, no. 1 (Summer 1990): 63–77.

Ramalho, Miguel Nunes. *Sidónia Pais: Diplomata e Conspirador, 1912–1917*. Lisboa: Cosmos, 2001.

Rankin, Nicholas. *Churchill's Wizards: The British Genius for Deception, 1914–1945*. London: Faber and Faber, 2008.

Redondo, Juan Carlos Jiménez. *Franco e Salazar: As Relações Luso-Espanholas durante a Guerra Fria*. Lisboa: Assírio e Alvim, 1996.

Reynolds, David. *In Command of History: Churchill Fighting and Writing the Second World War*. London: Allen Lane, 2004.

Rezola, Maria Inácia. *25 de Abril: Mitos de uma Revolução*. Lisboa: A Esfera dos Livros, 2008.

Roberts, Andrew. *A History of the English-Speaking Peoples Since 1900*. London: Weidenfeld and Nicolson, 2006.

———. *Churchill and Hitler: Secrets of Leadership*. London: Phoenix, 2003.

———. *Masters and Commanders: The Military Geniuses Who Led the West to Victory in World War II*. London: Penguin, 2009.

———. *Napoleon and Wellington*. London: Phoenix, 2001.

———. *The Holy Fox: The Life of Lord Halifax*. London: Phoenix, 1991.

———. *The Storm of War: A New History of the Second World War*. London: Penguin, 2010.

Rodrigues, Luís Nuno. *Salazar e Kennedy: A Crise de uma Aliança*. Lisboa: Casa das Letras, 2002.

———ed. *Franklin Roosevelt and the Azores during the Two World Wars*. Lisboa: Fundacao Luso-Americana, 2008.

Rohr, Isabelle. *The Spanish Right and the Jews, 1898–1945*. Brighton and Portland: Sussex Academic Press, 2008.

Rosas, Fernando. "Portuguese Neutrality in the Second World War." In Neville Wylie, ed. *European Neutrals and Non-Belligerents during the Second World War*. Cambridge: Cambridge University Press, 2002, 268–282.

———. *Lisboa Revolucionaria: Roteiro dos Confrontos Armados no Século XX*. Lisboa: Tinta-da-China, 2007.

———. *Portugal entre a Paz e a Guerra, 1939–1945*. Lisboa: Editorial Estampa, 1995.

Rosas, Fernando e Júlia Leitão de Barros e Pedro de Oliveira. *Armindo Monteiro e Oliveira Salazar: Correspondência Politica, 1926–1955*. Lisboa: Editorial Estampa, 1996.

Russell-Wood, A. J. R. *The Portuguese Empire, 1415–1808: A World on the Move*. Baltimore and London: John Hopkins University Press, 1998.

Ryan, John. "Election in Portugal." *Irish Monthly*. 1946, pp. 52–58.

Saraiva, António José. *Politica à Portuguesa: Ideias, Pessoas e Factos*. Cruz Quebrada: Oficina do Livro, 2007.

Saraiva, José Hermano. *Portugal: A Companion History*. Manchester: Carcanet, 1997.

Saramago José. *Small Memories: A Memoir*. London: Harvill Secker, 2009.

———. *The Notebook*. London and New York: Verso, 2010.

———. *Journey to Portugal: In Pursuit of Portugal's History and Culture*. San Diego, New York, and London: Harvest, 2000.

Scammell, Michael. *Koestler: The Indispensable Intellectual*. London: Faber and Faber, 2009.

Schellenberg, Walter. *The Memoirs of Hitler's Spymaster*. London: Andre Deutsch, 2006.

Schwarz, Reinhard. *Os Alemães em Portugal, 1933–1945: A Colónia Alemã Através das Suas Instituições*. Porto: Antilia Editora, 2006.

Sedgwick, Ellery. "Something New in Dictators: Salazar of Portugal." *The Atlantic Monthly* (January 1954): 40–45.

Selby, Walford. *Diplomatic Twilight: 1930–1940*. London: John Murray, 1953.

Shepherd, Naomi. *A Refuge from Darkness: Wilfrid Israel and the Rescue of the Jews*. New York: Pantheon Books, 1984.

Shirer, William L. *The Rise and Fall of the Third Reich: A History of Nazi Germany, Volume Three*. London: Folio Society, 1995.

Shrady, Nicholas. *The Last Day: Wrath, Ruin and Reason in the Great Lisbon Earthquake of 1755*. New York: Penguin, 2008.

Smith, Alfred. *Rudolf Hess: And Germany's Reluctant War, 1939–41*. Lewes: The Book Guild Limited, 2001.

Soutar, Ian, ed. "History Notes: Nazi Gold: Information from the British Archives." Historians LRD, Foreign and Commonwealth Office, rev. ed., January 1997.

———. "History Notes: Nazi Gold: Information from the British Archives: Part II, Monetary Gold, Non Monetary Gold and the Tripartite Gold Commission." Historians LRD, No. 12, Foreign and Commonwealth Office, May 1997.

Steury, Donald. "CSI: The OSS and Project Safehaven." www.cia.gov.library.

Stevens, Edmund. "Portugal Under Salazar." *Harper's Magazine* 205, no. 1227 (August 1952): 62–68.

Stone, Glyn A. *Spain, Portugal and the Great Powers, 1931–1941*. New York: Palgrave Macmillan, 2005.

———. "The Official British Attitude to the Anglo-Portuguese Alliance, 1910–1945," *Journal of Contemporary History* 10, no. 4 (October 1975): 729–746.

———. *The Oldest Ally: Britain and the Portuguese Connection, 1936–1941*. Woodbridge, Suffolk: Boydell Press, 1994.

Strachan, Hew, ed. *The Oxford Illustrated History of the First World War*. Oxford: Oxford University Press, 1998.

Streeter, Michael. *Franco*. London: Haus Publishing, 2005.

Sweeney, J. K. "The Portuguese Wolfram Embargo: A Case Study in Economic Warfare," *Military Affairs* 38, no. 1 (February 1974): 23–26.

Tarling, Nicholas. "Britain, Portugal and East Timor in 1941," *Journal of Southeast Asian Studies* 27, no. 1 (March 1996): 132–138.

Taylor, A. J. P. *The Origins of the Second World War*. London: Penguin, 1991.

———. *A History of England, 1914–1945*. London: Folio Society, 2000.

Teixeira, Nuno Severiano. "From Neutrality to Alignment: Portugal in the Foundation of the Atlantic Pact." *Luso-Brazilian Review* 29, no. 2 (Winter 1992): 113–126.

———. *O Poder e O Guerra, 1914–1918: Objectivos Nacionais e Estratégias na Grande Guerra*. Lisboa, Editorial Estampa, 1996.

Telo, António Jose. *A Neutralidade Portuguesa e o Ouro Nazi*. Lisbon: Quetzal Editores, 2000.

———. *Portugal na Segunda Guerra, 1941–1945*. 2 vols. Lisboa: Vega, 1991.

Thomas, Hugh. *The Spanish Civil War*. London: Penguin, 1990.

Trabulo, António. *O Diário de Salazar*. Lisboa: Parceira e A. M. Pereira, 2008.

Tremlett, Giles. *Ghosts of Spain: Travels through a Country's Hidden Past*. London: Faber and Faber, 2006.

Trevor-Roper, Hugh. *The Last Days of Hitler*. London: Macmillan, 1995.

Unger, Irwin, and Debi Unger. *The Guggenheims: A Family History*. New York: HarperPerennial, 2006.

Vail, Karole, ed. *The Museum of Non-Objective Painting: Hila Rebay and the Origins of the Solomon R. Guggenheim Museum*. New York: Guggenheim Museum Publications, 2009.

Vicente, Ana. *Portugal Visto pela Espanha: Correspondência Diplomática, 1939–1960*. Lisboa: Assírio e Alvim, 1992.

Walters, Guy. *Hunting Evil*. London: Bantam Books, 2010.

West, Nigel. *MI6: British Secret Intelligence Service, 1909–45*. London: Panther, 1985.

Wheeler, Douglas L. "And Who Is My Neighbour? A World War II Hero of Conscience for Portugal." *Luso-Brazilian Review* 26, no. 1 (Summer 1989): 119–139.

———. "In the Service of Order: The Portuguese Secret Police and the British, German and Spanish Intelligence, 1932–1945." *Journal of Contemporary History* 18, no. 1 (January 1983): 107–127

———. "The Price of Neutrality: Portugal and the Wolfram Question and World War II." *Luso-Brazilian Review* 23, no. 1 (Summer 1986): 107–127.

———. *Historical Dictionary of Portugal*. Metuchen, NJ, and London: Scarecrow Press, 1993.

———. "Fifty Years of Dictatorship by António Figueiredo." (Review Article) *The International Journal of African Historical Studies* 10, no. 3 (1997): 486–492.

———. *Republican Portugal: A Political History, 1910–1926*. Madison, WI: University of Wisconsin Press, 1978.

Wiarda, Howard J., and Margaret MacLeish Mott. *Catholic Roots and Democratic Flowers: Political Systems in Spain and Portugal*. Westport and London: Praeger, 2001.

Wigg, Richard. *Churchill and Spain: The Survival of the Franco Regime, 1940–1945*. Brighton and Portland: Sussex Academic Press, 2008.

Wilcken, Patrick. *Empire Adrift: The Portuguese Court in Rio de Janeiro, 1808–1821*. London: Bloomsbury, 2004.

Wills, Clair. *That Neutral Island: A Cultural History of Ireland during the Second World War*. London: Faber and Faber, 2007.

Woodward, Llewellyn. *British Foreign Policy in the Second World War*. London: Her Majesty's Stationery Office, 1962.

Wullschlager, Jackie. *Chagall: Love and Exile*. London: Penguin, 2010.

Wylie, Neville. "An Amateur Learns His Job? Special Operations Executive in Portugal, 1940–1942." *Journal of Contemporary History* 36, no. 3 (July 2001): 441–457.

Ziegler, Philip. *King Edward VIII: The Official Biography*. London: Collins, 1990.

INDEX

ANA BAIÃO

Neill Lochery, PhD, is a world-renowned source on Israel, the Middle East, and Mediterranean history. He is the author of five books and countless newspaper and magazine articles. He regularly appears on television in the UK, the USA, and the Middle East. He is currently based at University College London and divides his time between London, Lisbon, and the Middle East. For more information, go to www.Neill-Lochery.com.

PublicAffairs is a publishing house founded in 1997. It is a tribute to the standards, values, and flair of three persons who have served as mentors to countless reporters, writers, editors, and book people of all kinds, including me.

I.F. STONE, proprietor of *I. F. Stone's Weekly*, combined a commitment to the First Amendment with entrepreneurial zeal and reporting skill and became one of the great independent journalists in American history. At the age of eighty, Izzy published *The Trial of Socrates*, which was a national bestseller. He wrote the book after he taught himself ancient Greek.

BENJAMIN C. BRADLEE was for nearly thirty years the charismatic editorial leader of *The Washington Post*. It was Ben who gave the *Post* the range and courage to pursue such historic issues as Watergate. He supported his reporters with a tenacity that made them fearless and it is no accident that so many became authors of influential, best-selling books.

ROBERT L. BERNSTEIN, the chief executive of Random House for more than a quarter century, guided one of the nation's premier publishing houses. Bob was personally responsible for many books of political dissent and argument that challenged tyranny around the globe. He is also the founder and longtime chair of Human Rights Watch, one of the most respected human rights organizations in the world.

•　　　•　　　•

For fifty years, the banner of Public Affairs Press was carried by its owner Morris B. Schnapper, who published Gandhi, Nasser, Toynbee, Truman, and about 1,500 other authors. In 1983, Schnapper was described by *The Washington Post* as "a redoubtable gadfly." His legacy will endure in the books to come.

Peter Osnos, *Founder and Editor-at-Large*